Hemingway in the Digital Age

TEACHING HEMINGWAY

Mark P. Ott, Editor
Susan F. Beegel, Founding Editor

Teaching Hemingway's *The Sun Also Rises*
EDITED BY PETER L. HAYS

Teaching Hemingway's *A Farewell to Arms*
EDITED BY LISA TYLER

Teaching Hemingway and Modernism
EDITED BY JOSEPH FRUSCIONE

Teaching Hemingway and War
EDITED BY ALEX VERNON

Teaching Hemingway and Gender
EDITED BY VERNA KALE

Teaching Hemingway and the Natural World
EDITED BY KEVIN MAIER

Teaching Hemingway and Race
EDITED BY GARY EDWARD HOLCOMB

Hemingway in the Digital Age: Reflections on Teaching, Reading, and Understanding
EDITED BY LAURA GODFREY

Hemingway in the Digital Age

Reflections on Teaching, Reading, and Understanding

Edited by Laura Godfrey

The Kent State University Press   Kent, Ohio

© 2019 by The Kent State University Press, Kent, Ohio 44242
All rights reserved
Library of Congress Catalog Card Number 2019014329
ISBN 978-1-60635-381-3
Manufactured in the United States of America

No part of this book may be used or reproduced, in any manner whatsoever, without written permission from the publisher, except in the case of short quotations in critical reviews or articles.

URLs published in the print edition and hyperlinks included in the ebook edition of this book are provided as a convenience and for informational purposes only; they do not constitute endorsement or approval by the publisher. The publisher bears no responsibility for the accuracy, functionality, legality, or content of the URLs and hyperlinks.

Library of Congress Cataloging-in-Publication Data
Names: Godfrey, Laura Gruber, editor.
Title: Hemingway in the digital age : reflections on teaching, reading, and understanding / edited by Laura Godfrey.
Description: Kent, Ohio : The Kent State University Press, [2019] | Series: Teaching Hemingway | Includes bibliographical references and index.
Identifiers: LCCN 2019014329 | ISBN 9781606353813 (paperback)
Subjects: LCSH: Hemingway, Ernest, 1899-1961--Study and teaching--Technological innovations. | American literature--20th century--Study and teaching--Technological innovations.
Classification: LCC PS3515.E37 Z6186 2019 | DDC 813/.52--dc23
LC record available at https://lccn.loc.gov/2019014329

For Bruce

Contents

Foreword
    MARK P. OTT   ix
Acknowledgments   xi
Introduction: Hemingway in the Digital Age
    LAURA GODFREY   1

Virtual Hemingways

Virtual Papa: Ernest Hemingway's Digital Presence
    LISA TYLER   15
Beyond the Photographs: What the Images of Hemingway's Fish Don't Tell Us
    MICHAEL K. STEINBERG AND JORDAN CISSELL   22
A Meme-able Feast: Teaching Modernist Citationality and Hemingway Iconography through the Internet's Most Infectious Replicator
    KIRK CURNUTT   32

Hemingway for Digiphiles

How to Not Read Hemingway
    BRIAN CROXALL   57
"Concrete Particulars": The Suggestive Power of Physical World Details in *Across the River and into the Trees*
    MARK EBEL   92
Putting the Medium and the Message in Perspective: Teaching *The Sun Also Rises* in the Digital Age
    NICOLE J. CAMASTRA   105

Digital Resources for Teaching Hemingway

Using Digital Mapping to Locate Students in Hemingway's World
    RICHARD HANCUFF   119

Stories in the Land: Digital "Deep Maps" of Hemingway Country
    LAURA GODFREY AND BRUCE R. GODFREY   129

Using Digital Tools to Immerse the iGeneration in Hemingway's Geographies
    REBECCA JOHNSTON   146

Teaching Hemingway through the Digital Archive
    MICHELLE E. MOORE   157

Teaching Materials

Appendix A: English 482, Hemingway: End-of-Term Writing Prompts and Student Responses
    LAURA GODFREY WITH KELLY OWENS, RICKY BALDRIDGE, LEE J. BRAINARD, MARSHALL J. PALMER, AND ALLISON GNECKOW   167

Appendix B: *The Sun Also Rises* I-Search Project
    NICOLE J. CAMASTRA   179

Appendix C: English 296: Major Figures (Hemingway) Midterm Presentations
    LAURA GODFREY   183

Appendix D: Interdisciplinary Studies 250 Syllabus
    LAURA GODFREY AND ED KAITZ   185

Appendix E: INTR 250 Physical and Virtual Environments: Class Calendar
    LAURA GODFREY AND ED KAITZ   191

Appendix F: Directing Students toward Hemingway's "Concrete Particulars" and Intergenerational Connections
    MARK EBEL   195

Appendix G: How to *Not* Read Hemingway
    BRIAN CROXALL   197

Appendix H: Digital Resources for Teaching Hemingway
    COMPILED BY LISA TYLER   201

Works Cited   205
Contributors   221
Index   224

Foreword

Mark P. Ott

How should the work of Ernest Hemingway be taught in the twenty-first century? Although the culture wars of the 1980s and 1990s have faded, Hemingway's place in the curriculum continues to inspire discussion among writers and scholars about the lasting value of his work. To readers of this volume, his life and writing remain vital and meaningful and are still culturally resonant for today's students.

Books in the Teaching Hemingway series build on the excellent work of founding series editor Susan F. Beegel, who guided into publication the first two volumes, *Teaching Hemingway's* A Farewell to Arms, edited by Lisa Tyler (2008), and *Teaching Hemingway's* The Sun Also Rises, edited by Peter L. Hays (2008). In an effort to continue to be useful to instructors and professors—from high schools, community colleges, and universities—the newest volumes in this series are organized thematically, rather than around a single text. The series now includes *Teaching Hemingway and Modernism* (2015), edited by Joseph Fruscione, *Teaching Hemingway and War* (2016), edited by Alex Vernon, *Teaching Hemingway and Gender* (2016), edited by Verna Kale, *Teaching Hemingway and the Natural World* (2018), edited by Kevin Maier, and *Teaching Hemingway and Race* (2018), edited by Gary Edward Holcomb. This shift opens Hemingway's work to more interdisciplinary strategies of instruction—through divergent theories, fresh juxtapositions, and ethical inquiries, and often employing emergent technology to explore media beyond the text.

Laura Godfrey's *Hemingway in the Digital Age: Reflections on Teaching, Reading, and Understanding* speaks to fresh, pressing issues of intense interest to students and scholars today: How do we employ the emergent tools of the digital age to more deeply engage students with Hemingway's work? And how do we teach his writing to new generations of students, who often cannot put away their smartphones for the length of a class period? Hemingway never anticipated a world of "digiphiles," yet Godfrey's volume provides a range of pedagogical approaches to teaching Hemingway's writings to a generation that may prefer a digital text—and perhaps a digital world—to holding a paper text in their hands.

However, these digital tools can be used in exciting ways to bring Hemingway's work to life for a new generation of students. The expertise and insight Godfrey brings to this topic is manifest throughout this volume. These essays illuminate new strategies for employing digital photographs, archives, and maps to ignite students' curiosity in "Hemingway country," and the geographies that inspired texts as *In Our Time, The Sun Also Rises,* and *Across the River and into the Trees*. Godfrey brings forth a diverse range essays that not only explore Hemingway's fiction through the lens of the digital age but also revise our understanding of the complex cultural web that stimulated his imagination and his writing. Readers will quickly recognize that these digital tools create opportunities for enriching the textual experience and expanding the imagination of students.

Indeed, this volume demonstrates that Hemingway's work is being taught in more thoughtful, creative, and innovative ways in today's classrooms and lecture halls than ever before and that his work inspires vigorous debate and insightful discussion now more than ever.

Acknowledgments

Thanks must go first to the contributors within this volume for sharing their enthusiasm, their humor, and their astounding scholarly and pedagogical creativity. I am also deeply grateful for my colleagues at North Idaho College for their inspiration and support in creating the interdisciplinary course, INTR 250: Physical and Virtual Environments, in which the idea for this book first emerged: Lita Burns, Larry Briggs, Ed Kaitz, Lloyd Duman, Liz Adkinson, and Molly Michaud.

Special kudos also go to the brave students who took those original INTR 250 courses—as well as the students in my North Idaho College and University of Idaho Hemingway seminars—for their insights, their wit, their humor, and their intellect. This book would also not have been possible without the generous support of my home institution, North Idaho College, which awarded me a sabbatical leave as I completed the editing process.

Thanks also to Mark Ott, series editor for the Kent State University Press *Teaching Hemingway* volumes, who was encouraging and enthusiastic about this project from the beginning. At Kent State University Press, I owe a debt of gratitude to Susan Wadsworth-Booth, Will Underwood, Mary Young, Erin Holman, and Richard Fugini for working with me as the book moved through the channels to publication.

And last, thanks most of all to my family—my parents, William and Nancy Gruber, my husband, Bruce, and my two lovely daughters, Natalie and Julia, for always cheering me on every step of the way.

Introduction
Hemingway in the Digital Age

Laura Godfrey

The idea for this collection of essays came to me several years ago, when I team-taught an interdisciplinary capstone course at North Idaho College, titled "Physical and Virtual Environments." A member of the college's philosophy department (Ed Kaitz) and I created a reading list comprising major works of literature and philosophy, meant to help our students see the ways some of the world's greatest writers and thinkers have expressed what it means to *be in* the world. We chose readings that we hoped would help illuminate the ways that our ideas about being in (as well as our perceptions of) physical environments were shifting in the so-called digital age. To help define what we mean when we speak of "flourishing," we included in our syllabus selections from Plato's *Alcibiades I* and parts of Aristotle's *Nicomachean Ethics*. We studied Taoism, assigning Asian philosophers like Chuang Tzu and Lao Tzu, as well as the seventeenth-century Japanese haiku poet Bashō, to investigate the centuries-old quest for being "present" and for letting go of distractions. We read contemporary cultural critics like Sherry Turkle (*Alone Together*) and philosophers like Matthew Crawford (*The World beyond Your Head*), whereafter students engaged in heated debates about whether constant media buzzes, dings, pings, tweets, and other distractions were, as Crawford argues, making humans' mental lives "shapeless" (6). We spent one entire class period examining whether or not distraction was in fact the "mental equivalent of obesity" (16). My colleague and I worked hard to balance out the bleaker investigations of digital-age life by reading authors like Jane McGonigal, whose 2011 book, *Reality Is Broken: Why Games Make Us Better and How They Can Change the World,* looks at the positive social developments that come from various gaming behaviors. We incorporated real-world testimony from licensed family therapists about the benefits that digital devices and applications could offer to counseling patients, "including apps that promote self-care and social skills" (Keese-Hamm). And we read numerous articles that discussed the ways virtual or augmented realities are being harnessed to solve a host of problems as diverse as increasing access to education for underrepresented groups, preserving Native American oral traditions, curing postoperative pain, and easing posttraumatic stress disorder among veterans.

The literary selections we read during this semester allowed us a break from such direct examination of the darkness and light associated with living in the digital age. We selected several writers who for us have always embodied—both through craft and characters—the art of being fully immersed in a place, of paying close attention to the world. We read Thoreau's *Walden*, Willa Cather's *The Professor's House*, and Ernest Hemingway's *The Sun Also Rises*. And while the students appreciated Thoreau's prickly outrage at the bustling technological intrusions of the nineteenth century and loved Cather's vivid, lush prose paean to the American Southwest, it was Hemingway's novel that seemed to shake them up. We framed our discussions of the book around the question of how these characters were trying to live life "all the way up," the way Hemingway's bullfighters did. Which characters, we asked, were most engaged with the world around them? Which paid closest attention to others and to their environments? And did Hemingway seem to assign value to those who paid close attention? What could we, as twenty-first-century readers, learn from examining closely the ways these characters attempted to live fully in the world? Within this framework, Hemingway's 1926 Lost Generation novel emerged not simply as a chronicle of characters adrift in post–World War I chaos and misery. Instead, the book arose in stark relief as a work about the value—indeed, the necessity—of thoughtfully *trying* to consider, observe, and possibly even understand and connect with people and places. It became a book about the beauty of paying close attention.

We can define the often-used term *digital age* as an era during which the transfer of information moves at lightning speed. It is a time in which much of the world has undergone radical changes in the ways humans communicate and in the forms in which we encounter—and trust—information. New, intimate relationships with technology and increasingly digitally influenced selfhoods have swiftly emerged over these first two decades of the twenty-first century, states of being that Sherry Turkle describes as "new state[s] of the self, itself, split between the screen and the physical real, wired into existence through technology" (16). Our "new selves" often encounter the world with, and through, digital devices, smartphones in particular. Although access to digital technologies differs depending on a number of factors, ownership of a smartphone increasingly spans geographical, social, economic, and racial demographics, with projections that there will soon be 6.1 billion smartphone owners across the globe (Lunden). According to the Pew Research Center, 77 percent of Americans own smartphones and 94 percent of U.S. adults ages eighteen to twenty-nine own smartphones (Pew Research Center, "Mobile"). The Pew report data also demonstrates that "reliance on smartphones for online access is especially common among younger adults, non-whites, and lower-income Americans." For an ever-increasing number of people, then—including many of the students we teach—life in the twenty-first century involves the ownership of a digital device.

My lifetime thus far is about equally split between a pre-internet and internet world. My middle-class family didn't purchase a home computer until 1992, the year I was a sophomore in high school. I learned to type on an actual typewriter. Until I was halfway through my freshman year in college, I handwrote all of the drafts of my papers on lined notebook paper. In 1994, the year I enrolled as a freshman at Emory University, email was brand new; I remember going down to the basement of my dorm to send emails (at all hours of the night) to friends who were far away in other schools. Throughout my education, as I progressed from undergraduate to graduate study, I watched my professors learn—with varying degrees of success—to adapt some of the newest digital technologies to their classes. In 1995 my poetry professor, Harry Rusche, created his own website, still up and running, *Lost Poets of the Great War*: it was one of the first interactive educational web spaces I'd ever seen, and I loved using it. Five years later, in my MA program I was asked to compose biweekly discussion posts on Romantic poets within an online learning management system, a task I loathed, first, because the posts were clearly not being read by anyone, and second, because the digital format made my words seem shallow, decidedly un-Byronic, permanent, and unretractable. But by the time I had finished my PhD at Washington State University in 2005, I had acclimated: my campus and scholarly life were fully immersed in digital technologies. When I began my teaching career at North Idaho College a year later, all new faculty members were expected to develop "blended learning environments," mixtures of physical and virtual world pedagogies.

My relationship with technology and education, then, is multidimensional. I am not a "digital native"—someone who cannot remember a time without digital technologies—nor do I fully identify as a "digital immigrant," in Marc Prensky's characterization, someone who learns to "adapt to their environment" but who "always retain[s], to some degree, "their foot in the past" (2). I don't like to think of myself as having one "foot stuck in the past," because that makes me sound stuffy and intractable. I am neither digiphobe nor digiphile. I enjoy many of the changes that digital life brings about, and I adapt, more or less flexibly, to my twenty-first-century students and their constantly changing educational needs. I use digital technologies in my classes almost every day, and for years now I have participated in creating digital learning tools for my literature students, some of which are discussed later in this collection. But at the same time, there are still plenty of days when my students and I just spend time reading printed books and talking together about what we read. I have always believed that education is a luxury and a beauty to which everyone deserves equal access, but at the community college where I teach, plenty of my students have not had—for various reasons—any chance to enter the academy with anything remotely close to equality. Many of my students work multiple part-time jobs, are single parents with young children, and live in constant fear of not being able to pay rent or buy groceries or pay for a doctor visit. If my literature classes can provide these students a quiet space to read and ask the big questions—like "Who am I? What's worth fighting for? Who's lying to us? What's my purpose? What's the point of it all?"—then I sleep a little better at night (Ilgunas 243). Assigning them to read Hemingway's *The Sun Also Rises* or "Big Two-Hearted River" will not help these students pay for their parking permits or their groceries or their monthly smartphone plans (and yes, even my most economically disadvantaged students have smartphones), but reading Hemingway does help them see that their twenty-first-century struggles are part of a larger, intricate human web of suffering, anxiety, triumph, and magnificence.

There are two broad aims for the essays in the *Hemingway in the Digital Age* collection: to make available to high school, college, and university teachers a wide selection of the best techniques and contemporary digital tools for teaching Ernest Hemingway to twenty-first-century students, and to raise awareness of the ways that Hemingway's writing is increasingly useful for digital humanists and their own scholarly projects, projects that can in turn enrich the literature classroom itself. How do we uncover the dense complexities of Hemingway's seemingly simple prose to our twenty-first-century students? How can we highlight his characters' attachments to physical environments for classes often better attuned to virtual ones? Are there are other qualities of digital age life that make our students somehow *more* connected to Hemingway's life and his writing, connections between twenty-first-century "transhumanism" and twentieth-century modernism that are worth our time and attention? Contributors to this collection expose some of the interesting divisions—and the remarkable, unexplored parallels—between Hemingway's works and our own students' digital era, offering ways to bring those comparisons to life in the classroom. And several authors describe pedagogical opportunities made possible with digital applications or digital humanities approaches. I have found that Hemingway's world seems very remote to many of the students I teach—a disconnect mentioned by several of my students in the *Teaching Materials* section of the book—and these digital tools can help illuminate qualities of his work and life in ways that our twenty-first-century students will find immediately accessible.

The metaphors we once used for going online are no longer relevant. Gone from the common lexicon is the image of the internet as a vast ocean which we "surf," nor is "online" any longer a place one chooses to "go," a fact that reveals the first sentence of this paragraph as laughably old-fashioned. Instead, those of us and our students who live lives increasingly augmented by digital devices often live a hybrid existence, always fully or partially connected to the internet. In 1993, author Michael Heim wrote in his book *The Metaphysics of Virtual Reality* that "in the near future," our worlds would be enhanced with "reality augmentation": he defines this state of being as "inhabiting an electronic realm where reality and symbolized reality constitute a third entity: virtual reality" (77). We've arrived: Heim's predicted hybrid physical/virtual spaces exist all around us, across many corners of the globe.

If we also define our era as the "age of distraction" (this is again Matthew Crawford's term), then much of Ernest Hemingway's body of work can be presented as a counternarrative to distraction, as a testament to the art of disciplined, focused concentration on where we are and on the people right in front of us. As Scott Knickerbocker phrases it, "the power of close reading" Hemingway's writing "[serves] as an antidote to the technology-induced condition of our day: continuous partial attention" (212). In this twenty-first-century digital age comes an increasing vocabulary about the importance of being mindful, present, intentional, and engaged, and Ernest Hemingway's writing has become relevant for students of all ages in new ways. In the past few years, on secondary and postsecondary campuses across the country, diverse efforts for greater mindfulness have sprung up like mushrooms after a rain: we offer

"Mindful Meditation" sessions for students, staff, and faculty; in meetings we speak of "intentional advising"; we wrestle with syllabus technology policies in an effort to keep students' focus away from their devices without appearing too draconian; we work hard, too, to ensure that other students (who require technological assistance in our classrooms) have access to the tools they need. It is clear that a significant part of life for educators in the digital age is an anxiety about technological distractions, or about how to use technology to increase student access to education, or about how to harness digital technologies in useful ways to—as the common saying goes—"meet students where they are" without sacrificing rigor or straying from important content.

Hemingway had the ability—and the necessary melancholy—to recognize the ephemeral nature of any experience while still in the midst of the experience itself; mythologizing the moment was as regular a practice for him as it is for many of our digital-age students and for many of us. Similarly, we strive for such mythologizing of moments when we record events and upload them to our social media accounts, whenever we stop to take pictures of our meals, our clothes, our pets, our balcony sunset views, our friends and families. Increasingly, part of modern life seems to be the practice of experiencing while recording, and indeed, more and more twenty-first-century "experience" seems to happen *through* recording and sharing, whether that record be in the form of video or photograph or tweet or meme. But this, too, is an illuminating reminder of the past: "even in the late nineteenth century," writes Michael North, "when the camera had come to be an indispensable witness to both private and public life, the basis of modern media society was established" (180). Perhaps the main difference is that now there are simply more cameras. The thrill of capturing and sharing images of ourselves appears to be the same across the ages—North describes "the first real photographic craze, inspired by the *carte de visite* in the 1850s, [which] provided the peculiarly modern thrill of duplicating and transmitting oneself as an image" (179). Every time we post a photo on a social media platform or send one to friends and family from a personal device, we're participating in that same "peculiarly modern thrill."

The broad desire many of us have to record our lives is often tied to our need to share and showcase and thus preserve; Hemingway's desire to record often originates from that same impulse. The instinct behind his need to capture and record even the smallest details of his daily experiences surfaces in his essay "Monologue to the Maestro," an *Esquire* piece published in October 1935, where he instructs readers that all writers must train themselves in the art of paying attention:

Listen now. When people talk listen completely. Don't be thinking what you're going to say. Most people never listen. Nor do they observe. You should be able to go into a room and when you come out know everything that you saw there and not only that. If that room gave you any feeling you should know exactly what it was that gave you that feeling. Try that for practice. When you're in town stand outside the theatre and see how the people differ in the way they get out of taxis or motor cars. There are a thousand ways to practice. And always think of other people. (*By-Line* 219–20)

I have used this passage to introduce Hemingway's writing to undergraduate students for most of my teaching career, but his advice to writers has never felt more relevant.

Those of us who teach Hemingway know how the subtle textures of his prose can provide valuable training for contemporary students of all ages, students who need help learning to read slowly and with close attention to a literary text. In fact, the novelist Andre Dubus III touched on these benefits in his 2012 PEN Hemingway keynote address, remarking, "In this digital present where so many human faces are lit with the glow of one screen after another, a time when the notion of individuality and the truly real is beginning to blur, more than ever before we need the life's work of Ernest Hemingway" (15). Amid a buffet of terms emerging as terms for whatever cultural epoch exists after postmodernism—among the choices are *digimodernism, hypermodermism,* and *post-postmodernism*—scholars are increasingly using the term *metamodernism* to refer to the "emergent sensibility" of artistic production in the twenty-first century (Veremeulen and van der Akker). The metamodernistic sensibility is at once global and local, connected and disconnected, intimate and detached—think of your hyper-connected yet lonely, beleaguered student, smartphone in hand and the world of knowledge at her fingertips. She is barraged by a virtual firehose of information and connectivity, yet she is also paralyzed, unable to sort through the digital storm of data. The resulting ennui may call to mind Jake Barnes's comment to Brett Ashley in *The Sun Also Rises:* in the end, no matter what we do or say, "Nobody ever knows anything" (35). Too much information results in a mistrust of information itself.

There are many parallels between the tensions of twenty-first-century digital life and the cultural shifts Hemingway's generation underwent a century ago. "Because so much of the modern world," writes Paul Lauter, "seems 'open'—in part because of our greater control over the physical environment, our ability to travel further and more quickly, the systems of distribution, and so forth . . .

the modern self is sometimes confused by its own freedom" (949). In that observation, Lauter is characterizing the technological and cultural changes that led to new modes of artistic expression in early twentieth century, but he could just as well be chronicling life in the twenty-first century when he describes modern life as rife with confusion about core essences of "self," with constant "self-questioning," and with "deep-seated conflicts" about "social norms or political structures" (949). Our students witness and feel these same tensions, although they may originate from different sources. Bored, anxious, or restless students struggling to connect to the world of *The Sun Also Rises* (or any other Hemingway work) almost always come to life if we remind them how much their digital-age generation is chastised for the same behaviors that Hemingway and his early literary cohort were accused of demonstrating. These students pay close attention when we remind them of the parallels between the modernist era and the digital age: when we mention that "shitposting" (posts or memes that replicate a given community's posting patterns to the ludicrous extreme) is seen as the iGeneration's version of Dadaism or surrealism, or when we reveal that these students' multiform, carefully curated digital identities mirror the same interest in multiple focalizations that Hemingway explored throughout his entire career ("Shitposting"). Hemingway "rejected all apparently coherent and exclusive ways of perceiving the world," just as many of our students resist classification as one essential self, instead curating different versions of themselves for different virtual audiences (Trodd 8). Hemingway and his friends were also famously stereotyped as aimless and rootless, as are today's version of the Lost Generation, though the terms have changed—today we call them members of the iGeneration or Generation Z—raised with technology at their fingertips, sometimes seemingly adrift in a sea of digitized entertainments and distracting memes. But like most of our students, Hemingway had little patience for intergenerational prejudice: in a 1926 letter to Maxwell Perkins, his editor at Scribner's, he noted, "Nobody knows about the generation that follows them and certainly has no right to Judge" (*Letters* 3:158). And so it is my hope that this collection of essays stays firmly away from intergenerational culture wars, since it is clear that the temptation to be distracted is not at all limited to one demographic.

 An important note, now, about generational divisions. The authors in this book describe varying approaches for successfully teaching Hemingway's writing to students in the twenty-first century, and some of the pieces focus in on useful techniques for teaching iGeneration or Generation Z students in particular. Still, there is not a defined *age* range for digital-age students that binds the collection together. Instead of only targeting iGen students as being in need of particular pedagogical care and feeding, in this book, digital-age students are simply the students who we find signed up in our twenty-first-century classes, students who, like all of us, are navigating a physical world that grows increasingly blended with virtual spaces. Some are more adept at this navigation than others. Further, the authors here represent a diverse range of the educational spectrum; we have authors teaching at private college preparatory academies, technical and community colleges, private liberal arts universities, and large public universities. The students in our classes may range in age from sixteen to seventy-five—as I write this, I have among the students in my Hemingway major figures class a seventeen-year-old dual-enrolled high school student and three retirees in their early seventies.

Hemingway in the Digital Age: Thematic Sections

In the opening section of the book, "Virtual Hemingways," each writer considers the ways twenty-first-century Hemingway internet resources (and riffs) provide rich opportunities for seeing Hemingway in new light—in fact, for viewing him from multiple angles. When we put Hemingway's name into any basic search engine, like Google, hundreds of separate and fragmented identities emerge of him as a writer and a man. This is one of the most interesting and unmapped parallels between our own digital world and Hemingway's modernist era; both are moments in history in which we repeatedly see narratives built out of fragments, in which we witness a fracturing of core essences.

In her essay "Virtual Papa: Ernest Hemingway's Digital Presence," Lisa Tyler uncovers the versions of Hemingway that students see when they encounter his work through these disparate internet spaces, and she argues that the availability of many different internet "Hemingways" is helpfully disrupting the academy's "official totalizing narrative" on his life and writing. Next, Michael Steinberg and Jordan Cissell discuss the Hemingway photograph collections readily available online and what students can learn by using, in particular, the fishing photographs to conduct "historical ecological research." Steinberg and Cissell outline teaching practices that blend the use of digital photographs with literary and biographical analysis, a combination that helps steer students away from a mythological idea of Hemingway and toward a more astute understanding of his identity as an angler (and his influence on the Caribbean fishing industry of the 1930s).

Kirk Curnutt ends this section of the book with a fascinating investigation into Hemingway's "meme-ification." In this piece, Curnutt studies the ways the cyber-proliferation of humorous Hemingway memes and (often decontextualized) "inspirational" Hemingway quotes can help teachers clarify for students the practice of "modernist citationality" *and* the ways "canonical literature is reinvented by the platforms of [our] everyday experience." In Curnutt's essay, memes become important teaching tools in helping students see the complexity and humor of the many Hemingways that exist online.

The second section of the collection, "Hemingway for Digiphiles," addresses the different challenges—and surprising opportunities—that arise from presenting Hemingway's writing to students who have grown up in different textual ecosystems, so to speak. In his digital humanities investigation of Hemingway's entire body of writing, "How to Not Read Hemingway" Brian Croxall explains the differences between practices of "close reading" and "distant reading," tracing his use of Hemingway's writing in his Introduction to Digital Humanities classes and chronicling the surprising discoveries he and his students have made along the way. Croxall and his students have used twenty-first-century data-mining techniques to study Hemingway's entire oeuvre; their work generates important insights on how digital humanities approaches can illuminate, at times quite playfully, Hemingway's narrative techniques and thematic continuities.

Next, in "'Concrete Particulars': The Suggestive Power of Physical World Details in *Across the River and into the Trees*," Mark Ebel discusses the ways some of our students are often increasingly detached from the physical activities that Hemingway so enjoyed. As such, they require a new kind of basic training in interpreting material objects—duck hunting decoys and military insignia may be as mysterious to some twenty-first-century students as the most difficult of literary terminology. Ebel argues that strong, capable literary analysis of Hemingway's novel—and, indeed, of much of Hemingway's entire body of work—is made more accessible through detailed knowledge of the physical world Hemingway so carefully delineates.

Finally, the closing essay in this section is Nicole Camastra's "Putting the Medium and the Message in Perspective: Teaching *The Sun Also Rises* in the Digital Age," in which she outlines the important connections to be made between our twenty-first-century, fragmented digital selves and the characters within Hemingway's *The Sun Also Rises*, who similarly struggle with consuming large amounts of information and not fully understanding any of it. Camastra details the "I-Search Paper" assignment she uses to help students learn to better select, prioritize, and present information: skills more essential than ever in the digital age.

The final section of the collection, "Digital Resources for Teaching Hemingway," contains writing by authors who use varying types of digital creations and available tools to present Hemingway's life and writing to students in new and more digitally accessible ways. Three of these essays focus on digital mapping applications that help twenty-first-century students see Hemingway's geographical aesthetic with clearer eyes: Richard Hancuff's "Using Digital Mapping to Locate Students in Hemingway's World" discusses the spatial barriers between our contemporary students and the geography of Hemingway's Paris in the 1920s, and he outlines ways instructors can use Google maps to help uncover and untangle, at least partially, those spaces from the distant past.

My own essay, "Stories in the Land: Digital 'Deep Maps' of Hemingway Country" cowritten with my husband, Bruce Godfrey, chronicles our creation of a digital map that we use to help students better understand Hemingway's sensitive, astute geographical aesthetic. Rebecca Johnston continues the discussion of Hemingway's geographies as shown to students through the use of digital mapping tools. Johnston highlights the importance of teaching our students to see *beyond* the Hemingway internet mythos as "The Most Interesting Man in the World," and her essay details ways we can use digital tools like Google Maps and the Hemingway App to illuminate the complexity of a broad range of Hemingway's literary places. And finally, Michelle Moore's valuable essay, "Teaching Hemingway through the Digital Archive," provides a number of methods for instructors to use the vast number of digital resources (much more than just letters, photographs, and artifacts) to help students "think actively about literature and history and prompt[s] meaningful discussions about literary personas, the interpretation of texts through historical research, and the idea of a 'real' Hemingway."

We live in a period sometimes called the "transhumanist era," a cultural epoch in which humans have increasingly intimate relationships with their machines, a time in which our devices can become part of our bodies, our minds, and even our hearts. A frenetic, digitally infused energy often pervades our world and our psyches, and many of our students have been trained by habit and constant media exposure to follow website link after website link after website link in their pursuit of entertainment and knowledge. Today, the digital world has permeated the physical world in such innumerable ways that we often find ourselves referring to states of being in which we see a merging or blending of the digital world with the physical (think of the game Pokémon Go—where players run through the physical world to collect virtual prizes—as one of many possible examples). We speak casually of hybrid conditions of being, like *virtual reality* or *augmented reality,* and we pepper our communications with distinctions between our digital worlds and *IRL,* or *In Real Life.* Such gradations of the very definition of reality can blur our understandings of—or our confidence in—what is, in fact, "real" at all. In his book *The Singularity Is Near,* inventor, futurist, and Google-employed engineer Ray Kurzweil writes that the boundaries between human and machine are dissolving at such a rapid rate that "within several decades information-based technologies will encompass all human knowledge and proficiency, ultimately including the pattern-recognition powers, problem-solving skills, and emotional and moral intelligence of the human brain itself" (8). There is a growing body of transhumanists interested in the ways technology will allow us to extend beyond our human limitations. "For many transhumanists," writes Andrew Pilsch, "the availability of these [digital] technologies suggests an imperative to use them to remake ourselves into something more than merely human" (14).

Entrance into these techno-philosophical debates feels both intimidating and thrilling. Whether or not such a singularity is, in fact, near will not much matter to someone who needs to teach "The End of Something" or *The Sun Also Rises* to a class full of restless sophomores in two days' time. For teachers responsible for communicating the works of Ernest Hemingway to students who may be (partially or totally) immersed in these technologies, though, unique challenges emerge: how can we show students the need to slow down to the crawl that is often necessary to see the real power in the compressed language Hemingway uses to tell a story? How can we compare the twenty-first-century transhumanists' interest in making ourselves into "something more than merely human" with Hemingway's characters like Nick Adams, Jake Barnes, Brett Ashley, Frederic Henry, Catherine Barkley, Pilar, Robert Jordan, or Santiago, all of whom similarly wrestle within the bounds of their own mortality? How do we illuminate the parallels between Hemingway's ethos and emergent twenty-first-century narrative trends, the names of which are often born and debated online, like "hopepunk"—a genre that "isn't ever about submission or acceptance: It's about standing up and fighting for what you believe in"? (Alexandra Rowland, qtd. in Romano) How, in other words, can we expose some of the interesting divisions—and the remarkable, unexplored parallels—between Hemingway's works and our own digital era, and offer ways to bring those comparisons to life in the classroom? It is my hope that the essays in this collection will do exactly that.

Virtual Hemingways

Virtual Papa

Ernest Hemingway's Digital Presence

Lisa Tyler

Twenty-first-century students investigating any topic invariably begin their research online—and if they can get away with it, many of them will conclude their research that way as well, consulting online sources exclusively. Instructors wishing to introduce their students to the literary Hemingway (rather than the larger-than-life media celebrity or the tabloid fodder) might want to consider curating the sites their students use to research his life and work so that the Hemingway they discover is not (or at least is not exclusively) the name brand that sells Thomasville furniture or a doomed member of a supposedly cursed and tragically dysfunctional family, but the iconic American author of the twentieth century. Otherwise students researching Ernest Hemingway online will find an avatar of the Nobel Prize–winning author that, curiously, elides the work that made him famous.

The Hemingway whom students will encounter online is almost always someone whose public identity is already well known, even if the specific details of his life and work are not. Perhaps partly because he is a journalist who made good as a literary author, contemporary journalists seem to have a special affection for him and frequently report on the latest Hemingway-related book, museum exhibit, film, play, festival, or other manifestation in popular culture. A search for his name on any mainstream national media site (including ABC, CBS, *Chicago Tribune, Christian Science Monitor,* CNN, Fox News, *Huffington Post, The New York Times,* NBC, NPR, and *The Washington Post,* among others) turns up multiple relevant entries from the past five years. So does a search for his name on such international news sites as Al Jazeera,

BBC, CBC, *Le Monde, Moscow Times,* Reuters, and *Der Spiegel.* His stature in American culture is indicated by the space which he is given in larger web archives—the approximately 125 individual items available on *The New York Times* "Featured Writers" page devoted to Hemingway, for example, or the 34 Hemingway-related videos C-SPAN offers, or the nearly 300 Hemingway-related stories featured on National Public Radio's website.

Typically, in his online manifestations the quality of Hemingway's writing is taken for granted and therefore (unless the source is a book review) rarely demonstrated or even discussed at much length. To some extent, that is his own fault. As early as the 1930s, John Raeburn notes, "[Hemingway] began to publicize himself as someone more than a writer—indeed, it often seemed, as someone only incidentally a writer" (31).

Perhaps because Hemingway's estate polices its copyrights rigorously, the internet offers very few specimens of his work other than his early journalism (which is work made for hire and therefore copyrighted by the corporation that owns the newspaper, unlike his books, which are copyrighted by Hemingway and subsequently his estate); publisher-sanctioned excerpts from the most recent posthumously published books, such as *The Garden of Eden* and *True at First Light*; and brief quotations of particularly pithy lines from his fiction. The familiar passage "The world breaks every one and afterward many are strong at the broken places" from *A Farewell to Arms* (249) and the wildly popular "Never confuse movement with action," which Marlene Dietrich attributes to Hemingway, according to A. E. Hotchner's *Papa Hemingway,* are especially ubiquitous (28). Many of the quotations attributed to him are either apocryphal or mangled.[1] For example, both of these examples have variants online (e.g., "Never mistake motion for action" and "The world breaks everyone, and afterward, some are strong at the broken places"). On the Hemingway Society's blog, Steve Paul has formally debunked what is perhaps the most famous apocryphal quotation frequently attributed to Hemingway—"There is nothing to writing. All you do is sit down at a typewriter and bleed."[2] It's easier to find parodies of Hemingway's fiction online (James Thurber, E. B. White) than it is to find the fiction itself.

Instead, the virtual Hemingway who turns up in Google searches is frequently regarded as a legendary figure to emulate, one whose exciting adventures people long to have. His online avatar is frequently associated with place, from those sites the average American might envision as glamorous or exotic (Key West, Paris, Pamplona, Havana, and Sun Valley) to those one might view as more mundane (Oak Park, Illinois, and Piggott, Arkansas). He is often associated with specifically masculine physical activities, such as sport fishing, big game hunting, and (inevitably) running with the bulls. Each of his four wives has received individual attention online. One effect of these focuses (international travel, masculine adventure, and romance) is to suggest a James Bond–like identity, as if the author were the book nerd's version of the fictional gentleman spy.[3]

The web also offers students a sometimes prurient view of the Hemingways' well-publicized difficulties with mental illness, family dysfunction, and legal controversy. Sites explore the dubious legend of a Hemingway suicide curse (Marano); Mariel Hemingway's 2013 allegations, in the documentary *Running from Crazy*, that her father, Ernest's oldest son, sexually molested her sisters during their childhood (Landau); or the death in a Miami jail of Hemingway's troubled youngest son, Gregory, who is said to have undergone sexual reassignment surgery (Gumbel). Dark conspiracy theories about Hemingway's FBI file and his suicide also remain popular online.

Yet a persistent researcher *can* find many academically respectable sources. As already noted, copyright law limits primary sources. But the *Toronto Star* and the *Kansas City Star* have both ransacked their archives and published online every article they could find that Hemingway wrote during his tenure at their organizations; while *The New York Times* offers his dispatches from Spain; and *New Republic* contributes his pieces from Italy in 1927 and Spain in 1938 (Hemingway, "Italy, 1927" and "Hemingway Reports Spain"). *The Paris Review* has posted "The Art of Fiction," George Plimpton's 1958 interview of Hemingway online, while the *New Yorker* has made available Lillian Ross's controversial 1950 profile, "How Do You Like It Now, Gentlemen?" The official Nobel Prize website offers a recording of Hemingway reading his speech, which he was unable to travel to Stockholm to give because of injuries following two plane crashes in Africa in 1954. The FBI has posted its complete file on Hemingway. Even the Wikipedia page on Hemingway is surprisingly thorough and more accurate than some literature anthologies in its summary of his biographical details.

Family and biographical resources online include the John F. Kennedy Presidential Library site's digitized version of the family scrapbooks created by Ernest's mother, Grace Hall Hemingway, as well as memoir essays by Ernest's sister Marcelline Hemingway Sanford, his publisher Charles Scribner III, and his longtime friend A. E. Hotchner. Each of Hemingway's wives has also garnered individual attention online. Even during his lifetime, Hemingway's love life attracted media scrutiny: "The record of marriages and divorces among movie stars has been a staple of American journalism since about 1920, and the press attention given Hemingway's divorce from Pauline, his second wife, and his marriage to Martha Gellhorn shows how successful he had been in making himself the public equal of the more conventional popular celebrities" (Raeburn 107). The information about his marriages was often presented "in a manner suggestive of popular romance," Raeburn notes. Little has changed in more than ninety years.

Yet again, it is possible to locate academically respectable sources on each of Hemingway's marriages. Hadley's biographer, Gioia Diliberto, has written for the *Chicago Tribune* about the end of Hadley's marriage to Hemingway. Hadley's life with Ernest inspired Paula McClain's 2011 bestselling novel *The Paris Wife*, and McLain has discussed her extensive background research on Hadley in more than one video available online ("Paula McLain," "*The Paris Wife*"). Pauline Pfeiffer, Hemingway's second wife, worked as a fashion journalist for *Vogue*, so it's perhaps fitting that she has been defended in that magazine (Blume). The Hemingway-Pfeiffer Museum and Educational Center in Pauline's hometown of Piggott, Arkansas, celebrates both Pauline and her husband and offers a short biography of Pauline and a timeline of their life together. Martha Gellhorn has been profiled by *Salon* (Amdon), and her obituary appeared in *The New York Times* (R. Lyman). Examples of her journalism are available online. For example, Washington, DC, PBS station WETA posted a *Collier's* magazine article of hers from Madrid in 1937 because Gellhorn is featured in the station's 2003 documentary *Reporting America at War* (Gellhorn, "High Explosive"), and *The Atlantic* has posted her coverage of the trial of Nazi war criminal Adolf Eichmann in Jerusalem in 1962 ("Eichmann") and her article assessing the state of Germany in 1964 ("Is There"). The 2012 HBO film *Hemingway and Gellhorn* also garnered attention for Gellhorn and her place in Hemingway's life. Finally, Mary Welsh Hemingway, the writer's widow, also merited her own obituary in *The New York Times* (Mitgang). Her essay "At Harry's Bar in Venice," published in *Holiday* magazine in 1968, is available online.

Also available are essays by noted Hemingway scholars Carlos Baker, Scott Donaldson, Jeffrey Meyers, and Michael Reynolds. The Michigan Hemingway Society has published online a series of articles by Hemingway scholars on the importance of Michigan to Hemingway's fiction ("Publications by Members"). Also online are tributes to his writing by such distinguished fellow writers as Colombian novelist and fellow Nobel Prize winner Gabriel García Márquez, Tony Award–winning British playwright Sir Tom Stoppard, and American journalist and National Book Award winner Joan Didion, among others.

An astonishing assortment of additional Hemingway-related audiovisual resources is also available online. The University of Delaware Library curated "Ernest Hemingway in His Time," an online exhibition, in 1995, while the Key

West Art and Historical Society has created two online exhibits: "Hemingway in Key West" and "Depicting Hemingway: Guy Harvey Sketches *The Old Man and the Sea*." *The Guardian* offers a 2010 recording of British novelist Julian Barnes reading Hemingway's lesser-known short story "Homage to Switzerland." German artist Marcel Schindler has created a fascinating (and remarkably moving) hand-drawn, stop-action video of *The Old Man and the Sea*. Simon & Schuster, now Hemingway's publisher, offers videos of interviews with Hemingway's son Patrick and grandson Séan, as well as a series of reading-group guides for book clubs or first-time teachers of Hemingway's work ("Ernest Hemingway," *Simon*).

The internet abounds with personal testaments to the value of Hemingway's work by what Virginia Woolf liked to call "common readers," by whom she meant amateur readers like herself, who were reading for personal enrichment and pleasure—as opposed to professional readers who were reading for financial gain, professional ambition, and other unworthy reasons. (Woolf used the term *common readers* the way the Olympics has traditionally used *amateur athletes*—and in both cases, no disrespect is implied.) One particularly impressive example is The Hemingway Project, created by the late Wendy Simpson under the pen name Allie Baker. The site offers interviews with Hemingway scholars and family members and artists inspired by Hemingway.

The emphasis here is obviously on those sources that would pass muster with educators—primary sources; eyewitness testimonies; tributes by award-winning fellow writers; and works by researchers with academic credentials, previous publications, and distinguished reputations. With some exceptions, the sites recommended in this essay are those hosted by academic, government-sponsored, and cultural institutions, rather than commercial enterprises and private citizens.

But any search for "Ernest Hemingway" on the web, whether limited by the addition of a specific book title or just a general search for the author's name, will also turn up a plethora of wildly diverse sources, which in and of itself suggests the weight of Hemingway's reputation. Even the internet presence of so many study guides to his work, on sites like CliffsNotes, eNotes, SparkNotes, and the considerably more amusing Thug Notes, confirms Hemingway's stature as a canonical writer.

In a postmodern twist, however, there is perhaps a danger in seeing Hemingway as primarily or exclusively a canonical writer with a weighty reputation. In a discussion of Hemingway's posthumous celebrity in Key West, Russ Pottle notes a division between the respectful celebration of Hemingway as a literary artist and the more carnivalesque revelry commemorating Hemingway the man—in simpler terms, the split between the literary festival and the Hemingway look-alike contest:

> The look-alike contest is a reminder that the physical and material aspects of Hemingway's life were as meaningful and problematic as the intellectual or artistic ones. Perhaps one would rather remember the elegiac experiment of *Death in the Afternoon* than Hemingway worrying about his manhood and hitting Max Eastman. But both are important ways of remembering who Hemingway was and how he struggled both heroically and basely with himself for balance. (298)

Drawing on the work of Mikhail Bakhtin, Pottle suggests that in valorizing the artistic legacy at the expense of the physical human being, we lose some of the disruptive parodic energy characterizing the look-alike contest and that, culturally, both forms of commemoration have value.

By that standard, the many fan pages that celebrate Hemingway's life, the articles by journalists and ordinary people following in Hemingway's footsteps and running with the bulls or visiting Paris cafés, the photographs of Hemingway-inspired handmade artistic creations on the online marketplace Etsy, the discussions of Craig Boreth's *Hemingway Cookbook*, and the lively disputes about the proportions of alcohol and mixers in the author's favorite cocktails are all carnivalesque celebrations of Hemingway as a human being, commemorations that disrupt the official narrative of the academic elites to restore a vitality to Hemingway's popular reputation. Yes, some of these sites, like the annual Hemingway look-alike contest in Key West, verge on the ridiculous, while also commemorating that Hemingway was a human being before he was a writer.

The Hemingway whom students will find on the internet is not one unified representation, but many very different and sometimes seemingly incompatible Hemingways. While this multiplicity might well confuse students initially, it also reflects Hemingway's own self-divisions—the multitudes that he contained (and contains). As Hadley, his first wife, once said, "He was so complicated; so many sides to him you could hardly make a sketch of him in a geometry book" (Brian 52). Students who, wandering the web, discover or rediscover Hemingway's complex, multifaceted humanity and its power to inspire may be more prepared to look past the academy's official totalizing narrative about their assigned readings to see the vitality the iconic American novelist brought to both the writings that form his artistic legacy *and* his struggle to learn how to live in the world—how to live life all the way up.

Notes

1. See also Kirk Curnutt's essay "A Meme-able Feast: Teaching Modernist Citationality and Hemingway Iconography through the Internet's Most Infectious Replicator," in this volume.

2. For further examples, see also D. F. Lovett; Josh Jones, "(Urban) Legend"; and Garson O'Toole.

Interestingly, those are three of the identities Hemingway cultivated during his lifetime: "world traveler," "sportsman," and "manly man" (Raeburn 44). Other identities Raeburn identifies are "exposer of sham," "arbiter of taste," "*bon vivant*," "insider," "stoic and battle-scarred veteran," and "heroic artist."

3. For discussions of Hemingway's complicated, ambivalent, and often vexed relationship to his own celebrity, see John Raeburn, Leonard Leff, and Suzanne del Gizzo.

Beyond the Photographs
What the Images of Hemingway's Fish Don't Tell Us

Michael K. Steinberg and Jordan Cissell

When we ask students in our environmental literature class to describe the first image of Ernest Hemingway that comes to mind, a consistent reply is "fishing" or "fish." Their responses are no doubt biased; students in our class quickly learn about the first author's own obsession with fish and fishing. However, we are confident that the association of Hemingway with fish and fishing is broadly held among many people who are even vaguely familiar with the author and his work. These impressions are, of course, partially based on the success of *Old Man and the Sea,* published in 1952, which permanently cemented the connections between Hemingway, large fish, and the sport of fishing. The association is also supported by the large number of photographs taken of Hemingway standing next to large fish that he caught, images usually captured during his time in the Caribbean.

When one searches the internet using key words "Hemingway and fish" or "Hemingway and fishing," the vast majority of photos that appear are of him smiling, standing next to giant billfish or tuna on a dock near his boat the *Pilar.* Most of these photos were taken in Cuba, with some from the Bahamas or Key West. The Hemingway Archive at the John F. Kennedy Library provides a catalog of conquests with photos of 82 marlin, 21 bluefin tuna and 6 sailfish (Greenberg). The photos contain massive catches—fish so large they boggle the mind—that would be considered lifetime fish for any angler.

These photos, available via web search to any student, scholar, or teacher, serve not just as props that enhance Hemingway's image as a sportsman but also an important archival record of fish and fishing in the 1930s, the time they were

Ernest Hemingway posing with a marlin, Havana Harbor, Cuba, July 1934. (Courtesy of the Ernest Hemingway Collection, John F. Kennedy Presidential Library and Museum, Boston)

taken. Historical photographs similar to those found in the John F. Kennedy Library's Hemingway Archive have been used in a variety of historical ecological studies, which range from quantifying the recession of glaciers to the decline of fishing stocks and other marine resources. Other historical ecological tools— such as fishing logs, explorers' narratives, maps, letters, scientific surveys, and photographic archives—provide information that helps ecological researchers create a more detailed picture of past environments and the changing nature of human-environmental interactions. Exposing our students to this historical ecological research, using these materials, reveals how marine ecosystems and their resources have been altered and can also help guide present-day resource managers when developing conservation strategies.

In a digression from traditional modes of literary scholarship, then, teaching students to digitally search for, study, and use Hemingway photographs to learn about historical environmental conditions allows them to concentrate more on context than text. Such an endeavor also allows our digital-age students to understand the potential of new forms of environmental information that is increasingly available as more archives provide access via the internet. This digital information has the potential to expand the ways students can view and understand environmental change through access to previously unavailable information—as most students are unlikely to travel to a specific archive to view materials (See Drew et al. for examples of a digital research project published with students).

Our class begins with basic tutorials on search engines. We review library subscriptions, we describe how different lists are better for different project topics, and we discuss search terms that may yield the best results. Next, and most importantly for this chapter, we investigate online archival search engines. During this process, we try to show how simple Google searches can miss internal search engines, thereby limiting their success. The Hemingway Collection at the Kennedy Library provides a good example of how one must dig deeper, beyond simple searches and dependence on wiki. Once we reach archival sources, we discuss permissions and public domain and the process to get approval for the use of materials such as Hemingway's photographs. This is especially useful because many students are unaware of the rules surrounding the use of archival material found via the internet.

This type of historical data is also important because some historical ecologists have raised concerns that scientists have been measuring environmental changes over the course of their careers or lifetimes instead of across history (See Pinnegar and Engelhard; Daw; and Hanazaki et al.). In other words, what we remember based on our own experiences becomes a baseline to which we attribute scientific importance. This is problematic, because when researchers compare changes to already lowered baselines and degraded systems, they may underestimate the real magnitude of decline over many generations. This concept is known as "shifting-baseline syndrome" (Pauly). Incorporating previously described historical materials—including, for example, Hemingway's fish photographs—can help eliminate the shifting baseline by providing concrete baselines. In Hemingway's case, the baseline is very large billfish and Bluefin tuna in the 1930s off the coast of Cuba and adjacent areas.

Although the number of fish photographs found in the Hemingway Archive is relatively small, and thus lacks statistical significance, these images still point to a moment in time through which we can at least appreciate and actually measure (by noting the size of the fish) how fish and fishing have changed since Hemingway's exploits in the Caribbean. The size and number of fish Hemingway caught are largely unheard of today in the same waters. Billfish populations, like

Ernest Hemingway and his sons Patrick "Mouse" and Jack "Bumby," posing with a tuna at the docks in Bimini, Bahamas, circa 1930s. (Courtesy of the Ernest Hemingway Collection, John F. Kennedy Presidential Library and Museum, Boston)

those of so many other large open ocean species, have declined dramatically, compared with the first half of the twentieth century. By some estimates, large oceanic fish, including billfish, have declined by 90 percent worldwide, due largely to overfishing by commercial interests (Myers and Worm). And not only have overall numbers declined, but the size of certain species, including many billfish, have declined as well, as commercial fishing pressure harvests fish before they can reach maximum size (Jackson et al.; Myers and Worm). This is certainly the case in Cuba, where the state has subsidized unsustainable and unregulated fishing in its territorial waters, resulting in an overall decline of fishing stocks (Puga et al.). So the Hemingway photo archive reminds students of *what once was* in terms of fish size and abundance. Again, we cannot and should not suggest that students make quantitative statements about the declines in fish sizes and populations based on a limited number of photographs. However, the photographs can at least demonstrate what existed during Hemingway's Cuban years, illuminating their drastic decline in both size and number.

Building on observation from the photographs, the students are asked to investigate issues surrounding billfish conservation and fishing in the area from

Ernest Hemingway and friends aboard the *Anita*, with a marlin in Key West, Florida. *From left:* Ernest Hemingway, Carlos Gutierrez, Joe "Sloppy Joe"/"Josie" Russell (owner of the *Anita*), and Joe Lowe, circa 1933. (Courtesy of the Ernest Hemingway Collection, John F. Kennedy Presidential Library and Museum, Boston)

which the photo was taken. Students research today's environmental issues that might affect the sustainable management of billfish. To better understand the tournament's policies on harvest or catch-and-release rules, students are also charged with making contact with any local billfish tournaments. Thus, the photographs serve as a jumping-off point for larger-scale and present-day environmental research.

In our own class, we begin by viewing various Hemingway fish and fishing photos, followed by discussing what the photographs represent. We ask students to discuss what the photographs say about Hemingway and Hemingway's image. Most student responses typically revolve around giant fish, fishing, and Hemingway as a sporting icon. We then read various Hemingway works, such as *Old Man and the Sea,* and some of his early articles focused on fishing and the Gulf Stream, such as his work published in *Esquire* from 1933 to 1936. Students then analyze the connection and disconnection between the photographs and the writings. They are also asked to think more deeply about the text to identify environmental information not seen in the photographs and how environmental historians might use the photos. Finally, we also read and discuss an example of a published study that uses historical ecological information such as photographs or logs (for example, Drew et al.).

However, as important as the photographs are as both a record of Hemingway's fishing abilities and of the size of certain fish species in the 1930s, they can also create a misleading image of the man. The hyper-masculine image, crafted by Hemingway, his writings, and his handlers created an oversimplified character or caricature of the mid-century American male (Earle). Drinking, women, and death all fill his stories, yet important ecological information underpins many of these stories, and the environment was critically important to Hemingway personally. Therefore, it is important for the audience—and students, in particular—to look beyond the initial image of Hemingway that is portrayed in the photographs. In other words, we must help them see past Hemingway as a fisherman only concerned with catching and killing large fish. In angling circles, such a fisherman is known as a "meat" fisherman, someone who always kills his catch and is concerned with little other than catching big fish. By reputation, meat fishermen aren't known for their nuance regarding their appreciation of the sport or their sensitivity to the environmental conditions in which it takes place. We are certainly not arguing that Hemingway advocated for catch-and-release fishing. He didn't. (His use of a machine gun to kill sharks that sometimes fed on the billfish attached to his line contributed to his crude reputation in some angling circles.) However, even with his sometimes heavy-handed actions, Hemingway was an observant angler and certainly had a deep respect for and curiosity about the fish he sought and the environmental conditions in which he fished. He was more than a smiling meat fisherman with a large, dead trophy at his side. He obviously loved the environments in which he fished, as is clearly indicated by this poetic quotation from the *Green Hills of Africa* about the Gulf Stream:

> When, on the sea, you are alone with it and know that this gulf stream you are living with, knowing, learning about, and loving, has moved as it moves, since before man, and that it has gone by the shoreline of that long, beautiful, unhappy island since before Columbus sighted it and the things you find out about it, and those that have always lived in it are permanent and of value because that stream will flow, as it has flowed, after the Indians, after the Spaniards, after

Pauline Pfeiffer, Ernest, Jack "Bumby," Patrick "Mouse," and Gregory "Gigi" Hemingway with four marlins on the dock in Bimini, Bahamas, 20 July 1935. (Courtesy of the Ernest Hemingway Collection, John F. Kennedy Presidential Library and Museum, Boston)

the British, after the Americans and after all the Cubans and all the systems of governments, the richness, the poverty, the martyrdom, the sacrifice and the venality and cruelty are all gone. (102)

These words are powerful because they clearly show a deep appreciation of the physical environment and a keen awareness of time—not time in the human sense, but deep time, ecological time, time independent of people and our political and economic systems. Hemingway knows that when he was floating in the Gulf Stream searching for fish, he existed in system bigger than himself and all the human landscapes around him.

Even though Hemingway obviously enjoyed catching (and killing) large fish, he was also cognizant of the pressure that both early sport and commercial fishing were having on certain species. Again, the photographs don't tell the entire story. He was a founding member of the International Game Fish Association (founded in 1940) and warned the angling public about the dangers posed by increasingly sophisticated tackle (*Hemingway on Fishing*). He wrote in the introduction to Kip Farrington's *Atlantic Game Fishing*: "The development of big-game angling was retarded for many years by inadequate tackle," but is now "in danger of being ruined as a sport by the development of too efficient tackle" (xxiv). For Hemingway, the challenge of taking on a huge fish without overt advantages (or what he considered overt advantages) was part of the thrill.

This curiosity and knowledge about the fish and environment were also clearly on display in his correspondence and collaboration with Charles Cadwalader from the Academy of Natural Sciences in Philadelphia. Hemingway, Cadwalader, and academy ichthyologist Henry W. Fowler spent part of 1934 and 1935 on trips aboard the *Pilar* out of Havana and Cojimar. Hemingway continued to contribute specimens and scientific information for another year, during which he and the academy exchanged correspondence focused largely on fish taxonomy (Martin). Their 1934–35 letters document Hemingway's wide expertise as a citizen-scientist and are evidence of his lifelong role as a perceptive angler. Beyond his image as a celebrity, then, Hemingway held the respect of the academy scientists so much so that Fowler later named a new species of fish (a sculpin) after Hemingway (see Martin for a complete analysis of the correspondence and collaboration). If students who aren't familiar with Hemingway's varied portfolio and interests simply view photographs and don't dig deeper, they can easily overlook Hemingway's scientific contributions. The photographs, of course, provide other important information regarding specific fish, but again, this is only part of the larger picture.

When twenty-first-century students look closely at these photographs, they come to see that the Hemingway fish photos themselves, alongside the man's writings and his general image, all contributed to the birth of the big-game sport fishing industry in Florida and the larger Caribbean. The photographs, then, allow teachers to connect the complexity of his image as an author and a man to broader cultural and environmental changes in the early-to-mid-twentieth century. Yes, many individuals strongly associate Hemingway with fish and fishing. There is his literary connection to the subjects, of course, but there also exists a casual association. For example, the walls of any number of bars in Key West or Havana are decorated with grainy black-and-white photos of Hemingway standing by his enormous catches (the same photos found in the JFK Hemingway Archive). This may lead to the reader to ask if Hemingway's success led to the demise of the very fish he pursued by inspiring so many others to engage in his hobby.

"Portrait of author Ernest Hemingway posing with sailfish"—Key West, Florida. 194–. (Photo by Wright Langley, courtesy of the State Archives of Florida)

Initially, this perspective makes sense, given his ubiquitous image and widespread popularity. Hemingway did kill many large fish that would have produced larger fish if left unmolested. And no doubt other anglers, some inspired by Hemingway, have killed fish as well. While Hemingway was certainly a catch-and-kill angler, as the photos demonstrate today, billfish anglers and tournaments are at the forefront of catch-and-release angling. So while the sport has become more *popular* in recent decades, partly driven by Hemingway's image, the sport he inspired is more *sustainable* now than at any time in its history. That sport fishing, so loved by Hemingway, has led to more effective management of billfish species brings the issue full circle for many students. At first they view Hemingway as a hyper-masculine predator, but by the end of the discussion and analysis they realize he was far more complex than initially perceived and that one of his favorite hobbies (although we are reluctant to call it a mere hobby) had the opposite effect of what they initially understood.

By all accounts, including documentation in the photographs described here, Hemingway was an accomplished angler. He was not simply a wealthy individual who sat back, relaxed, and waited for a hired crew to do his fishing work. He was involved in and intimately familiar with all facets of this sport. As an experienced angler, the first author remains impressed with every reading of Hemingway's ability to weave the minute details of fishing into his story in such a way that it does not bore the non-angler. His descriptions of bait, the rocking of the boat, the reels and line, the angle and intensity of the sun are all important details, yet these could be boring and distracting if not written by a master who had equal command of the written word and a rod and reel. So in the end, the Hemingway photographs provide some interesting information about fish and fishing in the 1930s, but they only tell part of the story. Thus, to truly understand the depth and mastery Hemingway held regarding fish, angling, and the waterscape in which they were set, one must consider both the visual and written records.

A Meme-able Feast

Teaching Modernist Citationality and Hemingway Iconography through the Internet's Most Infectious Replicator

Kirk Curnutt

Like most teachers, I have felt continuous pressure throughout my career to be as entertaining as educational. Looking back over twenty-five years of annual evaluations at the same institution, I see that measuring my effectiveness in the classroom has never been a mere matter of demonstrating expertise or competency, displaying organization or preparation, or even promoting learning through such basic transactional pedagogies as classroom discussion. Rather, I have always had to convince supervisors and students that I "engage" classes in the material. In practical terms, what that means is I must prove I am not boring. Early on I learned tricks of the trade for keeping eyelids from clapping shut: have a sense of humor, do not come off stuffy or overly formal, do not read from lecture notes or from the book (call on students to read significant passages), do not chain oneself to the lectern or the blackboard (nowadays, the whiteboard), and—perhaps the single greatest influence on content presentation for educators my age—incorporate technology in the classroom.

Of course, technology itself is no guarantor of liveliness. I started teaching in the late 1980s as VCRs became ubiquitous and film scholars traded VHS tapes, many of them illegally dubbed from rental copies, despite that omnipresent FBI antipiracy warning. I well remember when the English department I enrolled in for graduate training bought several of the machines and made them available, along with portable televisions, as "instructional support." Mainly I remember being unimpressed. I had passed through middle and senior high school during the Dark Ages of the filmstrip, when students were expected to stare in rapt attention at static images while monotone narrators delivered facts and figures on an accompanying 33⅓ LP. In the earliest years of filmstrips, some will remember, teachers listened along for a *beep* that told them when to turn the knob to the next frame. Somewhere around the time I entered adolescence, manufacturers produced projectors with built-in cassette players that automatically advanced the filmstrip when that annoying 50-Hz tone bleated. That innovation freed teachers to stay at their desks and either grade or read the newspaper while knowledge wafted from speakers at us as unappetizingly as smells from the lunchroom. In some cases, our instructors were so detached from the hardware, calling upon students to spool the strips and hit *play* on the audio, that they failed to notice when a prankster substituted Van Halen or Ted Nugent for the correct cassette. The hail of laughter that greeted this practical joke was far more enthusiastic than any reaction the material ever sparked.[1] A decade later, I mostly felt about the VCR the way I did about filmstrips: somewhat prejudicially perhaps, I thought the only real benefit of the technology was to give teachers a break from actual teaching.

If that sounds like something a grouchy technophobe would say, I should note that today I regularly incorporate YouTube clips into my classes. I also enjoy showing students websites devoted to authors we study, if only to prove literature has relevance outside of the classroom. In a similar vein, I remain a devotee of software that most of my colleagues despise only a little less than they hate department meetings and fall convocations. I began creating Power-Point presentations for classes more than twenty years ago, when Microsoft's Windows 95 swept into desktop operating systems with all the thoroughness of Genghis Khan conquering Eurasia. I suspect my colleagues react with visceral loathing at the very mention of the name *PowerPoint* because this presentation tool is so associated with administrators. From its predesigned templates featuring straight-from-stock-photography golden sunsets and coastal paradises to its whirligig animations to its much-abhorred propensity for bullet points, the program seems designed for users whose aesthetics are firmly grounded in Hallmark cards and inspirational-quote wall calendars. For those of us who like to believe our cynicism and sarcasm are symptomatic of our rigorous critical thinking, PowerPoint can come off as coercively boosterish and cheerleader-y. I came to literature after studying magazine design and layout, however, and I immediately liked how clean and professional my slides looked projected on a screen. For me, PowerPoint was color TV compared to the black-and-white world of transparencies, which I avoided like the plague.[2] Selfishly, I appreciated the program because it saved my wrist the tedium of re-scrawling important terms, definitions, and characteristics on the board across multiple sections. It also saved students from interrupting me to ask what words my chicken-scratch penmanship had rendered illegible.

Among the design elements I especially like when creating slides are photographs. Even before I became a department chair in 2000, I cajoled my dean into buying me a scanner, whereupon I began uploading literary images from books into chatrooms in which I participated, blogs to which I was hired to contribute, and, much later, Facebook pages I helped manage. In scouring the internet for photos, I found myself drawn not to official author portraits but to funnier candids. Whenever I taught Ernest Hemingway, for example, I liked to decorate a slide with the 1935 photo of him wielding the submachine gun with which he famously fended off sharks during Bimini fishing expeditions on the *Pilar*—both the one of him aiming the Tommy gun directly at the camera and the one of him apparently passed out with it, drink in his other hand and his oldest son, John, or "Bumby," cradled at his knee (Figs. 1 and 2).[3] I was also fond of the 1952 photo of a shirtless Hemingway in the bathroom of his Cuban home, the Finca Vigía, wielding a shotgun to fend off prowlers after a series of break-ins (Fig. 3). These images succinctly embodied the stereotype of Hemingway that our classroom discussions of "Hills Like White Elephants" and "The Snows of Kilimanjaro" would inexorably complicate as we focused on textual nuance (*Complete Short Stories* 211–14, 39–56). The irreverence of presenting these unflattering photos seemed to set students at ease, the images' unintended humor relaxing barriers to learning by assuring the class their eminently serious instructor did not take either the author or the assigned writing *too* seriously—although I always made a point to end the discussion turning impiety to poignancy by noting the tragic place of alcoholism and suicide in Hemingway's life.

As the web proliferated and expanded, I gathered other examples of funny images to decorate my slides. I loved collecting caricatures of Hemingway, whether from masters of the form such as Miguel Covarrubias (1904–1957) and David Levine (1926–2009) or from anonymous clip-art illustrators. The internet is also a wonderful repository of "fan art." Whether comically bad, superlative, or inscrutably weird, these graphics make for great conversation starters. So, too, I find myself a connoisseur of Hemingway tattoos. The vast majority of this body art depicts the writer in his frailer senescent years, the renderings often based on Yousuf Karsh's famous 1957 close-up portrait of the writer sporting a "heavy turtleneck sweater from a Christian Dior Paris boutique that [his fourth wife] Mary had given him the previous Christmas"—the last formal photograph to capture Hemingway's commanding presence before

Figs. 1 and 2. These widely reproduced images of Hemingway on the *Pilar* in spring 1935 with his Thompson machine gun often help break the ice in classrooms by humanizing the author's image. (Courtesy of the Ernest Hemingway Collection, the John F. Kennedy Presidential Library and Museum)

Fig. 3. Hemingway defending the Finca Vigía, his Cuban home, from prowlers in 1952. (Courtesy of the Ernest Hemingway Collection, the John F. Kennedy Presidential Library and Museum)

depression and alcoholism sapped his vitality (Voss and Reynolds 45). Such artwork allows classes to discuss the enduring iconography of this later "Papa" image, which in the popular imagination swamps the more Clark Gable–like, matinee-idol charisma he exuded in 1930s photographs. Tattoos also encourage reflection on the range of body spaces on which people adorn themselves with their literary heroes, encouraging students again to recognize how fans publicize their literary passions.

Over the past few years, I have become a devotee of Hemingway memes that proliferate online. A recent online article about cyber-culture offers a basic definition of this term: "The majority of modern memes are captioned photos that are intended to be funny, often as a way to publicly ridicule human behavior. Other memes can be videos and verbal expressions. Some memes have heavier and more philosophical content" (Gil). The concept of a meme has deeper implications, however, than lolcats, arguably the first "captioned photo" series "intended to be funny." The term itself was coined decades ago by evolutionary biologist Richard Dawkins, best known today for his advocacy of atheism, often voiced through sweeping dismissals of religious faith that spark exhausting cycles of controversy and ire. In his bestselling study *The Selfish Gene* (1976), Dawkins recounts his search for a descriptor to convey how cultural concepts undergo the same evolutionary process by which DNA transfers and transforms during natural selection. Shortening the Greek word *mimeme* or "imitation" to *meme* because it is "a monosyllable that sounds like 'gene,'" Dawkins defines the term as "a unit of cultural transmission" whose primary characteristic is its ability to replicate: "Examples of memes are tunes, ideas, catch-phrases, clothes fashions, ways of making pots or of building arches. Just as genes propagate themselves in the gene pool by leaping from body to body via sperm or eggs, so memes propagate themselves in the meme pool by leaping from brain to brain in a process that, in the broad sense, can be called imitation" (192).

Two decades before the cyber age, Dawkins envisioned the human mind as the ultimate "vehicle for the meme's propagation in just the way that a virus may parasitize the genetic mechanism of a host cell" (192). Given its omnipresence since the turn of the millennium, the internet has become the more obvious mechanism for transmitting memes, usually through the act of posting or re-sharing them on social media. In some cases, popular memes become short-lived cultural phenomena, like Grumpy Cat, the Ermahgherd Girl (the subject of a *Vanity Fair* profile [King]), Epic Fail!, Evil Kermit, or Guy Checking Out a Girl (the subject of an admonishing *New York* editorial [Feldman]). Some users merely trade variations of these humorous conceits;

others flex their creativity and invent their own versions, whether through design software such as Photoshop or meme-generator websites that format memes for users. For cyber-surfers who fail to understand the joke of a meme, there is even a helpful reference site, Know Your Meme, that diligently explains each meme's meaning and chronicles its history.[4] Regardless of subject matter, memes evince how the internet as a platform encourages the replication essential to evolution. As "units of transmission," they illustrate the dual meanings of "infectious" in Dawkins's theory that the circulation of cultural ideas parallels genetic development: memes spread from user to user because disseminating them becomes socially irresistible—contagious even.

Many memes feature public figures, whether celebrities, politicians, sports heroes, or—yes—even famous writers. Not surprisingly, given his iconic stature in American culture, Hemingway is one of the most popular stars of literary memes. Through periodical Google searches, I have collected two types featuring him that I find useful teaching tools as I design PowerPoint slides. The more significant group features Hemingway quotes. These memes offer interesting devices for illustrating one of the fundamental premises of modernism—namely, its insistence that timeless truths exist beyond the contemporary rubble of meaning. The second group, less important but still highly effective for engaging students, involves humorous commentary on Hemingway's public image. Specifically, these memes visualize the outsized masculinity that can stereotype his reputation.

In the first case, memes that feature Hemingway quotations serve at least two complementary functions. The first is to provide an ad-hoc, online—not to mention free—alternative to *Bartlett's Familiar Quotations*, that venerable compendium of memorable sayings orators have called on for inspiration since its first edition in 1855. Incidentally, the eleventh edition of *Bartlett's*, published in 1937, was the first to feature Hemingway selections. As Philip Young first noted (517), editors Christopher Morley and Louella D. Everett included exactly four passages from the writer, three of them, weirdly enough, drawn from a single *Esquire* essay, "Notes on the Next War" (1935)—hardly the first text a reader then or now would think to peruse first for compelling quotes. (By contrast, the most recent edition, from 2012, the eighteenth, features nearly three dozen passages spanning the scope of Hemingway's career.) Thanks to these quotation memes, through the magic of one's preferred search engine, today an essayist or public speaker can bypass *Bartlett's* to sift through dozens of the author's most citable lines. Usually formatted as JPEG files, these digital

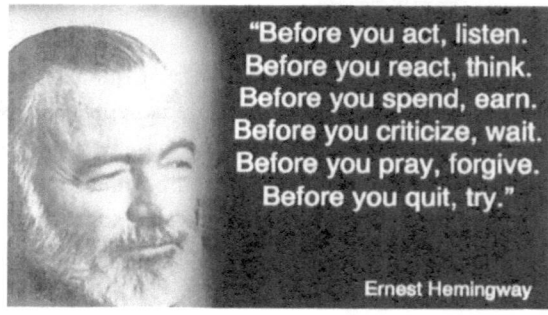

Figs. 4 and 5. Some memes readily available online may challenge even the most seasoned Hemingway scholars to identify their source. (Author's collection)

images often feature either a photo of the author or an eye-catching landscape, making them a perfect artistic embellishment for a PowerPoint slide. In some cases, the text is the only design element, rendered in an artful typeface and printed on a colorful backdrop.

Some of the most reproduced quotations are instantly recognizable: "All you have to do is write one true sentence" from *A Moveable Feast* (1964, 12) is a common meme, as is "*Man is not made for defeat.* ... A man can be destroyed but not defeated" from *The Old Man and the Sea* (1952, 76). Other memes may challenge even the most seasoned Hemingway scholars to guess their source: "There is nothing noble in being superior to your fellow man; *true nobility* is being superior to your former self" is a popular one, as is "Before you act, listen. Before you react, think. Before you spend, earn. Before you criticize, wait. Before you pray, forgive. Before you quit, try" (Figs. 4 and 5). I will return momentarily to the reason such quotations do not ring an immediate bell.

For now, I note that the purpose of most quotation memes seems inspirational. In excerpted form, the Hemingway passages resemble maxims, epigrams, or apothegms, offering insights on creativity, ethics, or interpersonal relationships.[5] Admittedly, looking to Hemingway for sage, uplifting advice puts a rather Pollyanna spin on his work. His ethos may strive for "grace under pressure," but his sensibility is far from buoyant or sanguine. For him, the question is not how one may triumph over defeat, fear, or death but how well one copes with these dark inevitabilities. The vaunted Hemingway code insists on stoic endurance, not on the power of positive thinking. The roseate view of Hemingway that quotation memes promote helps explain why several saturnine passages that are among his "greatest hits" are excerpted far less often than uplifting ones. I have yet to locate a meme, for example, featuring the fed-up Jig's admonishment in "Hills Like White Elephants" to the lover pressuring her to have an abortion ("Will you please please please please please please please please stop talking?" [*Complete Short Stories* 214]). Nor have I come across one that presents Brett Ashley's modest effort at exerting moral responsibility at the end of *The Sun Also Rises*, when she ends her affair with the young bullfighter Pedro Romero: "I'm not going to be one of these bitches that ruins children," she famously tells Jake (219).

It would be misleading, though, to argue that these memes turn Hemingway into a veritable Norman Vincent Peale or a Deepak Chopra. Some of his more existential assertions do appear in this online medium, such as the "our nada who art in nada" parody of the Lord's Prayer from "A Clean, Well-Lighted Place" (*Complete Short Stories* 291). Nevertheless, the vast majority read like wisdom from a life coach. Their epigrammatic quality calls attention to some intriguing idiosyncrasies. While most identify Hemingway as their author, only a small percent identifies the source text. As a result, a romantic reflection such as "*If two people love each other there can be no* happy *end to it*" may test devotees' ability to place the sentence. (I incorrectly guessed *A Moveable Feast*, but the line actually appears in *Death in the Afternoon* [122]). More importantly, not citing a title has the effect of decontextualizing the quotation, making its relevance universally applicable rather than thematically specific to a single text. Eliding the source enables the aphoristic potential of a statement to manifest more easily by making it sound like a timeless truth rather than a passing commentary on an adjacent thought or action. In some cases, decontextualizing a passage conveys a meaning that directly contradicts its original one. One popular Hemingway meme insists, "*Live the full life* of the mind, exhilarated by new ideas, intoxicated by the Romance of the unusual" (Figs. 6a and b). As fans of *Men without Women* (1927) know, this bit of hortatory

Figs. 6a and b. Two examples of memes that without irony cite an aphorism from 1927's "Banal Story" (from *Men without Women*), which in the story is meant to be facetious. (Author's collection)

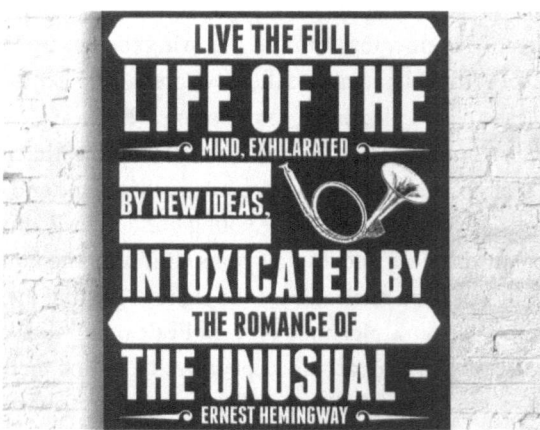

uplift appears in a minor prose effort called "Banal Story." The saying appears as part of a mock advertisement for a real-life periodical, *The Forum*, that the story parodies for perpetuating a fatuous worldview of middlebrow optimism and self-discovery (*Complete Short Stories* 275). In other words, Hemingway intended the line as an *ironic* maxim, yet memes present it as wholly sincere.[6]

In more extreme instances, memes do not just cite a passage out of context—they completely misattribute sayings to the writer. As Peter Hays has shown, the aforementioned line "There is nothing noble in being superior to your fellow man; *true nobility* is being superior to your former self" became associated with Hemingway thanks to *Playboy*, of all places. The quotation appears in a short compilation of the writer's supposed observations on life featured in the magazine's tenth-anniversary issue in January 1964 under the title "Advice to a Young Man" (153, 225–27). (This was the second such *Playboy* collection; a previous one, "A Man's Credo" [120, 124, 175] had appeared exactly a year earlier.) As Hays's impressive detective work documents, the magazine purchased the quotes from an entity called the Wisdom Foundation, which between 1956 and 1964 financed a glossy publication humbly titled *Wisdom: The Magazine of Knowledge and Education*. Hays makes a persuasive case that, rather than gleaning this and other "Kahlil Gibran–like" proverbs from Hemingway interviews conducted in the late 1950s as it claimed, the Wisdom Foundation manufactured some and simply attributed others to the author, in effect selling *Playboy* a bill of goods ("Hemingway's Playboy Interviews," 216–17). Although not widely remembered, both "A Man's Credo" and "Advice to a Young Man" enjoyed enough of an afterlife that in the 1990s, more than thirty years after appearing in print, their dubious contents made their way online.

In the case of the other unfamiliar quote cited above—"Before you act, listen; before you read, think," et cetera—some modest digging around reveals these are actually the words of the "Christian optimist" William Arthur Ward (1921–94), who made a lucrative career dashing off "pertinent proverbs" throughout the second half of the twentieth century. The point here is that attributing the saying to Hemingway rather than Ward illustrates a process Garson O'Toole outlined recently in his appropriately titled study, *Hemingway Didn't Say That: The Truth behind Familiar Quotations* (2017): "[Q]uotation superstars" like Hemingway (or Mark Twain, Albert Einstein, Yogi Berra, and others) "are so vibrant and attractive that they become hosts for quotations they never uttered. A remark by a lesser-known figure is attached to a famous host. The relationship is symbiotic and often enhances the popularity of both the host and the quotation" (10).[7]

The pedagogical value of these Hemingway quotation memes extends far beyond the simple lesson for students that the internet is often a "mélange of misinformation" or a "cacophony of conflicting information" in which "too often, accurate data is overwhelmed by inaccurate data" (O'Toole, *Hemingway Didn't Say That* 6). These memes illustrate a fundamental characteristic of modernism that allows classes to understand the movement's dedication to reinventing literary expression through experimentation—in other words, the commitment of its practitioners to "MAKE IT NEW," in Ezra Pound's famous phrase (*Cantos* 265).

As Shari Benstock argues, regardless of their political, religious, or aesthetic disagreements, most modernists shared a "sacred belief" in the "indestructibility of the bond between the Word and its meanings, between symbol and substance, between signifier and signified." Corrupt contemporary rhetorical practices had obscured this bond, but the various avant-garde techniques by which modernists challenged enculturated narrative norms marked their attempt to punch through the veils of hypocrisy and deceit to convey, however intuitively, "the power of Logos" and "the immutable and undeniable link between form and substance" (158–59). The chief means of approximating what T. S. Eliot in "Burnt Norton" (1936) called "the still point of the turning world" was to undermine or at least impede the temporality of human language (*Collected Poems* 219). Through some "inward turn," modernists transformed a text into a "verbal icon" or some comparable symbol of "spatial form," to borrow three famous critical images of the modernist project, by Erich Kahler (14–15), W. K. Wimsatt (x), and Joseph Frank (31–66). By doing so, modernists insisted the meaning of literature lay at a deep remove from the transitory flow of word sequences, fixed and unchanging because it is immanent instead of explicitly expressed. The particular devices creating this immutable form might be fragmentation and juxtaposition, as in Eliot's *The Waste Land* (1922, *Collected Poems* 67–96) or Pound's *Cantos* (1915–62); they might be the radical concision of Pound's earlier Imagism, which sought to present "an intellectual and emotional complex in an instant of time" (*Literary Essays* 4); or they might be Faulkner's endlessly digressive, involuted sentences, which as poet Conrad Aiken noted in 1939, transform the structure of narrative into a "*continuum* . . . a medium without stops or pauses, a medium which is always *of the moment*" (249).

Hemingway's central device for creating this deep structure, of course, was omission. His most famous image of the spatialized writing that resulted from his insistence on cutting any "scrollwork or ornament" in his prose (*Moveable Feast* 12) is the iceberg motif first presented in *Death in the Afternoon* (1932): "If a writer of prose knows enough about what he is writing about, he may omit things that he knows and the reader, if the writer is writing truly enough, will have a feeling of those things as strongly as though the writer had stated them. The dignity of movement of an iceberg is due to only one-eighth of it being above water" (192). As the image implies, explicit meanings do not need to be stated; readers intuitively infer them, as long as author and audience are attuned to the general truths of human nature that float below the verbal surface. The seven-eighths of submerged structure, in other words, is Logos, the source of common truth and knowledge, while the visible portion of the iceberg is human language.

Critics have debated just how well the iceberg principle works in practice. The aura of lost innocence may be foregrounded enough in initiation stories such as "Indian Camp" (*Complete Short Stories* 65–70) or "The Killers" (215–22) that readers do not need to be told outright that in each work Nick Adams's exposure to death irrevocably changes him. Other "submerged" truths are far less obvious. In my career, I have yet to meet a single student who guesses that the "thing left out" of "Out of Season" (133–40) is Peduzzi's suicide before I present my classes with the passage from *A Moveable Feast* in which Hemingway makes this claim (75). Similarly, the only time students speculate that Nick's numb affect during his fishing expedition in "Big Two-Hearted River" is a coping mechanism for surviving the trauma of war is when they read the story alongside the vignette also in *In Our Time* (1925), chapter 6, in which a wounded and under-fire Nick tells Rinaldi, his compatriot on the Italian front, that they have struck a "separate peace" (*Complete Short Stories* 105). When presented with the story by itself, students have never yet concluded that it is "about coming back from the war," although "there [is] no mention of the war in it" (*Moveable Feast* 76).[8] In reassuring classes that they have not overlooked essential textual clues to these omitted plot elements, I teach them meaning is rarely ever exclusively located within a narrative. Rather, readers depend on extratextual aids (such as autobiographies like *A Moveable Feast*, in which Hemingway reveals intentions we may or may not deem sincere) or intertextual sources (such as the additional half-dozen Nick Adams stories in *In Our Time*, or these and later ones Phillip Young specifically organized a Bildungsroman in *The Nick Adams Stories* [1972]). I also stress to classes that readers' inevitable reliance on information from outside of the work to make meaning complicates the somewhat simplistic idea that modernists were strict formalists. Modernists' use of allusion—a device, by definition, of intertextuality—insists that literary tradition is a font of truth that one can tap into through either citation or paraphrase: as Eliot implies in *The Waste Land*, allusions are "fragments" that the poet will "shore against [the] ruins" of the present (*Collected Poems* 69).

Yet as crucial as allusion is to the effort to establish a link to Logos that is, as Eliot puts it in "Tradition and the Individual Talent" (1919), "of the timeless and of the temporal together," modernists also employed a far less celebrated tool—and one that nearly a century later has proven, as we have already seen, conducive to memes (*Selected Essays* 5). I speak again of the maxim or aphorism, the concise assertion of moral principle that when repeated enough becomes an accepted cultural wisdom. Maxims are everywhere in modernism, in part because its poets and novelists were so fond of aesthetic decrees and manifestoes: Pound's previously cited admonition to "MAKE IT NEW," William Carlos Williams's "No ideas but in things" in "Paterson" (*Collected Poems* 263), Mina Loy's entire "Aphorisms on Futurism" (1914), which includes lines such as "Open your arms to the dilapidated, so you may rehabilitate them" (*Lost Lunar Baedeker* 149), and the 1929 *transition* call to arms "Proclamation: The Revolution of the Word,'" written by editor Eugene Jolas and signed by Harry Crosby, Kay Boyle, and Hart Crane, among others, are just a few notable examples. What the introduction to a recent edition of Pound's *ABCs of Reading* says of that collection's contents is true of many modernist efforts: "*ABC* itself is a compendium of the kind of inspirational maxims and pronouncements one might tape to the side of a computer monitor or pin to a bulletin board: 'More writers fail from lack of character than from lack of intelligence,' 'Incompetence will show in the use of too many words'" (Dirda 7–8). The same could be said of *Death in the Afternoon*, which includes, in addition to the definition of the iceberg theory, such memorable maxims as "All bad writers are in love with the epic" and "All stories, if continued far enough, end in death, and he is no true story-teller who would keep that from you" (54, 122). Assertions such as these are so prevalent throughout *Death* that on reading a draft John Dos Passos advised Hemingway to delete the parts where he seemed to "strap on the long white whiskers" to give "the boys the lowdown": "When you ... give them the low down about writing ... don't you think don't you think that's all secrets of the profession—like plaster of paris in a glove that oughtn't to be spilt to the vulgar?" (*Fourteenth Chronicle* 402–3). Despite the advice, from the 1933–36 *Esquire* essays on through *Green Hills of Africa* (1935) and all the way up to *A Moveable Feast*, such maxims appear more and more frequently in Hemingway's prose, not less.

A canny reader will note that the maxims cited above appear in nonfiction, not the novels or stories for which Hemingway is most famous. In general, it is true that during the 1910–30 heyday of high modernism, poets were more likely than fiction writers to employ maxims for a simple reason: poetry lends itself more readily than narrative to explicit offerings of wisdom. Indeed, part of the modernist project was to rid fiction of any authorial intrusion that even vaguely smacked of the preachiness of nineteenth-century literature, which is why Hemingway and fellow members of the movement eschewed the concluding morals commonplace to didactic fiction. One can, however, identify sentences early on that perform the same function as maxims or morals, even if they are not overtly stated. Joe's final thought in "My Old Man" (1923), for example—"Seems like when they get started they don't leave a guy nothing" (*Complete Short Stories* 160)—fulfills the two basic purposes of a storytelling moral: it both sums up the point of the plot and can be excerpted from the text to serve as a universal truth. Tense is one clue that reveals an assertion put to this use. Unlike the surrounding sentences, this concluding one in this apprentice story (often considered an imitation of Sherwood Anderson) is cast in the present rather than past tense. And not the punctual present, either, which describes passing actions, but the universal, or "timeless," present tense, in which the moral's truth is applicable in a twenty-first-century moment of reading as it was in its 1923 moment of writing. While this type of assertion is rare in Hemingway's early fiction, it becomes more common after 1930, much like in the nonfiction. The transition point is *A Farewell to Arms* (1929), when Hemingway has Frederic Henry extrapolate from Catherine Barkley's death a sense of universal defeat: "They threw you in and told you the rules and the first time they caught you off base *they killed you*. Or *they killed you* gratuitously like Aymo. Or gave you the syphilis like Rinaldi. But *they killed you* in the end. You could count on that. Stay around and they would kill you" (232). It should be noted that this passage is only in the past tense because Hemingway writes in the first-person voice of Frederic Henry, who looks back to 1918 from some undetermined time after the war. If the passage were rewritten in interior monologue, in which storytellers convey first-person experiences as they happen, it would be cast in the present tense as well. The larger point is that by the late 1930s, asserting the point become overt. The Hemingway of 1924, for example, would never allow a character such as Harry Morgan to make the dying declaration that stands as the moral of *To Have and Have Not* (1937): "No matter how a man alone ain't got no bloody fucking chance" (165). Nor would an earlier iteration of Robert Jordan in *For Whom the Bell Tolls* (1940) declare in a stream of consciousness rumination, "Dying is only bad when it takes a long time and hurts so much that it humiliates you" (407). By the time of *The Old Man and the Sea*, Hemingway was so fond of allowing characters to make such grandiose statements, whether in thought or in dialogue, that literary critic Dwight Macdonald complained that his "constant editorializing" creates the rhetorical "drone of a pastiche parable" as the writer strains for a "Universal Significance" that is "hollowly portentous" ("Masscult and Midcult," 41–42). Although Macdonald does not use the term *maxim*, the device is a key characteristic of what the critic lambastes as "Midcult" art—middlebrow writing that postures, often pretentiously, as high art.

Because memes are most apt to excerpt "inspirational" assertions, they provide a useful tool for illustrating how modernists articulated significance in their work. Typically, whether in a literature or creative-writing class, I ask students to break down a few pages of Hemingway, classifying individual sentences as either description, action, thought, or dialogue to help them understand how each functions in the texture of the text. I always provide two passages, one without maxims and one with. The contrast dramatizes the varying degrees to which even the same writer will either instill his main point through implication (as in "Big Two-Hearted River") or invest import in it by presenting it overtly

Figs. 7 and 8. Examples of the wide range of memes built around a famous passage from *The Old Man and the Sea*. (Author's collection)

as a universal truth (as in *The Old Man and the Sea*). As ardent web surfers, most students are well familiar with quotation memes, even if they do not make or send them. The device offers a uniquely eye-catching representation of the modernist view of Logos as a realm of free-floating principles that writers believed they could rearticulate if they could just shake up stolid expressive habits and restate them in revivifying ways. The lack of context implied by a simple box containing words visualizes this deep space of meaning, suggesting that truths exist in a continuum beyond the surface here-and-now of history. Even the misattributions that occur regularly in memes make the point: as O'Toole argues, crediting sayings to the wrong source implies that the truth asserted is more important than the person uttering them, inadvertently enhancing their authority (*Hemingway Didn't Say That* 10). So, too, the replicability of memes—the way the device inspires users to either share an existing JPEG or create a new version of a quote with a different design and/or image—helps students understand modernism's citationality, its desire to both cite and be cited. The sheer ubiquity that a saying gains online as it is replicated in meme-sharing creates pluripresence, the feeling that a quote is everywhere at once—something that a simple Google image search of a famous Hemingway aphorism nicely captures (Figs. 7 and 8). Repetition likewise lends meaning the appearance of timeless immanence: the more a quote is repeated, the truer its wisdom becomes, simply because it seems inescapable and unchanging.

In these various ways then, Hemingway quotation memes allow students to appreciate both the theory and practice of the modernist insistence that art articulates the Word. The theory holds that fundamental truths of humanity are perceptible if only we experience them through revolutions in perspective, perception, and expression. As many of the artists proclaimed, we need the shock of the new to reconnect with the old verities. In practice, though, modernists could only communicate through the very instrument they felt modernity had corrupted—language. For all the groundbreaking innovations in technique they developed to challenge readers' complacent interpretive habits, they also fell back on one of the oldest, most traditional rhetorical devices an artist can employ when claiming to speak a timeless truth: the maxim or aphorism. That so many choice sayings of modernists, including Hemingway's, make for popular memes suggests how desperately we still pine to believe in universals.

Inspirational quotations are only one type of meme internet users create and share. In general, humorous JPEG images and sayings are far more prevalent, although web searches seem to suggest the opposite is the case with Hemingway. For whatever reason, the range and variety of Papa jokes is relatively narrow compared to that of citations. Nevertheless, humor memes are useful additions to PowerPoint slides because they irreverently underline the qualities Hemingway symbolizes in American popular culture. Their comedy is a great device for dramatizing the idea of the carnivalesque, those practices and rituals popular culture produces to leaven if not outright counterpose the values handed down through official institutions and high culture. As Bakhtin wrote, carnival "is opposed to that gloomy and one-sided official seriousness which is dogmatic and hostile to evolution and change, which seeks to absolutize a given condition of existence or a given social order" (160). Again because a fundamental characteristic of memes is their replicability, their circulation encapsulates how everyday people challenge literary culture's glorification of individual artists by rendering the ideals they embody as relative instead of absolute. In this way, humor memes do the exact opposite work of quotation memes, which encourage us to view cultural wisdoms as universal and eternal. Using humor memes as teaching tools, I argue, does not diminish either the writers or the principles they stood for. Instead, the comedy allows students to appreciate how the public images of writers are often stereotyped by "absolutiz[ing]" them as avatars of their moral beliefs or aesthetics.

Consider two memes I often use on PowerPoint presentations—plus one I do not, for reasons of taste. The first plays off of the Cuauhtémoc Moctezuma Brewery's wildly popular Most Interesting Man in the World advertising campaign for its Dos Equis beer brand, in which a debonair globetrotter recounts his outlandish career adventures before declaring, "I don't always drink beer. But when I do, I prefer Dos Equis" and signing off with the tag line, "Stay thirsty, my friends." The connection to Hemingway is not accidental. As portrayed by actor Jonathan Goldman from 2007 to 2016, the campaign's fictional spokesman bears a physical resemblance to the weathered and white-bearded Papa of the 1950s. The particular meme I employ riffs on the campaign's slogan by featuring Earl Thiesen's oft-republished 1954 *Look Magazine* photo of an on-safari Hemingway posing with a dead leopard he presumably hunted and killed—though, as biographers note, it has never been established whether Hemingway or his friend and fellow hunter Mayito Menocal actually fatally wounded the animal (*1930s* 268). "I don't always go to Africa," the type superimposed over the image reads. "But when I do I survive two consecutive plane crashes" (Fig. 9). Student jaws often drop in amazement when I relate to them the story of how on January 23 and 24, 1954, Hemingway and his fourth wife, Mary, indeed walked away from a pair of serious aircraft disasters near Murchison Falls in Uganda. To classes, the improbability of not merely suffering but of surviving two consecutive crashes is exactly the type of tale the Most Interesting Man in the World boasts of in his ads; as I explain to them, the story elevates to near-superhuman levels the indestructibility of the thrill-seeking, fate-tempting adventurer that Hemingway embodied during both his 1933–34 and 1953–54 African safaris. The crashes allow classes to appreciate why the press of Hemingway's day found covering his travels so irresistible, all but outright calling the writer the Most Interesting Man in the World, especially after Hemingway emphasized his nerves of steel and nonchalance in a tone of "muscular jocularity" when interviewed during his Ugandan recovery (Raeburn 147–48).

The incidents further urge students to acknowledge the appeal of the Dos Equis ads, which simultaneously play to our fantasies of sojourning heroically through foreign worlds while parodying the preposterous immortality those Walter Mitty–like daydreams grant us—fantasies that, not coincidentally, account in no insignificant degree for Hemingway's continued popularity outside of academia. Yet the cartoonishness of this immortality turns poignant when I list the injuries sustained in these wrecks. Hemingway suffered from cerebrospinal fluid leaking from one ear, a loss of vision and hearing on the left side of his body, a dislocated shoulder, bloody urine, a damaged kidney and collapsed lower intestine, two crushed vertebrae, and a concussion—his fourth in ten years (Reynolds, *1930s* 274). Many observers suggest the brain trauma accelerated into chronic traumatic encephalopathy, hastening the depression and dementia that, among other factors, drove the author to commit suicide a short seven years later (Farrah x). The meme mentions none of these physical debilities, of course; the joke is on the public image, not the person. As we discuss the meme in class, we focus on the discrepancy between the two and how living up to the former proved so deleterious to the latter.

One string of memes I avoid using also dramatizes the baleful effects of the public image by addressing Hemingway's July 2, 1961, suicide. One variation of this strain features a tinted version of the Karsh photo with the caption, "Who Wants a Shot?" (Fig. 10). At the risk of belaboring this offensive joke, the meme puns on the dual meanings of *shot* as both a gun blast and as a serving of alcohol to link Hemingway's reputation as a heavy drinker

Fig. 9. This meme that references Hemingway's two near-fatal airplane crashes in early 1954 also alludes to the Dos Equis beer advertising campaign, associating the writer with the product's "Most Famous Man in the World" spokesman. (Author's collection)

Fig. 10. One of the more distasteful memes, joking about Hemingway's suicide. (Author's collection)

to his decision to end his life by one of the most violent means imaginable. As I read it, the dark humor here is less a comment on Hemingway than on the literary propensity for romanticizing self-destruction. The meme mocks our cultural tendency to celebrate both "getting wasted" and "wasting oneself" as expressions of the same unbearable anguish that supposedly drives artists' creativity. Broadly speaking, this is the Romantic notion of suicide, the glamorized insistence that life is "unequal to the demands of love, passion, and romance," and because it can never sustain or even realize the intensity of emotional craving, killing oneself remains the one "properly courageous way to exit this troubled existence" (Barry 75). Such a vision obscures more biological and genetic explanations for suicide, which is probably why the allure of self-negation remains a consistent theme in literature, music, and film. At its most basic, suicide for artists may be tragic, but it is also, undeniably, glamorized as a refusal to remain complacent or conformist.

A related meme about Hemingway's death makes the point. Featuring that aforementioned 1952 photo of Hemingway brandishing his shotgun in his Cuban bathroom, the image reads, "Hipster Hemingway: committing shotgun assisted suicide before it was cool" (Fig. 11). Here the object of ridicule is less Hemingway than the cultural stereotype of the "hipster," a "media stereotype commonly associated with young middle-class adults who share certain interests or values in alternative cultures" that since the early 2000s has been "predominantly used as a pejorative label to describe someone who outwardly seeks nonconformity through niche consumerism and boycott against mainstream culture" (DeLand). Because suicide is the ultimate act of nonconformity, a number of cultural figures who have killed themselves have been appropriated alongside Hemingway to ridicule hipsters' supposed boycott of middle-class convention, including writers as different as Sylvia Plath, Virginia Woolf, and Yukio Mishima. If I were a braver teacher, I might use such memes as a tool to punctuate classroom discussions of suicide in literature, but the truth is the insouciance is to me unprofessional. Although I like to think I have a funny bone at the lectern, I would no more treat suicide irreverently in the classroom than I would crack a sexual assault joke.

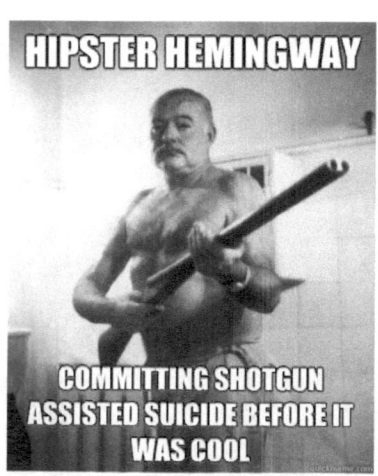

Fig. 11. Here the 1952 photo of Hemingway protecting his Cuban home from prowlers (see fig. 3) is doctored to refer both to his suicide and the hipster figure widely ridiculed in contemporary culture. (Author's collection)

Instead, the most useful meme I have located centers on Hemingway's masculinity. Again featuring the Karsh photo, the caption this time reads, "Manliest looking guy ever. Wrote the only Book that ever made me cry" (Fig. 12). The joke here zeros in on a supposed contradiction between a writer looking "manly" and his prowess at arousing enough emotion to wet readers' eyes. The meme does not need to name a specific title for the humor to make sense; it can apply to *The Sun Also Rises*, which ends with Jake Barnes and Brett Ashley imagining how they might have enjoyed "a damned good time together" if only love in the modern age were possible ("Isn't it pretty to think so? " [*Sun Also Rises* 251]), or to *A Farewell to Arms*, in which, again, a stunned Frederic feels powerless at the hands of the hostility of the universe after the death of Catherine and his infant son, or even *A Moveable Feast*, in which Hemingway

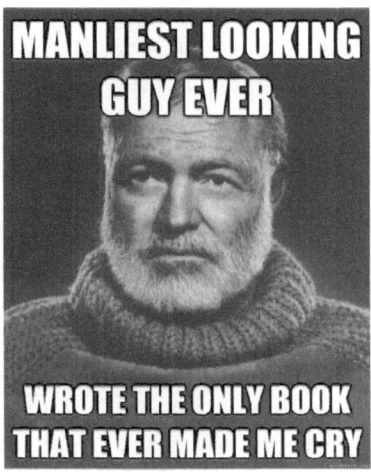

Fig. 12. A humorous meme built around Yousuf Karsh's famous 1957 portrait of Hemingway plays to the masculine sentimentality of his prose. (Author's collection)

regrets committing adultery and ruining his first marriage, to Hadley Richardson ("I *wished I had died* before I ever loved anyone but her" [210]). In these and other instances, Hemingway is not repressing emotion as his macho reputation would have us believe a swaggering male writer must. Rather, he indulges in a certain powerful types of emotion—specifically, poignancy and/or nostalgia. In other words, Hemingway's ability to make a reader tear up as this meme humorously claims is rooted in what Allen Tate in his 1926 *Nation* review of *The Sun Also Rises* identified as the core incongruity of his fiction: "It is not that Mr. Hemingway is . . . hard-boiled; it is that he is not hard-boiled enough." Instead, Tate accused Hemingway of appealing to an emotion that "betrays the inner-machinery of his hard-boiled attitude": sentimentality (94–95). As I explain to classes, sentimentality was verboten in modernism because emotional responses to art were considered crass, populist, and superficial, unlike the intellectual grappling with depth that irony and depersonalized imagery supposedly prompted. It was also redolent of the floridness associated with Victorians. Of course, gender stereotypes also tainted perceptions of emotion, with sentimentality dismissed as feminine and objectivity celebrated as masculine. As Tate's review suggests, though, few male modernists completely eschewed feelings—they simply prompted *certain types* of them, mostly involving a sense of loss and disempowerment. In discussing this reality with classes,

I like to make the point with a quote from Henry Miller: "I've always felt this about the hard-boiled writer...: Underneath they are tender as babies, they're all lambs; this is all compensation for their extra-tender qualities. All tough men I know are like this" (70). The meme thus offers a tool for dismantling the idea of manly reticence as a repression of emotion to recognize the very real feelings motivating that tight-lipped exterior. The conversation in turn allows students to recognize how simplistic cultural definitions of both Hemingway and masculinity are and to rehabilitate sentimentality from the limiting idea that its expression involves excessive or verbose demonstrations of feeling. In many cases, the meme relaxes students' resistance to exploring their own emotional responses to Hemingway, whether positive or negative, and to appreciate how all writing styles—even hard-boiled ones—provoke reader feelings.

The length and depth I go into here might seem to suggest that I teach classes on memes rather than literature. I feel confident I spend just as much time on theme and technique as the old-guard instructors who remain convinced that the only technology they need in the classroom is a piece of chalk. I won't claim that all of my students are impressed or even care about my efforts to demonstrate how literature lives outside the classroom, but I do find the majority appreciate seeing canonical literature reinvented by the platforms of their everyday experience. Memes may not seem as ambitious an artistic undertaking as a Hollywood movie about Hemingway, or even an amateur YouTube video of the type high school teachers seem to assign to technologically savvy students these days. Yet as "units of cultural transmission," as Dawkins defines them, memes do illustrate in more commonplace or even mundane ways literary authority and status circulate in the real world. Maybe even more than graffiti or body art, memes are the ultimate populist form of expression: anyone with internet access can make one and circulate it, and no one need claim authorship if he or she chooses not to. Whether inspirational or humorous, their ability to replicate in the culture makes them their own type of moveable feast. Only time will tell if there is ever any end to them, but for this moment they offer an intriguing mode of social communication, and most make Hemingway photos and quotes look damned good and professional—

Even in PowerPoint.

Notes

1. As easy as filmstrips are to mock, it is useful to remember that they, too, were once considered cutting-edge technology that could deliver pedagogical benefits. See, for example, the 1952 article by Lottick, who recommends them for their affordability

and creativity, encouraging teachers to create their own soundtracks. The author's final words suggest the downsides of technology in the classroom have not changed much in seventy years: "Let's use A-V in teaching, but let's not allow the procedure to become the 'Big Top.' A-V can only be, at best, a circus wagon or a motor truck for use in 'setting the stage.' Then it is that learning begins—not before" (327).

2. I note as well that I have taught online since 1996, long before platforms such as Blackboard or Canvas were available. In the early years, when we simply uploaded files onto a university server, PowerPoint was essential for creating professional-looking lecture files with a modicum of visual appeal, as opposed to providing students simple MSWord files with only text blocks and white space. For a good discussion of why we should not avoid this technology just because it seems like the George Babbitt of presentation tools, see Gallo.

3. The story of Hemingway and his Tommy gun has become a legendary chapter of his biography, most entertainingly narrated in Dos Passos's memoir, *The Best Times* (1966), where "the Old Master," as Dos Passos derisively dubs Hemingway, hatches various attempts to finagle the submachine gun in Bimini in May 1935 from its original owner, the millionaire yachtsman Bill Leeds Jr. (234). Shortly after doing so, Hemingway strafed sharks attacking a thousand-pound black marlin hooked by his friend Mike Strater, exciting a feeding frenzy that whittled what should have been Strater's prize catch down to a veritable toothpick. Hemingway wrote about the incident in his July 1935 *Esquire* article, "The President Vanquishes," omitting his responsibility for the attack. Strater was already annoyed that the grandstanding Hemingway had pushed himself to the center of photographs taken when the marlin was brought ashore and hoisted on hooks; the article's flagrant fiction so irritated him the incident effectively ended the pair's friendship. See Hendrickson 299.

4. The website is www.knowyourmeme.com. *The New York Times* recently documented how it tracks the life and death of memes. See Bromwich.

5. I use these terms interchangeably, recognizing their differences: a maxim is typically a moral principle, an epigram a witty saying, and a proverb a religious/spiritual wisdom. In practice, these and comparable terms like *aphorism* tend to be obscured by their common purpose, which is to assert a so-called timeless truth.

6. In meme form, for example, an assertion such as "The fun of talk is to explore" attains gravitas. No longer is it the first half of a complex sentence that actually qualifies the value of extemporaneous chatter ("but much of it and all that is irresponsible should not be written," reads the second half of the passage). No longer is it a defensive 1958 dismissal to *The Paris Review* of an offhand claim made four years earlier in an p interview with George Plimpton that "imagination could be the result of inherited racial experience," a belief that Hemingway now attributes to the aftereffects of the concussions suffered in 1953 when he survived two airplane crashes in two consecutive days (*Conversations* 115). Decontextualizing the declaration enhances its assertiveness: it becomes a statement of principle.

7. The Hemingway misattribution O'Toole is centrally concerned with in his book is the infamous "For sale: baby shoes, never worn" six-word short story that is erroneously credited to the writer. O'Toole traces the origins of this tragic plot back as far as 1906

(186) and demonstrates how it became associated with Hemingway largely thanks to sci-fi writer Arthur C. Clarke, who wrote an essay commending the pure brevity of the anecdote included in his 1999 collection *Greetings, Carbon-Based Bipeds!* (188, see Clarke 354).

8. The definitive study showing that Hemingway rarely ever employed the iceberg theory in practice is investigation of several manuscripts, including "Big Two-Hearted River" and "Out of Season" ("Hemingway's Early Manuscripts"). The essay was one of the first to make use of the newly accessible drafts and discards made available to scholars by the opening of the Hemingway Collection at the John F. Kennedy Presidential Library and Museum in Boston in 1980.

Hemingway for Digiphiles

How to Not Read Hemingway

Brian Croxall

> What we really need is a little pact with the devil: we know how to read texts, now let's learn how *not* to read them.
> —Franco Moretti

Like almost all writers, Ernest Hemingway very much wanted to be read. When *The Old Man and the Sea* was published, for example, he "read all the reviews his clipping service sent him [and] commented to friends on some of them" (Reynolds, *Final Years* 259). His keen interest in following the critical fortunes of *The Old Man* was perhaps predictable, given that his previous novel, *Across the River and into the Trees,* had earned scathing reviews. Although sales figures had suggested people *were* reading *Across the River*—or at least putting it on their shelves—Hemingway believed those who had written about the novel in public forums were misreading it, missing the point, or both. In *Hemingway: The Final Years,* Michael Reynolds suggests that it was Hemingway's desire to be read astutely that led him to cultivate relationships with scholars like Carlos Baker, Charles Fenton, and Philip Young (240). Hemingway "needed intelligent response," he told Baker in letters, despite being "always embarrassed" by this same need (Reynolds, *Final Years* 240). But if Hemingway was keen to know that he *was* being read—and read carefully—and therefore corresponded with researchers, it is also clear that he also disliked *how* these scholars read his work. His irritation with their insistence on analyzing his work becomes plain in letters to friends who, while editors or critics, were decidedly not researchers. For example, writing to Harvey Breit on 23 July 1956, Hemingway clearly articulates his complaint with literary scholars: "But all these guys have theories and try to fit you into the theory" (*Selected Letters* 867). This was not an isolated comment; four years previously, in a 21 February 1952 letter to Wallace Meyer, Hemingway was already describing the criticism of scholars like Young or Arthur Mizener as "getting all mixed up with a combination of the Junior F.B.I.-men, discards from Freud and Jung and a sort of Columnist peep-hole and missing laundry list school" (751).

On the one hand, Hemingway appears to have been seeking private assurances, delivered by scholars via letters, that his work was being read and that particular symbols and structural innovations were being noticed. On the other hand, he was perpetually exasperated with the literary analysis that Baker, Fenton, and Young produced, telling the last's editor, Thomas Bledsoe, in a 9 December 1951 letter that understanding his work "is not as simple as" Young's book made it out to be (745). What accounts for the differential in these two contradictory responses to the same group of scholars? I suspect it has to do with the key word, twice repeated, in his letter to Breit: *theory*. A scholar's theory was, as Hemingway put it, something that an author would be "fit" to, much like a guest to the Procrustean bed. Applying a theory—or an algorithm, if you will—to one of his novels emptied it of its multiple meanings, which were brought about by the rich ambiguity of language that persisted both in spite and because of his style and diction. While a scholar was in fact a good reader, theory turned him or her into a reductive one. What's more, a scholar's theory demeaned the hard work required to produce writing in the first place since it suggested, in essence, that all writing proceeded from source A ("the wound," in the case of Young) or muse B (his time on the newspaper in Kansas, in the case of Fenton). Thus, when Carl P. Eby notes that Hemingway "despised all theories about his work," we can trace the affective response, once again, to the concept of *theory* and its alchemical power to explain "it all" by radically overlooking nuance (1).[1] Theories are, too much of the time, answers simply looking for confirmations.

Happily, given Hemingway's cathected response to such "Junior F.B.I." tactics, I am pleased to report that I do not have a theory. Instead, I have begun to wonder about new methods for reading his work. Such a statement is not idle wordplay, where I am simply substituting "method" for "theory." Rather, I am increasingly cognizant of the fact that almost sixty years since Hemingway's death, we live in a very different reading ecology than he could have ever imagined. I am as likely to read *The Sun Also Rises* on my iPad as

I am to turn through the pages of the print copy on my shelf. I read 99 percent of the news I encounter on the screen of a phone which, amazingly, has a permanent connection to satellites in space and therefore keeps me up to date on the weather in Key West, the bulls in Spain, and the price of tinned mackerel in France. When I assign my students Hemingway's short stories, they inevitably download the texts from the university library and read them as PDFs on screens, the size and shape of which vary widely. Reading, it turns out, ain't what it used to be.

Given this transition to a digital age, how can our experience of reading Hemingway change? What new questions could we ask about his work when it makes the leap from the printed page to the malleable world of the digital? In what ways do ninety-year-old stories about fishing, bullfighting, war, and eating and drinking both submit to and resist the digital? Since 2014, I have been trying to investigate with my students how we have tended to read Hemingway and how we could read him differently today.

Despite my classes' focus on method (the *how* of reading) and our avoidance of any one particular theory, I'm still not convinced that Papa would like what I'm going to share. And that's because the central question my students and I have been exploring is what we can learn by *not* reading Hemingway. What do I mean by this? What does "not" reading look like? That is exactly what my students wonder when I introduce this project in my digital humanities courses.[2] Digital humanities, as I explain it, is the use of computational methods to find patterns in texts, followed by the interpretation of those patterns.[3] Humans are, of course, very good at finding patterns; computers cannot easily find many of the patterns humans can, like allusion or metaphor, but they excel at recognizing other forms that humans are ill equipped to tackle, such as the frequency of a particular word in a novel. What's more, computers can "read" much faster than humans, provided the texts are formatted properly. I place *read* in scare quotes since computers do not read the same way as humans. They do not know what different words or phrases *mean*. Instead, they are like the Tralfamadorians in Kurt Vonnegut's *Slaughterhouse-Five* (1969), able to see all of the words in all of their books at once, having perfect recall. More recently and in our own universe, digital humanists such as Franco Moretti have described the sort of "not reading" that computers make possible as "distant reading." Distant reading, Moretti argues, "is a condition of knowledge: it allows you to focus on units that are much smaller or much larger than the text: devices, themes, tropes—or genres and systems" (*Distant Reading* 48–49). In short, a computer can read all of Hemingway in the blink of a byte and allows my students and me to look for different patterns than a traditional, close reading approach would enable. Again, I do not think this approach would excite Hemingway, but what does prove thrilling is the sense of adventure that my students bring to a textual encounter that has been loosed from its normal bounds thanks to the digital age. What's more, their unfettered access to *all* of Hemingway—a number of pages we would be unable to read even in a whole semester—has led to them asking new questions, a marked departure from the theories or readymade answers he so despised. So while Hemingway probably wouldn't love us "not reading" his work, I think he would appreciate our emphasis on curious questions and the fact that my students have reached genuinely new insights through this method.

Reading before Not Reading

Although my project is playfully titled "How to *Not* Read Hemingway," I think it critical for my students to begin, in fact, by reading some Hemingway. While many of them have encountered a short story here or there, reading a selection of texts (re)acquaints them with Hemingway's style and some of his recurring themes. To this end, I plan three days of reading that draw from *The Complete Short Stories*. The first day features what could easily be termed "classic" Hemingway: "Big Two-Hearted River, Part I," "Big Two-Hearted River, Part II," "Now I Lay Me," and "Hills Like White Elephants." These stories provide an opportunity to discuss the iceberg aesthetic and how it manifests itself in Hemingway's prose. They also introduce Nick Adams and several of Hemingway's frequent themes: war, the outdoors, and strained relationships, whether romantic or familial.

The second day includes what I playfully refer to as "weird" Hemingway. By "weird," I mean stories that do not necessarily accord with themes that the general public would consider typical of "classic" Hemingway. The texts I have chosen for this day include, variously, "The Sea Change," "Mr. and Mrs. Elliot," "A Simple Enquiry," "Cat in the Rain," and "God Rest You Merry, Gentlemen." Hemingway scholars will, of course, identify shared motifs among these stories and those mentioned above: failed and failing relationships, characters who are authors, religious allusions, and settings that are both exotic (Paris) and mundane (the Midwest and Plains in the United States). What students see, however, are stories that foreground non-heteronormative gender roles and performances as well as a fairly disturbing hospital emergency room. For those who think of Hemingway as the domineering, manly man of the Michigan wilderness, the Floridian boxing ring, or the European battlefront, these small dramas that explore sexuality and misplaced religious fervor open new vistas for understanding the range of his concerns.[4]

If the first two days of reading allow me to give my digital humanities students a guided tour of two of Hemingway's sides, the third day points to where the class is headed with the assignment. While reminding them that the purpose of our reading *some* Hemingway is to understand his style and themes, I ask them to consider that the seven or so stories we have read out of the 650 pages of *The Complete Short Stories* might not be representative. After all, we have read fewer than 40 pages of Hemingway's stories, or approximately 5 percent of the total. What's more, everything that we have considered to this point was subject to my selection biases. To avoid these further influencing us, I propose that we read a random sample of the remaining stories. There would be many ways to produce such a sample, but I present the class with a simple online poll that lists the titles of all the texts we have not read. Students vote for up to four stories, and we read those that get the most votes. They should base their selections, I tell them, solely on which titles appeal to them or make them curious. Unsurprisingly, the most popular choice always ends up being "A Very Short Story." (Students, it turns out, are quite rational.) In addition to this story, one year we read "The Butterfly and the Tank," "Black Ass at the Cross Roads," "The Doctor and the Doctor's Wife," and "Summer People." Another year, the students also chose "The Snows of Kilimanjaro" and "The Doctor and the Doctor's Wife." Most recently, the students added "The End of Something" and "The Killers."

In the end, my students and I spend three class periods discussing ten stories as students in a literature class would normally do: with a focus on close reading. From their encounter with *The Complete Short Stories*, they already know that there's simply too much Hemingway to read, especially in the three weeks that I dedicate to the project. Their knowledge about the impossibility of reading all of Hemingway is made more certain when I bring his other fifteen books to class. At that point, we are ready to "*not* read" the rest of his oeuvre.

Turning Pages into Files

When I ask my students to "not read Hemingway," what I am actually asking is for them to engage with a different method of reading, one made possible by computers. A distant reading approach allows one to consider an author's works at an entirely different scale and to see patterns that might not be so obvious when reading in a conventional manner. What's more, this form of "reading" is exponentially faster, given the differences between the way computers and humans process text. But for all their speed, computers encounter a serious problem when you ask them to read all of Hemingway: they can't turn the pages. More to the point, the codex and the print on its pages is not in a form that is ready for digital processing. The first task for my students and me, then, becomes preparing digital copies of Hemingway's works.

Digital editions of some authors' texts are easy to come by. Anyone can download all of Shakespeare or Jane Austen from Project Gutenberg with no trouble. Each edition of Walt Whitman's poetry has been carefully prepared in electronic form by scholars at the Universities of Iowa and Nebraska–Lincoln. Similar repositories exist for the works of William Blake, Dante Gabriel Rossetti, and others. Hemingway, however, is not so readily available, since all of his works remain under copyright.[5] Without preexisting digital editions, my students and I have to digitize everything he wrote. Luckily for us, however, this is not nearly as difficult as it sounds. As mentioned, I bring copies of all of Hemingway's books to class, each of which I purchase specifically for this assignment. These in hand, my students and I set off for the library's preservation department.

Contrary to what someone might expect, university libraries almost always have a book guillotine. These devices are not used for dispatching banned books—or students with late fines who attempt to graduate—but instead for removing the spines of books prior to their receiving a new binding. In less than ten minutes, we go from having fifteen books—nine novels, five nonfiction volumes, and one very large collection of short stories—to several thousand loose pages, which we quickly secure with binder clips. Each student receives approximately two hundred pages of text for which he or she is responsible. As a participant, I get my own stack of pages.

For the next stage of the assignment, each individual turns his or her pages into a usable digital format. Accomplishing this requires two steps. First, we scan our pages and turn them into PDFs. Second, we convert the scanned pages into machine-readable text. The first step is surprisingly simple. We have access to the large business copiers found in many university libraries. These include a document feeder and the capability to scan both sides of a page and email the results. In less than five minutes each, we convert all of our pages into PDFs. Of course, if you want a computer to help you read, a PDF is not much better than a printed page. It is true that the former is a digital file, and therefore a computer can open it in a way that it cannot open a print codex. But as far as a computer is concerned, the PDFs we create are just inscrutable images with light and dark areas. The second step, then, is to transform the page images into something the computer can, in fact, "read." To do this, my students and I use optical character recognition (OCR) software, which "looks" at a page covered in letters and does its best to determine what each of those letters are. Several commercial OCR products exist, and after testing a number of them, I chose Prizmo (creaceed.com/prizmo), which produced excellent results while also being affordable and having a simple interface.

After scanning our pages, we open the PDFs in Prizmo. With a few clicks, we set the OCR engine to work on each of our pages. The results are presented in a side-by-side view that features the original page image on the left and the extracted text on the right (Fig. 1). The latter is editable, so we can compare the extracted text to the original scan and make corrections as needed. Prizmo also marks, with red underlines, words that it does not recognize. With these highlights, it is easy to find most of the problems. We could also quickly remove entire regions of the pages, such as chapter titles or page headings.

Although most of the text is correctly recognized, creating a perfect corpus of Hemingway's books would require checking every word. That sort of brute force endeavor was outside the scope of what I wanted my students to learn, either about Hemingway or digital humanities. Instead, I asked them to do only three things for each page. First, they have Prizmo skip any page regions that

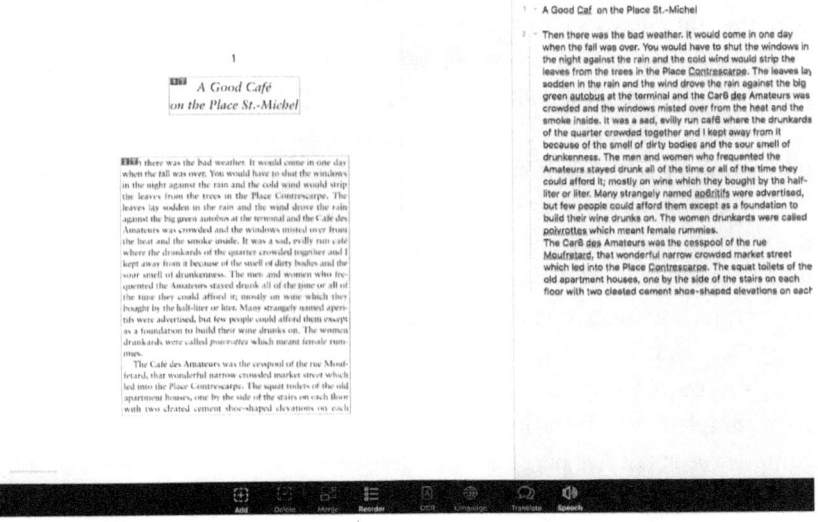

Fig. 1. The Prizmo interface.

are not the body of the text. Second, they correct any words that Prizmo had marked with a red underline as misspelled; for example, they would change *ap6ritifs* to *apéritifs* (see Fig. 1). Students have to be careful, however, as these underlined words are sometimes spelled correctly and instead fall outside Prizmo's dictionary. This happens most often with character and place names or words from other languages, as with *Contrescarpe* or *poivrettes* in Fig. 1. In these cases, the students can add the words to Prizmo's dictionary and avoid having to check them in the future. Third, they quickly cast their eyes over the text for any random characters that stand out. In Fig. 1, for example, a student will hopefully notice the (non)word *Car6* at the beginning of the second paragraph, despite its not being underlined, and fix it to the appropriate *Café*. Once they complete these three tasks for one page, they move on to the next. After completing all of their pages, they send me their extracted pages in plain text, which I compile into their individual volumes.[6] At last, we have something the computer can manipulate.

While this process does not produce a perfect transcription of Hemingway's books, it creates a *good enough* transcription. Good enough to work from, with, hopefully, a minimum of effort. And to make sure that the students believed that I really meant it when I said they did not need to check every single word, I asked them to spend no more than four hours scanning and OCRing their pages. Since this was a lablike experience, I canceled two classes, accounting for two and a half of the hours I had asked them to work on the project. During these class periods and at other times, I made myself available to consult with the students as we worked through our pages.

Over the years, I have learned that it is normal for new assignments to present unexpected difficulties; with a project that has as many moving parts as this one, I was not at all surprised to find that everything was more complicated in its first iteration than I could have imagined (Croxall, "Tired of Tech"). Problems arose during both the scanning and the OCRing stages of the process. These ranged from students simply forgetting to scan both sides of the page to the fact that we actually had to lower the quality of the scans to prevent Prizmo mistaking the grain of the page for commas, apostrophes, and stray diacritics. We were able to catch and correct many of these issues while the project was underway, but some only surfaced after a student's four hours were complete. When my first class finished the project, in 2014, we only had complete scans of five texts. We had accomplished significant work on all of the remaining fiction: sometimes only a handful of pages were missing. But in fewer than 80 person-hours, twenty students and I had created a "good enough" corpus that allowed us to do some text analysis.

A year later when I did the assignment again, I was able to set the students and myself up for much more success, thanks to the lessons I had learned the first time around. That second year, my goal was to get all of Hemingway's nonfiction digitized. Additionally, I surveyed the fiction that had not been finished and incorporated those pages into what I distributed to the students. This time, I was able to help the students avoid most of the problems in digitization, which meant that at the end of another 80 person-hours our corpus was almost complete, although, for a number of reasons, we were still missing *For Whom the Bell Tolls*. When I returned to the assignment most recently, in 2017, my students and I tackled the remaining pages and fixed some additional holes. At this point, I am confident that our corpus is as "good enough" as it can get. Granted, 240 person-hours is a considerable span of time, amounting to a month and a half's output for a single individual. But what we learned about both digitization and the sheer size of Hemingway's output could not have been achieved by any other means.

Asking Questions without Reading

Having read some Hemingway and having done the work necessary for our computers to read all of Hemingway, my students and I are ready to move on to the second half of the project. This half, of course, involves us *not (close) reading* Hemingway; instead, we rely on the computer to help us ask questions about Hemingway's work as a whole.[7] Such distant reading, hopefully, brings to the surface patterns for interpretation. Any number of different tools and methods can be used to perform computational text analysis, but I need something both simple enough for my students to use and flexible enough to provide them with the means to chase their specific questions.

The right tool, in this case, in Voyant (available online at voyant-tools.org), a suite of web-based text analysis interfaces developed by Stéfan Sinclair and Geoffrey Rockwell of McGill University and University of Alberta, respectively. That Voyant is freely available on the Internet means that it is accessible to students whether they are working on their personal laptops or on a computer in the lab; my students did not, in other words, have to install a text analysis package. Moreover, Voyant provides a simple, graphical user interface (GUI) rather than requiring students to interact with the command line, as many text analysis packages do. With only a fifteen-minute demonstration, I can get my students using the tools and returning their focus to Hemingway. While Voyant's ease of use is helpful for this project, its flexibility proves far more important. Writing in their book *Hermeneutica: Computer-Assisted Interpretation in the Humanities,* Rockwell and Sinclair indicate that they "tried to make Voyant a tool worth thinking *with*" (10). Voyant should, they claim, "augment reading rather than replace it" and make possible "interpretive reflections assisted by tools" (Rockwell and Sinclair 17, 12). One of the keys to Voyant's flexibility is the large number of interactive interfaces—more than two dozen of them—it provides my students.[8] These tools range from simple statistics (*Summary*), like counts of words in a corpus; to word clouds (*Cirrus*), which visualize the most frequent terms in a text, with the term's size determined by its frequency in the corpus; to graphs (*Trends*) that plot the frequencies of terms across either intervals of one text or the different works in a corpus (see

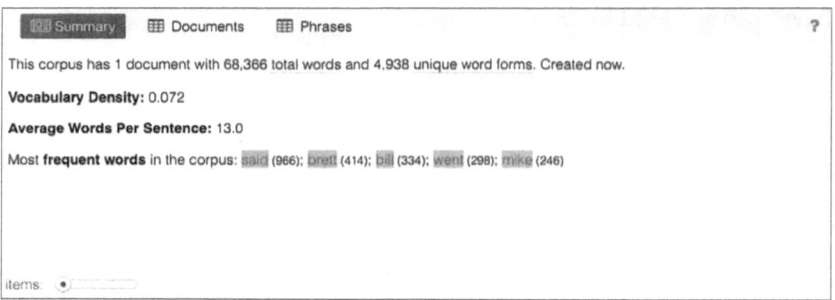

Fig. 2. Voyant's Summary tool for *The Sun Also Rises*.

Fig. 3. A word cloud of the most common terms in *The Sun Also Rises,* with stop words removed. (In this visualization, I have used Voyant's standard English stop-words list, plus the word *said.*)

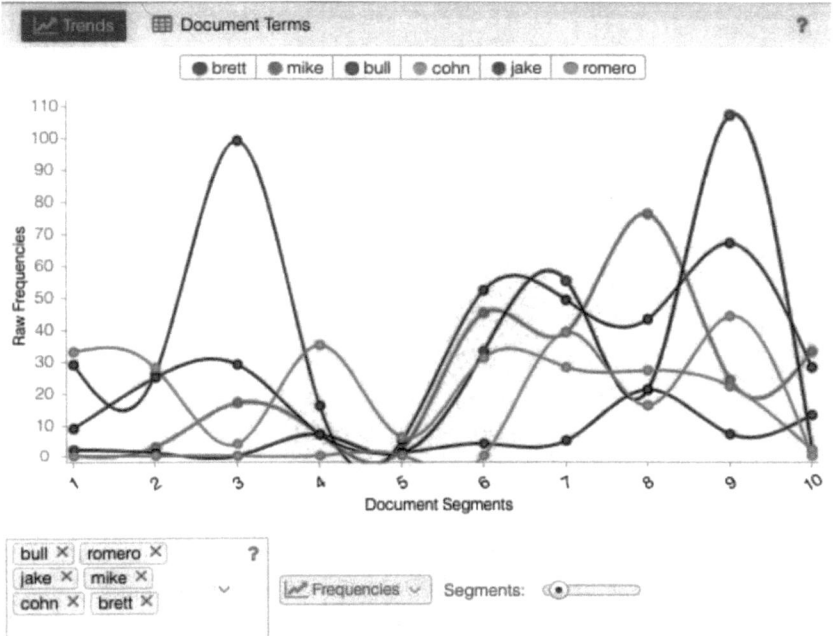

Fig. 4. Voyant's Trends tool for *The Sun Also Rises*, which has been segmented into ten equal portions. The chart displays the raw frequencies (i.e., the total counts) for the terms *brett, bull, cohn, jake, mike,* and *romero* in each of those segments. (Voyant ignores the case of the word when searching.)

Figs. 2–4). Rockwell and Sinclair call the different interfaces *toys* because the term "rhetorically ... invites playing around with the text by means other than reading" (17). This deliberate playfulness is precisely what I want to encourage as my students encounter all of Hemingway.

I take a number of steps to further encourage the playfulness of this portion of the project. First, I instruct students to work in groups of four or five. Collaborating with peers provides opportunities to brainstorm questions to explore in the corpus while simultaneously providing companions who are also learning Voyant's interface. As groups huddle in different sections of the room, it is clear that they are exploring both the texts *and* the tool, as various students take turns pulling everyone over to look at their screens and see what they had found. Second, I compress the "not reading" into a fixed amount of time: the final exam. In the weeks leading up to the final, we create our library of digitized Hemingway, but we do no analysis whatsoever until the beginning of the exam. As a result, the groups have only 2.5 hours to play, find patterns,

Fig. 5. The default view of Voyant—including the tools Cirrus, Reader, Trends, Summary, and Contexts—after loading the short stories and novels.

and, crucially, write up short interpretations of what they find. I emphasize that the compressed time for "not reading" Hemingway is intended not to stress them out but instead to provide clear bounds to an experimental process. Third, I underscore my commitment to play by providing clear guidelines for how their work will be graded. They are not assessed on what their group learns about Hemingway's work, since, after all, I do not know what they should find. Instead, they are graded on whether they accomplished all the parts of the assignment and how engaged they are with the work. In short, they are rewarded for asking interesting questions and not on their abilities to get answers.

Assigned to their groups, the students load all of Hemingway into Voyant (see Fig. 5) and began to play, thinking about what questions they might ask while not reading. Again, the reading the students have done help them have a sense of Hemingway's themes, diction, and style, with the result that they can investigate the extent to which such usage persists across the rest of his corpus or across divides such as fiction/nonfiction or texts published while he was alive or posthumously.

Finding Answers without Reading

Equipped with our digital files, Voyant, and two and a half hours, my students can finally start investigating everything they'd ever wanted to know about Hemingway but had been unable to ask. In many cases, their initial questions grow out of the short stories that they have read. For example, having read

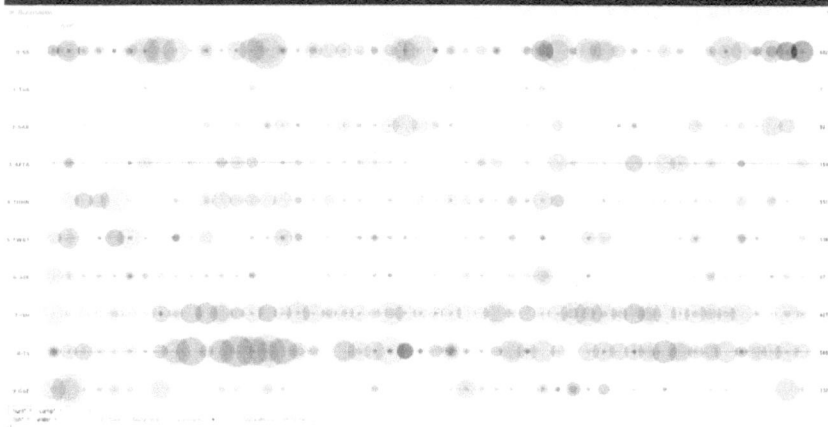

Fig. 6. Voyant's Bubblelines tool displaying the terms *fish**, *water*, *camp**, and *hunt** in the short stories and novels.

"Big Two-Hearted River" and "Now I Lay Me," more than one group have suspected that outdoor activities would continue to occupy a significant portion of Hemingway's output. Using a Voyant tool called Bubblelines, the students easily visualized where words like *fish**, *camp**, *hunt**, and *water* appeared across all of his fiction.[9] Bubblelines segments each text into fifty equal parts and represents the text along a line. If a term appears in a particular segment, the tool creates a bubble at the appropriate place in the line; the more often the term appears within the segment, the larger the bubble grows. The number at the end of the line shows how many total hits for all terms appear in that one text.

With a quick glance, the students could see how frequently Hemingway's characters were engaged in hunting, fishing, and camping. They were not surprised that *The Old Man and the Sea* emphasized fishing and water, as many of them had basic knowledge about the plot of that book. But this visualization helped them see that *Islands in the Stream* might have some similarities. A more important discovery, however, was that so many of the novels simply did not include outdoor activities to the same degree that their small sample of stories had led them to believe. There was a chance, of course, that Hemingway might use different terms than the ones they had searched for, and the students acknowledged that *water*, in particular, was a vexing term, insofar as it can be either a noun or a verb and might as easily refer to a beverage served in a Parisian cafe as it might to Nick standing in a river. Nonetheless, Bubblelines

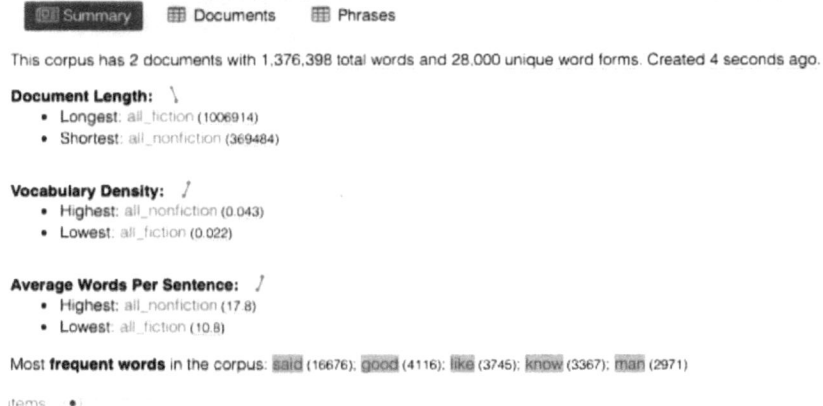

Fig. 7. Voyant's Summary tool of the "all_fiction" and "all_nonfiction" corpora.

provided a reminder that the students had *not* read Hemingway and that their sense of his preoccupations might be incorrect.

Other students, cognizant of a major divide in Hemingway's prose—fiction vs. nonfiction—turned their attention to Voyant's Summary tool to look at overarching differences. As these divisions interest me as well, I had already prepared blocks of the texts to make them easier to investigate. Given that our corpus contained ten texts of Hemingway's fiction and only five of his nonfiction (*Death in the Afternoon* [1932], *Green Hills of Africa* [1935], *A Moveable Feast* [1964], *The Dangerous Summer* [1985], and *True at First Light* [1999]), the students were not surprised to see that the fiction corpus was considerably larger: 1,006,914 words compared to 369,484 words (see Fig. 7).[10] But two other measures from Summary proved more unexpected: while there was simply less of the nonfiction, it had both a higher vocabulary density and longer average sentences. Vocabulary density is a measure of how many unique word forms there are in a corpus (e.g., *truth* and *truths* are different word forms) divided by how many total words appear in the corpus. Hemingway's nonfiction has 15,879 unique word forms and his fiction has 22,611. Although the fiction has a greater number of different word forms, when it is divided by the number of total words in the novels and short stories, the vocabulary density is measured at 0.022; the density of the nonfiction, however, is 0.043.[11] Since the same person authored both the fiction and the nonfiction, what could account for Hemingway's introducing new words into his nonfiction at almost twice the rate that he does in his fiction? We hypothesized that the subjects of his nonfiction books—two about bullfighting, two about safaris in Africa, and one about Paris in the 1920s—would lead to his using specific vocabulary as a way of simultaneously being accurate and, more importantly, showing his expertise in these areas. Flipping through the sundered pages of *Death in the Afternoon* corroborates this, as it includes an explanatory glossary so readers can easily refresh their memories of bullfighting terminology. Importantly, however, we had chosen to *not* scan the glossary, as it did not seem part of the text proper. While one may argue with my choice here, it does means that higher vocabulary density of the nonfiction is not attributable to the presence of objects like the glossaries or image captions. My students also conjectured that Hemingway's fiction might use less unique word forms as a hallmark of his sparse aesthetic. Hemingway's style depended on his reusing simple words, as we had seen in his "classic" stories.

During our discussion of these stories, the students had also remarked on the brevity of many of Hemingway's sentences, such as in "Big Two-Hearted River: Part I": "He had not been unhappy all day. This was different though. Now things were done. There had been this to do. Now it was done. It had been a hard trip" (*Collected Short Stories* 167). Accordingly, they were not surprised to discover that his fiction averaged short sentences: 10.8 words per sentence. Without having read his nonfiction, they did not have specific expectations for how the sentences in those volumes might differ from the rest of his work. But with an average length of 17.8 words per sentence, the average nonfiction sentence was 64.8 percent longer than that in the fiction. My students conjectured that if we actually *did* read all of Hemingway we would observe clear stylistic differences between the fiction and the nonfiction—both in the words he used and in the shape of his sentences.

Voyant's Summary also allowed students to explore another critical division in Hemingway's books: those published while he was alive and those published posthumously (see Fig. 8). Less familiar with Hemingway's life, the students were a little surprised to see that more of his nonfiction—as measured by total number of words—had been published posthumously than when he was alive. They also observed that while the average length of Hemingway's "living" sentences (for lack of a better term) in his fiction was 10.5 words per sentence, his posthumous fiction sentences averaged 11.8 words; meanwhile the living nonfiction sentences averaged 20.0 words and the posthumous nonfiction averaged 16.3 words per sentence. This change amounted to a 12.4 percent increase in sentence length in the posthumous fiction but a 19.5 percent decrease in sentence length in the posthumous nonfiction. The best hypothesis that the students could offer for an increase for one type of prose and a decrease for the other was that Hemingway might have had different approaches for editing and revising his fiction and his nonfiction. His process might have led him to more frequently trim sentences in his fiction as he moved from drafts to publication, and he might have similarly expanded sentences in his nonfiction. But the Summary measure that most caught my students' attention here was the vocabulary density. Whereas the densities of the living and posthumous nonfiction remained relatively close at 0.063 and 0.055, there was a significant difference between the densities of the living fiction (0.025) and the posthumous fiction (0.046). On average, in other words, the posthumous fiction used 84 percent more word forms than the living fiction. What could account for this difference? A group of my students—Kelly Burdick, Alex Lyman, Liz Pickrell, Stephen Rackleff, and Amanda Vite—wrote, "This could be the result of different editing procedures between editing the works of a living author and the works of a dead one. It may be that the posthumous editors might not have captured the between-the-lines feel that Hemingway is known for. . . . This is obviously conjecture, but much of our takeaways from Voyant are" (Burdick et al.). As studies of the manuscripts of *Islands in the Stream* and *Garden of Eden* have made plain, considerable editing took place at Scribner's before the texts were published. But if the density of the vocabulary in these two volumes is any indication, it appears that the process produced significantly different results than when Hemingway edited his other novels. Another possibility that we considered was the chance of a "late" style, that Hemingway might have stopped being so parsimonious with his language in the manuscripts of these last two novels.[12] Neither my students nor I were

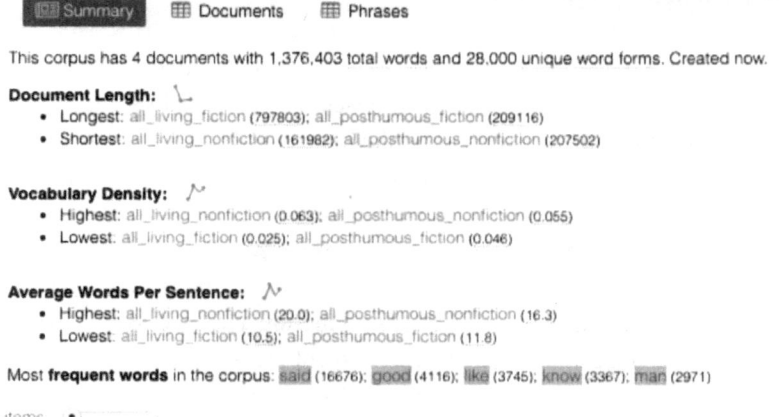

Fig. 8. Voyant's Summary tool of the "all_living_fiction," "all_living_nonfiction," "all_posthumous_fiction," and "all_posthumous_nonfiction" corpora.

in a position to determine which of these choices might be right, but Voyant provided us with insights about Hemingway's style that we would have never reached even if we *had* read everything he had written.

As Fig. 5 depicts, Summary is one of the first tools one sees after loading texts into Voyant. Another default tool is Trends, which displays the frequency of one or more words across the corpus you have loaded. If your corpus has more than one text, each point in the Trends chart will represent the frequency for the term in that particular text. If you load only a single text, Trends will divide that text into ten equal parts, similar to Bubblelines, and plot points for the frequency of the term in each of those ten segments. The segments are not meaningful; Voyant simply splits the text into ten equal-sized chunks. Upon opening a corpus, Trends will display graphs for the most frequent terms. Across the whole of Hemingway's corpus, the most frequent word—apart from the most common or "stop words" in English—is *said*.[13] As a result of seeing it so prominently displayed, a number of groups have explored this term and others related to it (see Fig. 9).

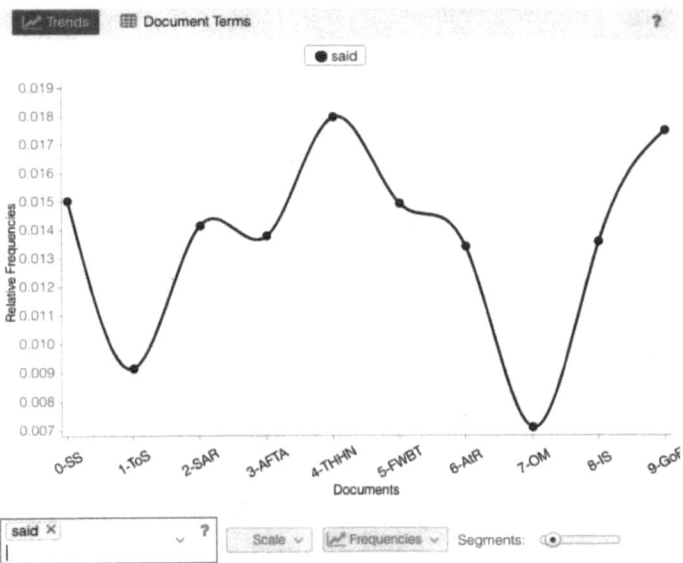

Fig. 9. Voyant's Trends tool displaying the relative frequency of *said* across the fiction corpus. This graph displays "relative frequencies" (i.e., percentages). In other words, *said* makes up 1.5 percent of the words in *The Complete Short Stories* and 0.9 percent of the words in *The Torrents of Spring*. Note that the Trends tool employs "smoothing," which accounts for the curves in the line that moves across the chart. Smoothing makes it easier for the human eye to see the patterns at play, but it is algorithmically determined. The only "real" data in this chart and the others from the Trends tool are the individual points.

Having read some short stories, the students already know that Hemingway tends to introduce dialog with the word *said*, if he uses an introductory word at all. *Said* therefore becomes a rough proxy for understanding how much dialog actually takes place in his different fiction. My students are always quick to point out that *The Old Man and the Sea* probably does not have much dialog because there are only—as far as they know, not having really read the text—an old man and the sea.

But when students start to add other terms alongside *said*, Trends becomes much more interesting. For example, students in one group wanted to see if they could explore the relationship between external speech and internal narration, so they plotted *said*, *thought*, and *think* (see Fig. 10).[14] Given which Hemingway stories they had read, my students were not terribly surprised to see that his characters did not spend much time in thought or, rather, that the narrator of the different texts did not report on the thoughts of the different characters very often. In other words, Hemingway prefers his readers to deduce a character's motivations and inner state from dialog rather than being informed by an omniscient

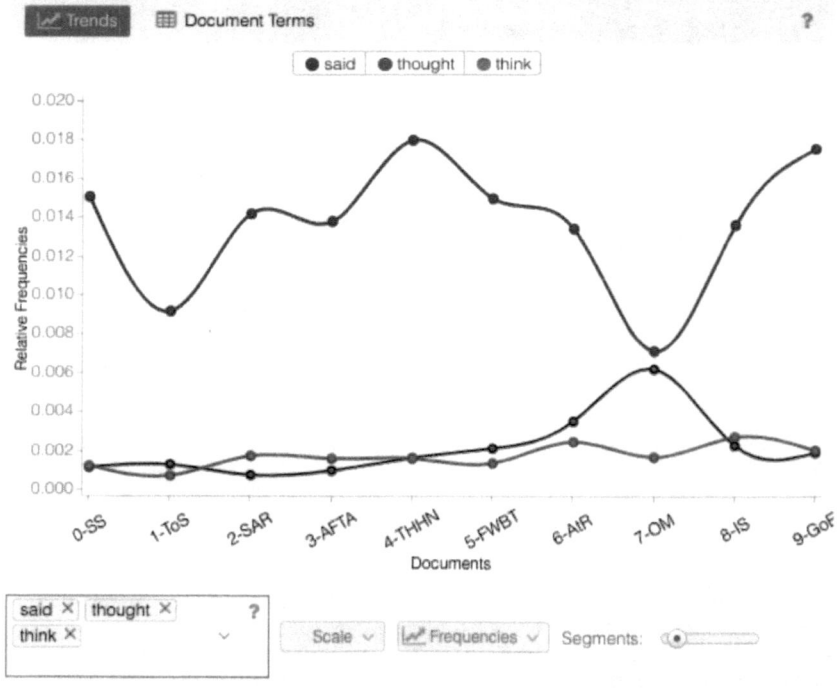

Fig. 10. Voyant's Trends tool displaying the relative frequency of *said*, *thought*, and *think* across the short stories and novels.

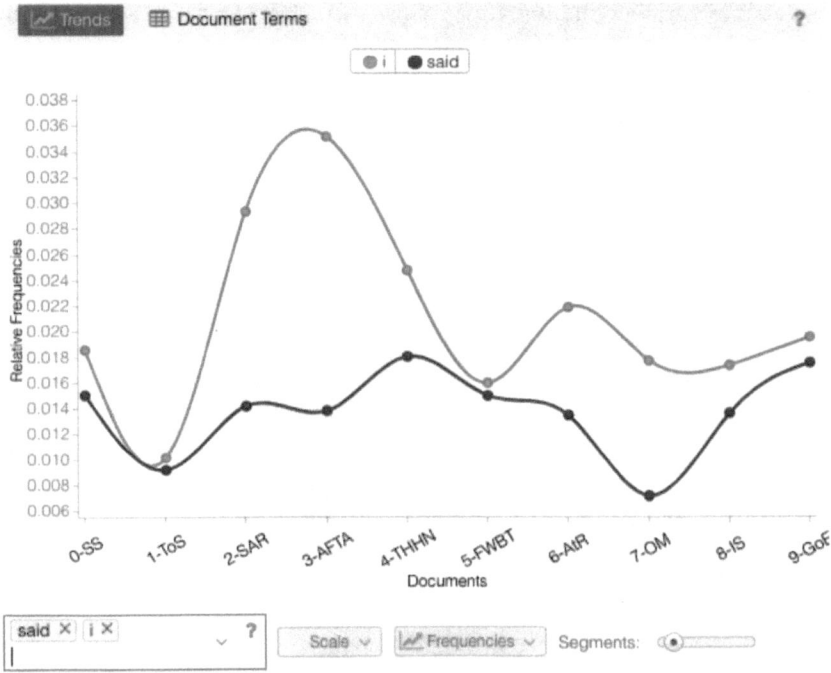

Fig. 11. Voyant's Trends tool displaying the relative frequency of *i* and *said* across the short stories and novels. For this visualization, no stop words were used.

narrator. A striking deviation from this pattern occurs in *The Old Man and the Sea*, where there is a sharp increase in *thought*. *Thought*, they hypothesized, appears much more often in this work than in his other fiction because it replaces the dialog that simply does not exist. In this case, Hemingway has no choice but provide interior monologue in order to help his readers understand Santiago.

Another group graphed *said* against the personal pronoun, *I* as an attempt at gauging which novels might use the first person (see Fig. 11). They correctly intuited that *The Sun Also Rises* and *A Farewell to Arms* would be first person, but it was more difficult to tell with *To Have and Have Not*, which is in first person, and *Across the River and into the Trees*, which is not, facts they could verify by quickly opening the files we had created from each of the novels. Hemingway scholars, of course, know that his early novels use first person, *The Torrents of Spring* notwithstanding, and that his later novels all use third person, and indeed it takes all of fifteen seconds with each of the books for a non-scholar to learn the same thing. But my students were able to observe much of this perspectival shift in Hemingway's writing without having read him.

Intrigued by their findings, this group—Shelbi Davidson, Chris Dichmann, Miles Farnsworth, Elizabeth Harper, and Clarissa Thiriot—began to explore the relationship of character names and *said* throughout the corpus of fiction. They discovered that if they loaded a single text into Voyant the most frequent terms tended to include character names. Thus, they could find main characters without reading. When they loaded *The Torrents of Spring*, for example, they quickly determined that Scripps and Yogi were two of the principal actors. What surprised them was Scripps's dominance in the first half of the novel and Yogi's rise in the second half (see Fig. 12). What's more, they observed that the transition between the two characters (at segment 6) was accompanied by one of the lowest instances of *said* throughout the text. Without reading *The Torrents of Spring*, they could not offer more than this observation, but they suggested that the middle of the book might feature an important change in the narrative. The group then tried a similar approach with *The Sun also Rises*, trying to determine who the main character—besides the first person *I* of Jake Barnes—might be (see Fig. 13). They write, "The character that closest matches

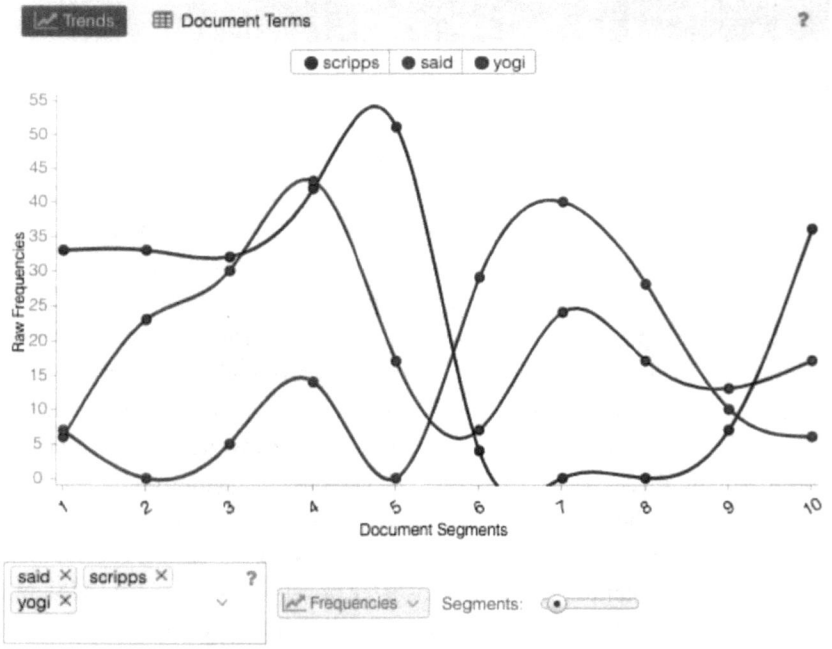

Fig. 12. Voyant's Trends tool displaying the raw frequencies of *scripps*, *yogi*, and *said* across *The Torrents of Spring*, which has been broken into ten segments.

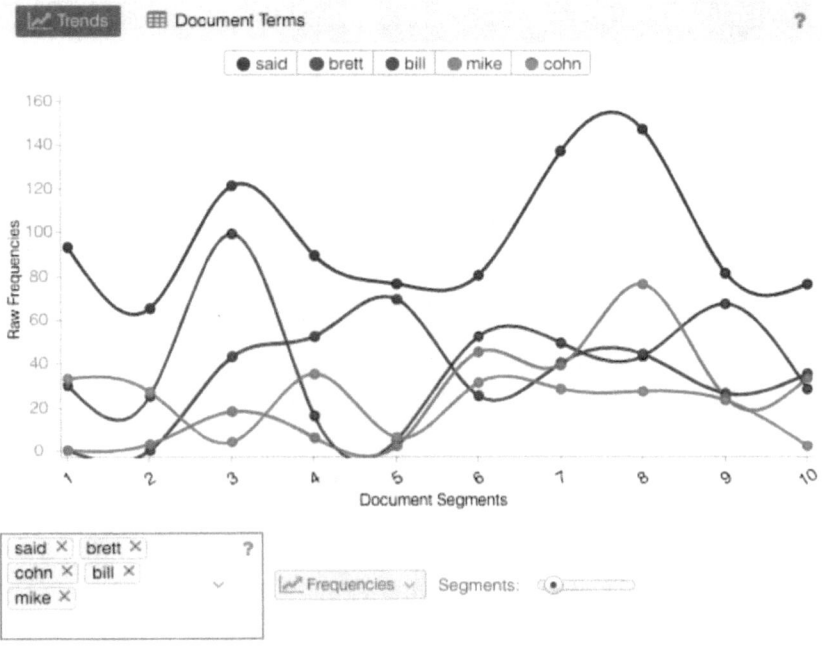

Fig. 13. Voyant's Trends tool displaying the raw frequencies of *said, brett, bill, mike,* and *cohn* across *The Sun Also Rises*, which has been broken into ten segments.

'said' is Brett, the dark green line that nearly matches [said's' rising and falling," and they conclude that she is likely the second most important character (Davidson et al.). Again, this is a conclusion one might easily reach after reading only a few pages of *The Sun Also Rises*, but without reading my students not only discovered the same thing but did so after they identified an interesting question to ask. While learning that Brett is an important character might not seem not terribly revolutionary, what really matters is that my students had the opportunity to explore the texts in a different way that encouraged them to find questions that intrigued them and that could be answered using the tools and the corpora at hand.

After moving through as many novels as they could in this manner, these students had amassed a list of Hemingway's characters. They then plotted all of the names across the whole fiction corpus (segmented fifty-one times) and made an interesting discovery. In addition to learning that Hemingway reuses particular character names, such as *Robert, David,* and *Catherine,* across several texts, they observed that two pairs of names mirrored each other very closely:

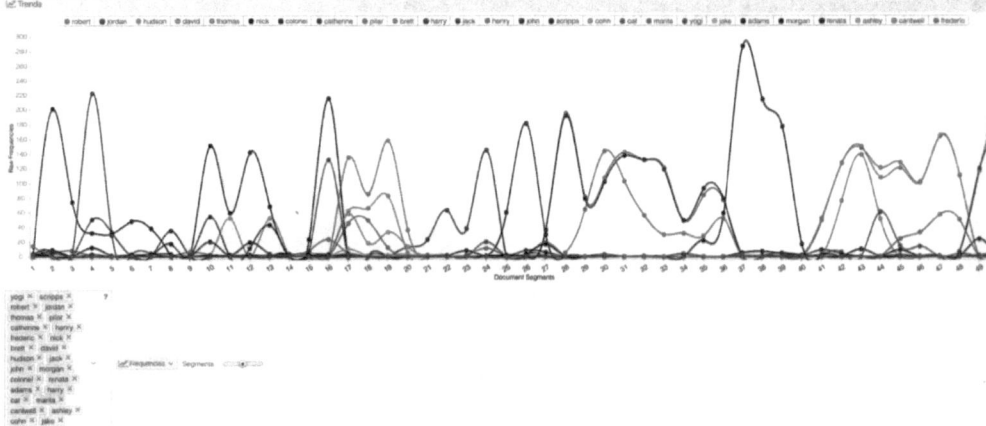

Fig. 14. Voyant's Trends tool displaying the raw frequencies of various character names across the "all_fiction" corpus, which has been broken into fifty-one segments.

Robert and *Jordan,* in one case, and *Thomas* and *Hudson* in another. (In Fig. 14, you can trace the mirrorings of *Robert* and *Jordan* from segments 28–36 and *Thomas* and *Hudson* from 41–48.) Upon turning to the texts themselves, the students naturally discovered that Robert Jordan and Thomas Hudson are the central characters of *For Whom the Bell Tolls* and *Islands in the Stream,* respectively. What their work isolated, in other words, is Hemingway's decision in these two books to use the character's name in full at almost every mention. By reading digitally and at a distance, they could identify a key stylistic feature of two of Hemingway's novels and easily demonstrate how they departed from his other work. What's more, they observed that Hemingway was not perfectly consistent with his usage of full names; about *Robert Jordan,* they wrote, "Later in the book, the names are still consistently used together, but there's a little more variety between just using first or last name" (Davidson et al.).

The Trends tool provided opportunities for other groups to quickly investigate how terms change over the course of Hemingway's work. One group wanted to know if Hemingway preferred wine or beer—at least in his narration. They learned that the preference depended on the novel (see Fig. 15). What's more, with a little more knowledge of the texts, it became apparent that wine dominates in novels set in Europe and beer is the choice of novels set in North America and the Caribbean.[15] A related search answered the question of whether Hemingway's characters are more likely to eat or drink (see Fig. 16). Apart from *The Torrents of Spring, For Whom the Bell Tolls,* and *The Old Man and the Sea,* drinking proves

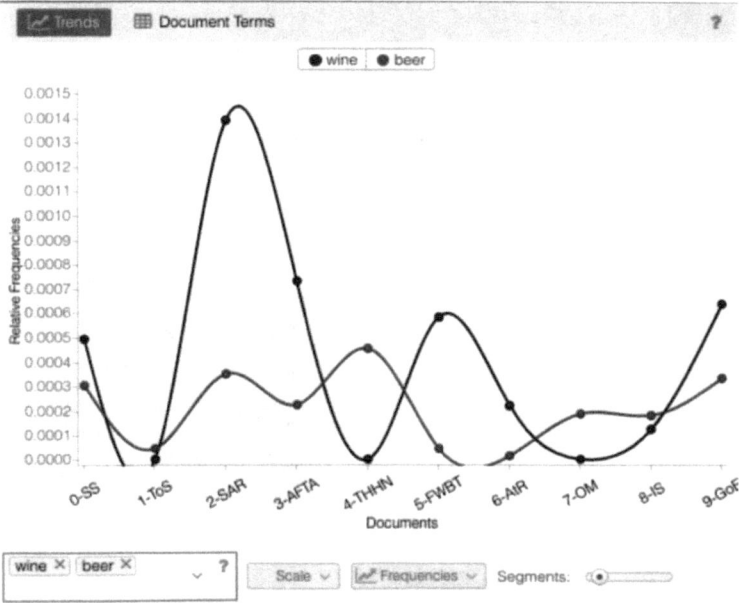

Fig. 15. Voyant's Trends tool displaying the relative frequencies of *wine* and *beer* across the short stories and novels.

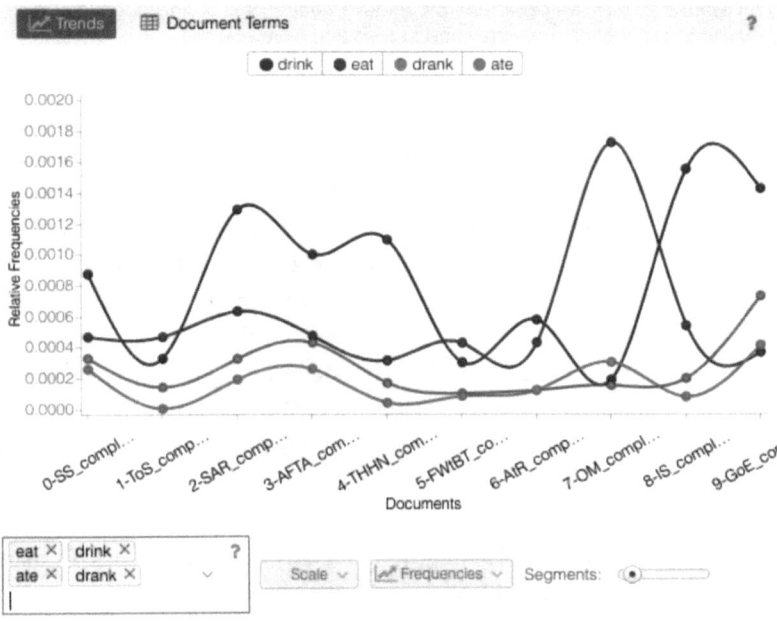

Fig. 16. Voyant's Trends tool displaying the relative frequencies of *ate, drank, drink,* and *eat* across the short stories and novels.

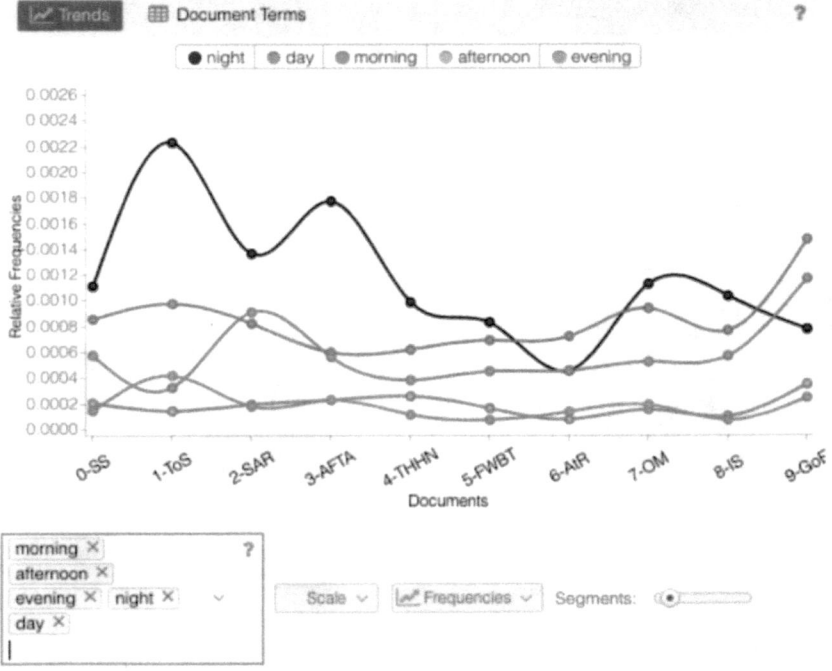

Fig. 17. Voyant's Trends tool displaying the relative frequencies of *afternoon, day, evening, morning,* and *night* across the short stories and novels.

more popular than eating. The importance of food in *The Old Man and the Sea* makes particular sense insofar as almost all the novel's action takes place out of the range of anything worth drinking. Of more significance is that the present-tense *drink* and *eat* appear more regularly than the past-tense *drank* and *ate*. This might suggest that Hemingway's characters talk about food and beverage more often than the narrative directly relates their repasts. Another search in Trends reveals that Hemingway is fonder of *morning* than *afternoon* or *evening* but that *night* is by far his preferred time of day (see Fig. 17). And surprising none of my students, who had read "Hills like White Elephants," Trends helps confirm that Hemingway tends to call his adult male characters "men" and his adult females "girls" (see Fig. 18).

In each of these cases, Trends provides a quick way for students to ask a range of questions about all of the Hemingway that they have never read. In many cases, the answers they find will not surprise those who have indeed read all of Hemingway, but the questions do differ materially from what undergraduate students are typically able to do with a single author's work. Moreover, the work

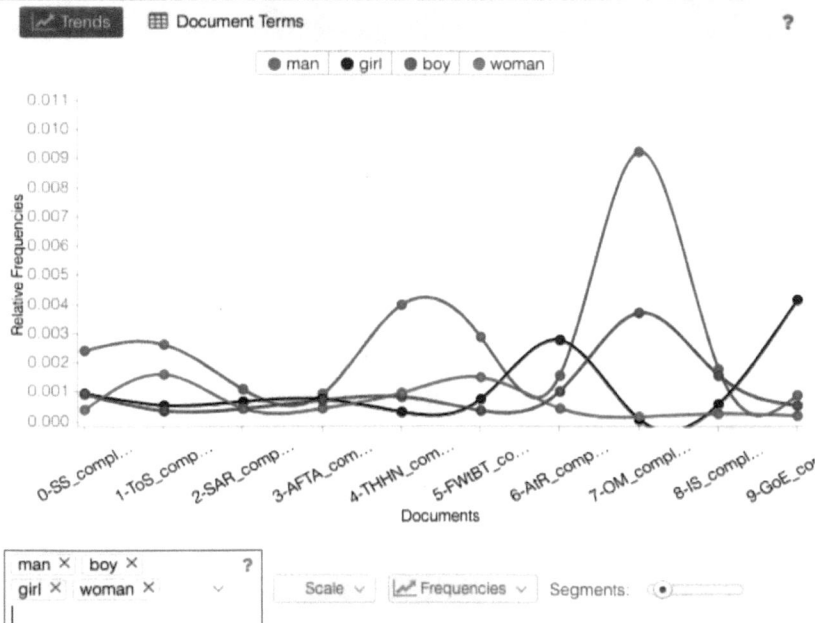

Fig. 18. Voyant's Trends tool displaying the relative frequencies of *boy, girl, man,* and *woman* across the short stories and novels.

they are doing is inherently inductive by nature rather than the rote deployment of deductive methods (aka "theory") that Hemingway was so set against. My students may arrive at a theory of Hemingway after working with Trends, but they do not begin with a theory in mind.

A final Voyant tool that my students explored was Mandala. Mandala, as Sinclair and Rockwell write in the Voyant documentation, "is a conceptual visualization that shows the relationships between terms and documents. Each search term (or magnet) pulls documents toward it based on the term's relative frequency in the corpus." In other words, instead of showing term frequencies in a manner in which the terms do not affect one another, as is the case with Trends, Mandala makes it possible to see which texts are more closely associated with a particular term (see Fig. 19). Dane Whitaker, one of my students who was working on his own, had observed that "knowing" was a central thematic concern in Hemingway's short stories. He therefore wanted "to pursue the themes of thought, knowledge, and truth" in the corpus of fiction and used Mandala to this end (Whitaker). Whitaker writes,

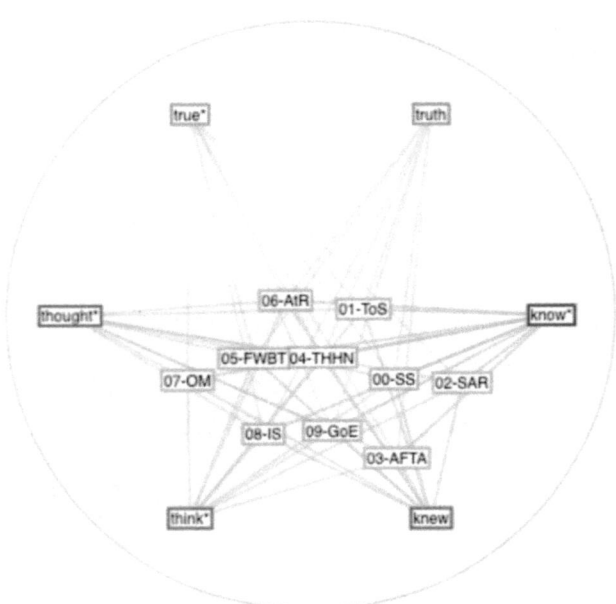

Fig. 19. Voyant's Mandala tool displaying the short stories and novels, with the terms *true**, *truth*, *thought**, *think**, *knew*, and *know** acting as magnets.

[Using] the Mandala tool I realized all volumes of Hemingway's fiction contain all of these six search terms, except for *OM [The Old Man and the Sea]* and *SAR [The Sun also Rises]*, both of which are lacking only "truth." Curiously enough, these two works are also the most polarized on the thinking-knowing spectrum. *OM* falls towards thinking and *SAR* falls towards knowing. In fact they mirror each other almost perfectly in their coordinates. *THHN [To Have and Have Not]* seems to be the most balanced between thinking, knowing, and truth.... I tentatively conclude that Hemingway sees thinking and knowing as related activities which are not entirely associated with truth. The relative infrequency of "truth" and "true" may show that he regards truth with some reverence, as a rarely glimpsed object—or perhaps that truth is conveyed better through concrete detail than abstraction.

Whitaker's analysis of these texts is, as he says, tentative, and that is just as well, since, of course, he has not read the novels he is commenting on. Yet his nuanced reading of the Mandala visualization would provide him with an interesting point of departure for reading Hemingway in the future.

Of all the activities my students engaged in, perhaps the most playful took place outside of Voyant. Right as my most recent class was beginning its work on Hemingway, a new Harry Potter chapter was published. What made this chapter unique was that it was not authored by J. K. Rowling. Instead, "a community of writers, artists, and developers" working under the collective name of Botnik had trained a predictive keyboard on the dialogue and prose passages from the popular series (Botnik, *Botnik*). A number of participants used the keyboards to generate sentences in the style of Rowling, and an editor strung them together to present a chapter from a new Harry Potter novel, entitled (also algorithmically) *Harry Potter and the Portrait of What Looked Like a Large Pile of Ash* (@ NatTowsen). Botnik made its predictive keyboard available for others to use, and one of my students, Alex Lyman, trained the keyboard with the text from the "living fiction" corpus. He then used the keyboard (botnik.org/apps/writer/?source=57514759240f9cb3eda367f8faee84cb) to produce a short story:

> I don't know how he was riding all day through fields of the poppies. He was very embarrassed and he could remember how he had started the motor car with his flat face. You mustn't ever tell him. They do it.
>
> Nick felt so very impressive. It's the car.
>
> We'll see her husband in the dining room. Liz wanted some breakfast and she wanted it now. There was always a chance to be born. She loved Africa until the last night. Nothing happened.
>
> Oh do you think we might try to go fishing? That's Mr. Robert buffalo. He knew how you died. You just got in the ring that night and went absolutely rigid. Exactly what I said.
>
> Nick swung his feet over the bull's head. Still he thought it was very uncomfortable.

Lyman's story might not make it into *The Best of Bad Hemingway* (1989), but I'd submit it for inclusion in *Pretty Good Bad Hemingway*. As a response to an assignment that asked students *not* to read Hemingway, generating a new story that Hemingway never wrote seems fair and appropriate, and it highlights what is possible when you teach Hemingway in the digital age.

Reading after Not Reading

It probably would not be fair to expect Hemingway, were he able, to read what my students wrote since, after all, we did not really read him. If he did, however, he might accuse us of being "Junior F.B.I.-men," as he did Baker, Fenton, and Young (*Selected Letters* 751). But I believe what my students and I have done is distinctly different from the theory-driven readings those scholars produced.

To Hemingway, theory seems to have been reading with a narrow lens of interpretation, a search for evidence to confirm what one has already decided must be there, whether that be The Code, The Wound, The Twin Sister, or The Hair Fetish. The theorist encounters Hemingway's texts with an answer already found; my students, however, approached Hemingway's writing with questions rather than answers. They knew that they did not know his oeuvre well enough to make informed readings. Instead, they extrapolated on observations they had made from a very small sample and then observed whether those observations were confirmed or radically upended. I have been amazed at the number and variety of things they have thought to ask—many, many more than I have been able to report here. Indeed, my students have asked questions Hemingway scholars have never thought of, and they have been able, without too much trouble, to obtain what appear to be some convincing answers.

The opportunity for my students to ask new questions and, in particular, ones that I as their professor do not know the answer to is perhaps the most important outcome from this assignment. In the context of my Introduction to Digital Humanities course, it is useful to have them learn how to digitize materials and perform distant readings. But in the context of a *humanities* course, what is far more valuable is the process of formulating questions and trying to figure out how to ask them in a new environment.[16] Insofar as I do not know the answers and can only serve as an imperfect guide to my students' explorations, one might suggest that I am failing to instruct and instead am just letting my students play haphazardly at literary analysis. Such play is, however, what Stephen Ramsay has called "the hermeneutics of screwing around": "It is ... to ask whether we are ready to accept surfing and stumbling—'screwing around,' broadly understood—as a research methodology. For to do so would be to countenance the irrefragable complexities of what 'no one really knows.' Could we imagine a world in which 'Here is an ordered list of the books you should read,' gives way to, 'Here is what I found. What did you find?'" (7). Ramsay's essay is the first thing my digital humanities classes read, and his invitation to confront the unknown in our reading—or our not reading, as the case may be—is, I believe, something that Hemingway, always an adventurer, would have welcomed.

Along with developing students' capacity to ask questions, this assignment's departure from close reading allows us to escape the canonicity of Hemingway's works. In *Distant Reading*, Moretti argues that "the trouble with close reading (in all of its incarnations, from the new criticism to deconstruction) is that it necessarily depends on an extremely small canon" (48). The great majority of the world's published literature never gets considered. Measured against these millions of unread volumes, what Moretti has called "the slaughterhouse of literature," Hemingway's books have received more than their fair share of attention (*Distant Reading* 65–66). But that attention is not evenly distributed. In survey courses of American literature or even more focused courses on the twentieth-century short story or novel, one tends to find the same "classic" stories being taught alongside *The Sun Also Rises*. Semester-long seminars on Hemingway expand the number of texts that can be taught but still cannot cover everything. For example, the first purpose of Alex Vernon's Fall 2016 Ernest Hemingway Seminar is to "immerse [students] in Hemingway texts (*though we only have time for roughly half of his creative work*)" (emphasis added). A quick search of the more than one million syllabi gathered at *The Open Syllabus Project* (*opensyllabusproject.org*) indicates that while *The Sun Also Rises* has appeared on 599 syllabi, *Across the River and into the Trees* has been assigned just twenty-two times, *Green Hills of Africa* nineteen times, and *The Torrents of Spring* has only appeared on a single syllabus within the entire database. In short, most of the fifteen books that formed my classes' corpus are assigned so infrequently that one could say without much exaggeration that they simply are not taught. While the assignment to not read Hemingway might well arouse the suspicions and ire of those who worry that reading is endangered in a digital age (see National Endowment for the Arts, "Reading at Risk"; Bauerlein; Carr), it turns out that much of Hemingway is already not being read. When I asked my students to "not read" fifteen of his books with a digital approach, they inadvertently came into contact with more Hemingway than any other class on earth.

This digitally enabled (non)encounter with all of Hemingway's writing produced, as mentioned above, questions that other readers have never before thought to ask about Hemingway's work. But perhaps these questions have gone unasked because they are not the most critical for understanding Hemingway's contribution to American fiction. At the beginning of *Hemingway's Fetishism*, Eby acknowledges that his theory "ignores innumerable extremely significant issues in Hemingway's work" and that the "psychosexuality underpinning so much of it" is by no means "the most important thing about his fiction" (2). The same is true of the distant reading that has engaged my students and me. Along with knowing our contributions may be relatively minor, I remain deeply aware that what we have found does not amount to conclusive proof. Just because we have used a computer, counted words, and produced some lovely graphs—all with the help of a fabulously simple tool—does not mean that we *know* anything concretely. Reading Hemingway in the digital age is not, in other words, a positivistic endeavor—just as reading Hemingway has never been. Indeed, Rockwell and Sinclair caution against trusting the empiricism that text analysis appears to possess: "Ultimately, word lists, like distribution graphs, do not prove anything about the text. However, they can encourage the formation and exploration of new hypotheses" (40). Digital approaches to reading, are, in the end, most similar to other reading methods in that they ultimately produce more questions than answers. Since, as Rockwell and Sinclair argue, "indexing and concording have always been tied to re-reading," what *not* reading Hemingway in a digital age does is give us new reasons to return to his books (53).[17] In the end, our job after not reading Hemingway is to once again read, ask questions, and see what the encounter reveals.

Notes

For larger, color versions of the figures in this chapter, visit https://www.briancroxall.net/publications/how-to-not-read-hemingway-images.

This chapter would not have been possible without the work of students in three of my Introduction to Digital Humanities courses. They not only worked with me to scan and OCR all of Hemingway but also came up with many of the questions that I report on here. Some of the images I have used are recreations of their original work. The students, who each year asked whether I would credit them if I ever wrote about the project, are

> Spring 2014 at Emory University, Jacob Albrecht, Daniella Bloch, Nathan Briones, Celia Curtis, Connor Dillman, Jeffrey Dillon, Andrew Drumm, Tiffany Gesang, Angelica Gonzales, Adriti Gulati, Shilpa Jhol, Omair Kazi, Eryn Levine, Abe Lim, Mitchell Lo, Matt O'Connor, Heba Qureshi, Cara Stechmann, Dennis Valerstain, Jonathan Weiss, and Saier Zeng;
>
> Spring 2015 at Emory, Maida Ahmad, Hana Ahmed, Joyce Au, Caroline Adams, David An, Savannah Bacon, Elyssa Brezel, Matt Casseday, Nancy Chung, Ashley Glenn, John Keuler, Lily Kronfeld, Daniel Lim, Justine Nurse-McLeod, Erin Penney, Brandon Pownall, Abby Schreiber, Nicholas She, Noreen Siddiqi, Jayme Smith, Hannah Teetor, and Ben Woodworth;
>
> Fall 2017 at Brigham Young University, Sadie Anderson, Paul Bunker, Kelly Burdick, Maddie Calder, Shelbi Davidson, Chris Dichmann, Miles Farnsworth, Elizabeth Harper, Mike Kim, Alex Lyman, Liz Pickrell, Stephen Rackleff, Tara Sampson, Clarissa Thiriot, Amanda Vite, and Dane Whitaker.

At Brown University, I worked with Lloyd Kevin Sy, then an undergraduate, to clean the corpus and begin topic modeling it; he is now pursuing his PhD in English at the University of Virginia. I owe a great debt of gratitude to Stéfan Sinclair for always being a quick and affable respondent to any questions I've had about Voyant. Finally, my teaching has been influenced by many colleagues who publicly share their syllabi, assignments, and experiences. In particular, my thanks go out to Jason B. Jones, Mark Sample, Miriam Posner, Ryan Cordell, my fellow ProfHackers, and Paul Fyfe, who directly inspired the title of my assignment and, subsequently, this essay.

    1. Nancy R. Comley and Robert Scholes also write about the problem with theories:

> [Edmund] Wilson emphasized the psychic wounding or trauma that, in his view, constituted the origin of art, and he has been followed in this by Philip Young and other commentators on Hemingway. Hemingway himself hated this reduction of his achievement to a traumatic reflex.... Looking for The Wound is like looking for The Code: it is an attempt to reduce a complex textual phenomenon to an excessively simple formula. (8)

    2. The particular course that I include this assignment in is Introduction to Digital Humanities, which, as the name suggests, is an overview of methods and concerns within the field. The Hemingway project serves as a summative experience for the class, where the students apply many of the concepts we have studied throughout the semester, including digitization, text analysis, and, importantly, how to ask questions in a new information environment. This class was taught within the English department at Emory University and the Office of Digital Humanities at Brigham Young University. In both situations, while many of my students have been humanities majors, not all of them were.

    3. *Digital humanities* has, of course, many other definitions than the one that I find useful with my students. The term also includes the consideration of digital culture, media, and more through humanistic lenses. Those who define *digital humanities* also frequently include aspects of scholarly communication and digital pedagogy. Those interested in the term's rise and its different meanings would do well to begin by consulting Matthew G. Kirschenbaum's 2010 essay "What Is Digital Humanities and What's It Doing in English Departments? " and his subsequent essays "Digital Humanities As/Is a Tactical Term" (2012) and "What is 'Digital Humanities' and Why Are They Saying Such Terrible Things about It?" (2014). Other essential reading includes the essays in part 1, "Defining the Digital Humanities," in Matthew K. Gold's edited volume *Debates in the Digital Humanities* (2012) and Gold's entry on the subject in *The Johns Hopkins Guide to Digital Media* (2014). Those who want still more definitions and are feeling playful might visit Jason Heppler's *What Is Digital Humanities?* This website randomly serves the reader one of 817 definitions written by digital humanists over the period 2009–14.

    4. It is no mistake that I have already cited both Comley and Scholes's *Hemingway's Genders* and Eby's *Hemingway's Fetishism*. For the last forty years, and especially since the publication of *The Garden of Eden,* scholars have increasingly considered the role of gender and sexuality in Hemingway's work, revoking what Peter Messent called the author's "automatic... and simpl[e]" consignment "to the 'cult of masculinity'" (qtd. in Eby 3). In addition to Comley and Scholes, Eby, and Messent's 1992 *Ernest Hemingway,* one must also mention Aaron Latham's "A Farewell to Machismo," Kenneth Lynn's 1987 biography, Mark Spilka's *Hemingway's Quarrel with Androgyny* (1990), and Richard Fantina's *Ernest Hemingway: Machismo and Masochism* (2005).

5. One of the few bright lines of US copyright law is the year 1923. All copyrightable works published in the United States prior to 1923 are in the public domain. Works that were published after 1923, on the other hand, have a much more complicated status. Apart from his newspaper reporting, Hemingway's first publications were the vignettes that appeared in the Spring 1923 issue of *The Little Review*. The publication date of these vignettes, which would eventually become part of *In Our Time,* means that everything that is neither journalism nor juvenilia remains under copyright.

6. As mentioned, all of Hemingway's works are in copyright at the time of my writing and this in-copyright status was one reason why the assignment has to happen as I conduct it. That said, I consulted with the copyright offices and librarians at both universities where I carried out the project, and the assignment was also designed with US Copyright Law (USC title 17) in mind, specifically section 107 which focuses on fair use. Our use of Hemingway's work was in the context of a "nonprofit educational purpose" (title 17, section 107). The assignment used a large and substantial portion of Hemingway's work (as all text mining must), but the assignment was deliberately constructed so that the reproductions we produced were tightly controlled to minimize "effect of the use upon the potential market for or value of the copyrighted work" (title 17, section 107). Since students were only given 200 pages, almost no student had an entire work in her or his possession. The students created both PDFs and extracted plain text of their assigned pages and then emailed them to me. The PDFs were never distributed to the students. The compiled, plain text files were made available to the students through my own private server for the purposes of the assignment only, and they were removed from the server directly after the completion of the assignment. Students were instructed not to distribute any of the texts further.

7. The inspiration for this assignment originally comes from Jason B. Jones, who asked his students "to read 3 Victorian novels in 2.5 hours." For his assignment, Jones had his students use freely available novels from *Project Gutenberg* and asked them to create word clouds for each chapter and then use text analysis recipes from the Text Analysis Portal for Research (TAPoR). Paul Fyfe was inspired by Jones when he taught his students "How to Not Read a Victorian Novel." His students also got their texts from *Project Gutenberg* and used a combination of word clouds and TAPoR. But Fyfe's students went a step beyond Jones's: each wrote a full paper about "what they learned about their chosen text and about this kind of 'distant reading'" (87). In building on Jones's and Fyfe's assignments, I added the scale of tackling an entire author's works and the goal of creating the digital corpus from print originals.

While my project was inspired by Jones's and Fyfe's assignments, those interested in similar endeavors should read about Leslee Thorne-Murphy's students who preceded mine in the creation of a corrected corpus via OCR, which Thorne-Murphy describes in an essay written with Michael C. Johnson. Her approach differed from mine in both scale and the level of correction students were requested to perform. And Fyfe cotaught with Richard Menke a class across their two campuses (North Carolina State University and the University of Georgia) that featured a collaborative distant reading of Charles Dickens's *David Copperfield*. Students "develop[ed] a hypothesis for a data-driven exploration of the novel" and then "share[d] the labour of collecting the 'data' from the novel" (Fyfe and Menke 563). Fyfe and Menke's assignment foregrounded, as did mine, the importance of formulating questions and developing a means to test their hypotheses.

8. It's worth noting that Sinclair and Rockwell have designed Voyant at least in part as an opportunity to experiment with different forms of visualization. The result is that some of the tools are immediately easier to understand than others. The word cloud Cirrus (voyant-tools.org/docs/#!/guide/cirrus), for example, enables a user to quickly see which words are most prominent in a corpus. At the other extreme are visualizations like Bubbles (voyant-tools.org/docs/#!/guide/bubbles), which reads a text from beginning to end, creating bubbles for each word that grow incrementally bigger each time the word is repeated. At the same time, the computer plays a tone that corresponds to how frequent the term is; higher frequency words get higher tones. What Bubbles allows a user to do, then, is to *hear* the frequency of the words in a text. While Bubbles is a novel object and one that I certainly demonstrate to every class I introduce to Voyant, it is less useful for answering questions about the text.

9. Voyant allows for wildcard searching. This means that *fish** will return *fish, fishes, fishing,* and so on. *Water,* without the asterisk, however, will return *water* but not *waterfall* or *watering.*

10. The last of the five nonfiction texts in our project corpus may be the most controversial since in its introduction Patrick Hemingway describes *True at First Light* as "a fiction" and Scribner's places it, as per the back cover of the current edition, in the Scribner Paperback Fiction series (9). Yet Patrick Hemingway also writes, "Ambiguous counterpoint between fiction and truth lies at the heart of this memoir" (9). In this way, *True at First Light* is similar to all of Hemingway's nonfiction. Given the overlap in material between it and *Under Kilimanjaro* (2005), I included only the former in the corpus, in part because it was an easier text to scan. Future iterations of this project might lead to my students and me scanning *Under Kilimanjaro* and then replacing *True at First Light.*

One might also question my decision to include *The Dangerous Summer* in the list of posthumous works insofar as large portions of it were published in *Life* in 1960. However, the 1985 publication contains more of the text and provides, as James A. Michener writes in his introduction, "an honest rendering of what was best in [the] massive affair" of the 120,000 words Hemingway originally produced (13).

Finally, one might wonder why our nonfiction corpus does not include Hemingway's reporting. While it is undoubtedly nonfiction and naturally related to *The Dangerous Summer,* I have decided to treat Hemingway's journalism as a separate genre to be tackled in subsequent assignments.

11. It is worth noting a complication for these measures: in general, the longer the corpus, the lower its vocabulary density will be since it will tend to reuse word forms more often (see Koizumi 60–61).

12. Recent stylometric work by Jonathan Pearce Reeve on twelve authors, including Hemingway, provides early evidence that the concept of late style, as discussed by Theodor Adorno and Edward Said in "Late Style in Beethoven" and *On Late Style: Music and Literature against the Grain,* may not actually exist.

13. Voyant autodetects the language of a corpus and then applies a stop-word list. Stop words are the most common words in a language, such as *and, the,* or *I* in English. Linguists often remove stop words before analyzing a text, as they are less significant for understanding the unique properties of a corpus. As such, Trends and other tools in Voyant display the most frequent terms in the corpus that are *not* part of its stop-word list. It is very simple to edit Voyant's stop-word list, either adding or removing terms, or to remove the filtering altogether and simply display all words forms in a corpus. Unless otherwise noted, the figures in this chapter were created with the standard English Voyant stop-words list applied.

14. Knowing that fiction is almost always narrated in the past tense, the students wanted to look for *thought* as a corollary to *said*. Both of these terms would convey the narration. They included *think* knowing that the present-tense form of the verb would appear within dialogue. It is important to remember that these Voyant charts are scaled according to what terms one searches for. If one looks at the Voyant's Trends tool for *the*, which accounts for approximately 6.5 percent of the total words in each of Hemingway's novels and the short stories, and *said*, the peaks and valleys of the latter flatten out considerably.

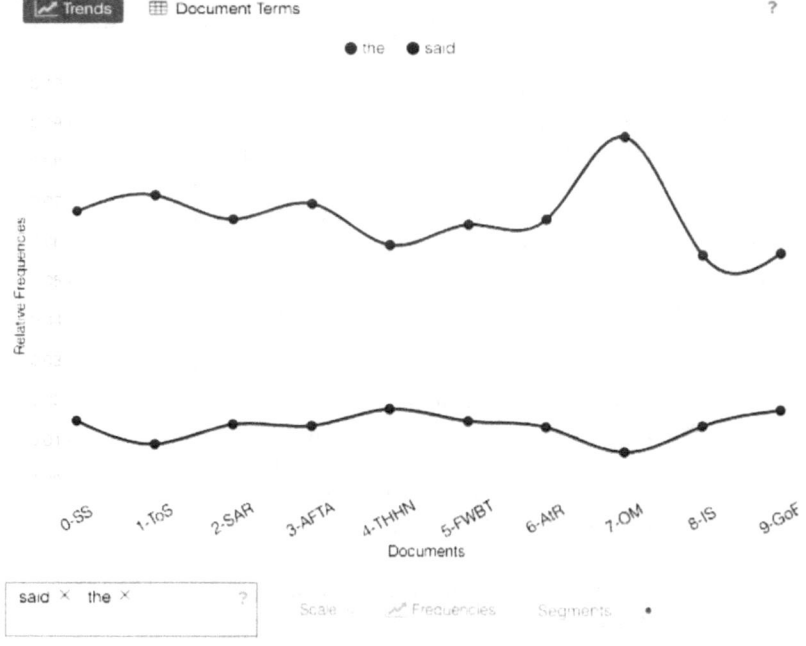

15. Of course, Hemingway preferred to have his characters drink something more specific than simply *wine* and *beer*. He was far more likely to provide specific varieties or brands as he prided himself on knowing the right thing to drink at the right time. Samuel J. Rogal's *For Whom the Dinner Bell Tolls* provides a detailed index to everything

people consume in Hemingway's work. Coupled with Rogal's research, Voyant might provide a simple interface for understanding Hemingway's provender.

16. In "How to Not Read a Victorian Novel," Fyfe similarly argues that his distant reading assignment "teach[es] students to ask good questions and to embrace the interrogative as a condition of knowledge" (88).

17. In the second chapter of *Graphs, Maps, Trees,* Moretti also suggests that distant reading can ultimately lead us back to a closer reading of the texts in question. Making maps—a distant reading process—is "a good way to prepare a text for analysis" (53). What makes maps so powerful, he argues, is how they "may bring some hidden patterns to the surface" (54). But—and this is critical to recall in all distant reading—the map and its patterns are *not* an explanation; rather, they "show . . . us that there is something *that needs to be explained*" (39). Making a visualization of a feature that we find in a single novel or millions of novels does not explain anything. Instead, the visualization points us to the thing that needs to be interpreted; hence, my definition of digital humanities as the use of computational methods to find patterns in texts followed by the interpretation of those patterns.

"Concrete Particulars"

The Suggestive Power of Physical World Details in *Across the River and into the Trees*

Mark Ebel

Critics have judged Hemingway's novel *Across the River and into the Trees*, published in 1950, as his least successful, attacking the book and sometimes Hemingway with a vengeance. Yet, perhaps trading on Hemingway's fame as a writer, this was his only novel to reach the top of the *New York Times* bestseller list, where it remained for seven weeks (Bear 47). Only a few writers, such as Tennessee Williams, recognized the artfulness of the novel, but even Williams's judgment is tinged with apparent contradiction: "It is the saddest novel in the world about the saddest city, and when I say it is the best and most honest work that Hemingway has done, you may think me crazy." This essay offers an analysis and teaching methodology for the "story beneath the story" in *Across the River and into the Trees*, specifically the framing narrative of the first and last several chapters describing how the protagonist (referred to initially as simply "the shooter" and later as the Colonel) goes duck hunting in a low-lying area of canals, lakes, and lagoons known as the Veneto in northeastern Italy.

Why spend time focusing students' attention on the duck hunt frame in *Across the River and into the Trees*, just a small episode in the context of the larger narrative? The increasingly obscure nature of duck hunting, a sport in decline among young people, coupled with the foreign aspect of the Veneto, may limit the accessibility of the duck-hunt frame story to some iGens (the term for younger digital-age students coined by Jean Twenge), alike. "Hunting participation" nationally, writes Natalie Krebs, "peaked in 1982, when nearly 17 million hunters purchased 28.3 million licenses," but in 2016, the US Fish and Wildlife Service reported just "11.5 million people [who] hunted, "a mere "4 percent of the national population." Still, I strongly believe that twenty-first-century students will find Hemingway's hunting frame story more intriguing, challenging, and rewarding than the popular reading of the novel, namely as the story of one man's efforts to face death gracefully while engaged in a May–December romance. First, a focus on the frame story avoids the novel's "stumbling block," as Kathleen Verduin describes it, namely the arrogance and self-preoccupation justly ascribed to the main character, Colonel Richard Cantwell (633). In his critical study of Hemingway's novel, *Reading Hemingway's* Across the River and into the Trees, Mark Cirino notes, "One of the pleasures of reading a novel of any kind is its invitation to the reader to experience vicariously the growth, development, and lessons of the protagonist" (xii). In Cirino's interpretation, Cantwell does not change as a character; rather, he "experiences no insight, no epiphany, no moment of change during the action of the novel" (xiii). However, this is only true of the middle part of the novel; the interpretation ignores the duck-hunt frame story, in which Cantwell, in an interior monologue, acknowledges his own frailties while accepting those of others: "'I'm sorry that I shot. I shot in anger.' I have done that myself sometimes, the Colonel thought, and did not ask him what the anger was about" (259).

Hence, teachers and students have much to gain by committing to a careful reading and discussion of the often ignored duck hunt frame narrative. Hemingway's frame contains classic examples of "concrete particulars" of the physical world that suggestively communicate important narrative details to careful readers (Owens-Murphy). While I am not by any means arguing that iGeneration students have not developed the analytical skills necessary to unlock meaning from buried or understated narratives such as this, I do think that our twenty-first-century world of instantaneous information makes the patience for *reading* particulars more difficult to model and practice. In 2018, the *Chronicle of Higher Education* commissioned a survey about faculty satisfaction of over a thousand professors across America, and the results showed that "nearly two-thirds of the faculty members agreed with a statement that students are harder to teach than students of years past" (June). The ecosystem of higher education, the survey respondents reported, had for various reasons changed so significantly in the last five years that it led to "more students who are unprepared for college, unwilling to read the required texts, and are unmotivated to participate in class" (June). Compounding these challenges with student engagement, too, is a cultural diminishment of what Glenn Adamson calls "material intelligence: a deep understanding of the material world around us, an ability to read that material environment" (4). He goes on to argue—convincingly, I believe—that "as a culture, we are in danger of falling out of touch, not only with objects, but with the intelligence they embody: the empathy that is bound up in tangible things" (4).

Hemingway's writing can return us to those "tangible things" in literary form. We can use Hemingway's frame narrative to guide twenty-first-century readers through a natural, physical world from which some of us may have consciously or unconsciously distanced ourselves. Characters in the duck-hunt frame story have something valuable to teach to contemporary students who may struggle—as have students for ages—to connect imaginatively with characters and places drastically different from their own experiences. At first, the boatman and shooter fight each other every step of the way out to the duck blind: "All right you surly jerk, the shooter thought to himself. We are going to get there. We've made two-thirds of the way now and if you are worried about having to work to break the ice to pick up birds, that is altogether too bad" (12). In later actions, however, after an apparent change of heart on each man's part, they "worked together in complete coordination" (272). Hemingway's creating of this change of attitude is an apparent epiphany for the Colonel. A discussion of the subtle, "concrete particulars" which initiate the transformation, then, are the focus of this essay. Such careful reading of the duck hunt story illuminates that the protagonist does indeed experience change—it represents a small moment within the larger broader narrative, yet one in need of examination.

The Concrete Particulars of Duck Hunting

In the opening paragraphs of the novel, Hemingway identifies two characters, one as "the shooter," who is paired with a hunting guide, alternately identified as "the poler" or "the boatman." Students unfamiliar with Hemingway's fiction may presume that the relationship between boatman and shooter would be harmonious or at least amicable. But this is often not the case—in short stories such as "The Short Happy Life of Francis Macomber and "Out of Season," and in the novel *To Have and Have Not*, the relationship between a hunting or fishing guide and his client are strained by differences in personal history, nationality, or social class.

The narrative begins as "[f]our of the boats went toward the big lagoon to the north" (11). As boatman and shooter ply the shallow, partially frozen waters of a system of canals and lagoons where the duck hunting actually takes place, they leave behind the earthly world and enter a less substantial one of air and water. Hemingway takes readers into a realm with which he, as a duck hunter and a writer who draws from his hunting experience, is intimately familiar, but with which many readers, especially today's students, may not be, given the national decline in hunting participation (Krebs). Yet the physical transition from solid ground of terra firma to the watery world of the Veneto is important because it creates an otherworldly ambience that immediately suggests change and intrigue.

There are many such simple elements in the duck hunt narrative that belie the greater complexity of Hemingway's characters and places. The narrative continues, "'Get your back into it, jerk,' he said in English. 'What?' the boatman asked in Italian" (13). This simple conversation underscores sharp cultural distinctions between the two characters. Though he could be from any English-speaking country, the shooter, one presumes, is an English-speaking American, as are most of Hemingway's protagonists, while his guide is an Italian, presumably native to the area. Teachers can explain that this presumption may be made based on the fact that Hemingway's fiction contains characters crafted in his own likeness, with stories based on his own life experiences. Readers may also infer that the season is winter—"It was all ice, new-frozen during the sudden, windless cold of the night"—even though the shooter is "sweating in his heavy clothes" (11, 12). To help twenty-first century students visualize the characters and setting, teachers can provide supplemental visual information, such as photographs easily available online, of Hemingway duck hunting in Italy, which present a scene very suggestive of Hemingway's frame story. Teachers may also wish to access a relevant video, which Caorle Chanel + Venice posted on YouTube, that features aerial views of the Italian Veneto and evocative images of the precise area where Hemingway's fictional duck hunting scene is set. The video, an excellent accompaniment to Hemingway's text, contains passages from the text of novel, spoken in Italian with subtitles in English.

As American society becomes increasingly urban and habitat for duck hunting (or any hunting) becomes scarcer, teachers can expect that fewer twenty-first-century students will have had hunting experiences similar to those Hemingway enjoyed and about which he wrote (Rott). Of course, this depends greatly on the geographical area in which an instructor teaches, but the national decline in hunting "is expected to accelerate over the next decade" (Rott). Therefore, teachers may want to include background information on the particulars of duck hunting in their lesson plans. One way for us to take students right into Hemingway's setting is to provide visuals that are as authentic to Hemingway's time and experience as possible and to ask questions about the scene of the duck hunt that develop both concrete and mental imagery in students' minds. We can provide students with relevant facts about the setting—its geographical features—that require them to use their visual imaginations to understand what may not be seen, but implied.

While previous generations of students may have shared a familial attachment to hunting, an activity often passed on from one generation to the next (as was the case with Hemingway, his own father, and Hemingway's three sons) such attachments have dwindled, in part because of the considerable loss of habitat necessary for hunting due to urban sprawl and industrial agriculture (Rott; Krebs). In turn, these factors mean a wide swath of the American population has limited access to the natural world, a process that began in Hemingway's time but has since greatly accelerated. The number of hunting permits for most states is on a slow decline (Carson). Young people, then, are taking up the sport in much smaller numbers than did previous generations. Thus, teachers can safely assume that their students will benefit from being provided with both visual images such as those in the aforementioned video in order to facilitate a dialogue whereby they may gain an understanding and appreciation for this duck hunt frame narrative. The physical logistics pertaining to duck hunting can be explained for students to help them grasp the full meaning of the story.

The following questions could be posited as discussion prompts about the "concrete particulars" of duck hunting: Why is a hunting guide necessary? What are the duties of a hunting guide? What are decoys? Are live decoys necessary? Why is a dog aboard the boat? Why are ducks hunted in winter? What are the distinguishing characteristics of a shotgun that make it preferred for duck hunting? A teacher might ask students to prepare responses to these questions following an initial reading of chapter 1 of the novel, leading into a more detailed discussion of Hemingway's writing.

Because the shooter is hunting on unfamiliar ground, he has engaged the services of a local guide who knows the terrain and habits of the game being pursued. As such, the boatman would know things that the shooter, not being familiar with the area, could not know. The boatman would know that it was unnecessary to break the ice, because the water would likely refreeze quickly, while the commotion would alert the ducks to the hunters' presence. But the shooter, unfamiliar with local conditions, would not have known this. Moreover, he would have assumed that the boatman knew his business and would behave as a professional, as suggested in this earlier passage, "This is his trade isn't it?" (14). He thus remains unsuspecting of the boatman's true motives, which, as we learn in a later chapter, are aimed at revenge.

Students unfamiliar with duck hunting are also unlikely to know that it would also be the guide's responsibility to select a shooting spot that is concealed from view from above but overlooking a patch of open water, large enough to attract birds flying overhead. They must learn also about decoys, replicas of ducks that are placed in nearby, open water so as to appear to incoming birds like a flock of ducks resting or feeding. Some of the decoys referred to in Hemingway's story may have been carved from wood; such handmade artifacts have become collector's items, as wooden replicas have been replaced by ones made from synthetic materials such as foam or plastic. They are secured by a weighted line and placed in open water near the blind to attract ducks flying overhead. To maximize the shooter's chances of success, the guide must also calculate the travel time accurately so they arrive at the blind predawn. Yet this crucial step isn't taken in Hemingway's text; as the shooter notes, "I said let's go. It's going to be light" (13). This delay provides another subtle yet important example of the guide's plan to sabotage the hunt.

Ducks begin to fly at sunrise, which is also when shooting can begin legally, and if there is commotion around the blind, the ducks will not come in. Any guide should provide and handle a dog to retrieve killed and wounded ducks. The guide may carry a shotgun, but he is only expected to use it to kill cripples that the dog cannot recover. When Hemingway's fictional boatman shoots at a flock of ducks coming into the blind—"It was the boatman shooting at ducks that would have come to the Colonel" (258)—his action can properly be interpreted as another act of sabotage. But again, this fact is only apparent to readers if they know the logistical particulars of duck hunting.

A guide would be expected to attend to his client's physical necessities, with water being principal among them. However, when the shooter asks for water, the boatman uncaringly replies, "No water" (13). This constitutes another act of subversion, and it may have produced another adverse effect on the shooter's already declining health. Lacking water, the Colonel washes his medications down with the only liquid at his disposal. He "took two tablets from a bottle and a sip of gin from his flask" (258). Hence the Colonel ingests a combination of "mannitol hexanitrate" (alluded to on page 18) and alcohol, a practice strongly warned against by medical personnel. Given Cantwell's fragile health, the lack of water and resultant dehydration and possible drug-alcohol interplay may be considered contributory to his impending physical collapse.

One more unusual feature of Hemingway's narrative is that the men use live decoys in addition to the artificial ones. While not common, live decoys do increase the shooter's chances for success by adding movement and sound to the sensory environment of a duck blind. A live duck is tied to a weighted string so that it cannot fly but remains active and vocal among the decoys.

Working dogs such as Labrador Retrievers are essential for recovering ducks after they fall into the water. Sometimes ducks fall to the water dead, and other times they are only wounded and can escape. Dogs are trained to track them by sight and smell and retrieve them and return them to the shooter unharmed. To illustrate the particulars of the scene's physicality, teachers might even provide teaching props to their students, such as miniature duck decoys (Campugan). Strong, capable literary analysis of Hemingway's writing—and not merely in this one novel—is thus made more accessible with full knowledge of the physical world he so carefully delineates. It is up to twenty-first-century teachers to convey that knowledge to their classes.

A basic understanding of hunting practices and equipment is also essential for students. So as to provide for a harvest of ducks and other game that will not adversely harm the overall populations, individual nations usually set and monitor hunting regulations. The season for duck hunting is fall and winter, when ducks are migrating; along with other waterfowl, ducks generally fly from colder regions to warmer ones during these seasons then return north to breed in the spring. Wild game is generally hunted with either a rifle or a shotgun. A rifle discharges a single bullet, making it more suitable for stationary or large, slowly moving land targets, such as deer and elk. The shotgun is preferred for small game such as pheasants, ducks, and quail. These birds are shot on the wing, that is, while in motion, at distances of forty yards or more. It would be almost impossible for even an expert marksman to hit a distant, rapidly moving bird with a single, small bullet. A shotgun, however, discharges a cartridge filled with dozens of tiny, steel pellets that disperse into a small cloud into which the birds fly.

The Veneto's natural features include vast expanses of open water and natural vegetation, surrounded by mountains. In Hemingway's time, it was a haven for all sorts of migratory birds and waterfowl, a duck hunter's dream. However, we might remind students that today these are the species that have suffered most in population declines, due to industrialization, urbanization, and consequent loss of habitat. Hemingway was born in the late nineteenth century and grew up the early twentieth century, a time when Theodore Roosevelt and his hunting prowess rose to international prominence (Reynolds, *Young Hemingway* 28–29). Roosevelt's prestige, coupled with his dedication to hunting as a part of the "strenuous life," increased hunting's popular acceptance and the awareness of the need for conservation. Concurrently, the perception of hunting in Hemingway's era was divided into two camps: those who subscribed to Roosevelt's notion that hunting was an integral part of "the strenuous life" and those who, as Kevin Maier notes in his contribution to *Ernest Hemingway in Context,* viewed it as "a celebration of machismo, weaponry, and death" (275). Twenty-first-century teachers may wish to query their classes in order to initiate discussion about if and how this dichotomy plays out today as well as how it emerges in the novel. Teachers may note that near the end of the novel, Cantwell returns with just four ducks, a reasonable take for one hunter but an apparent disappointment for Cantwell: "You shot very few, he [the boatman] said to the Colonel. "With your help" (257).

Following up on this thought, twenty-first-century teachers may ask why Cantwell is disappointed having killed that number of ducks. The possibilities are several. Was it frustration with the boatman's many attempts at sabotage? Was it the Colonel's competitiveness with other shooters? Instructors might then ask students—in contrast to the Colonel's hunting experience—to focus on the quite different hunting experience enjoyed by Cantwell's friend, the Barone Alvarito, who killed more than forty ducks. The Colonel, an upper-middle-class American, has his hunting experience thwarted by an Italian boatman, presumably a member of the lower class; while the Barone, a representative of European nobility, takes game greatly in excess of what would be considered reasonable numbers, at least by American standards. Patrick Hemingway provides useful background information for this tension in the foreword to *Hemingway on Hunting:* "Italian duck hunters, most of whom are very rich industrialists or titled agricultural landowners, who are not particularly known for their adherence to conventional democratic conservation principles, are very proud of Puccini the duck hunter." In *Across the River and into the Trees,* Ernest Hemingway thus produces an authentic, multidimensional treatment of hunting as a thematic element, an effect Maier notes, writing that "Hemingway seems uniquely tuned into the ways a hunter's image is stretched in many directions, and his work explores the nuances of this image" (274). Hemingway correlates the integrity of hunting practices with the distinctions of class, and readers may infer the assumptions of culpability to each for succeeding or failing to practice good conservation.

While some may wonder why Hemingway chose to weave a hunting frame story together with a story of romance, he may have found a very definite connection between the two. Though the countess does not join the shooter on the duck hunt, the relationship between their romance and the Colonel's adventure in nature is implied. Presaging his own death, the shooter wishes to spend his remaining time with the two great passions of his life: Renata, the young woman, and duck hunting, his final adventure in the natural world. This eloquent passage by Aymer Maxwell suggests such a relationship: "Who shall say that the hunting spirit, the desire to match one's own wit against the wariest of wild fowl, is a lower motive than the softer attractions of a young May moon and a fair companion" ("Ten Greatest Waterfowling Quotes.") Hemingway combines these two seemingly disparate elements—an older man's love for a much younger woman, a woman of noble class, with an enduring desire to reconnect with boyhood memories of duck hunts. Cantwell describes the proposed hunt to his surgeon: "Good shoot. Real ducks. Mallard, pin-tail, widgeon. Some geese. Just as good as at home when we were kids" (19). For Cantwell, then, a successful duck shoot proves as desirable and often unobtainable as his impossible love with Renata.

The "Patch": Material Objects and Their Meaning

A number of other small yet significant material details within Hemingway's duck hunting story may be lost on twenty-first-century students without a teacher's guidance. Consider this passage, where Hemingway mentions "an old combat jacket, with a patch on the left shoulder that no one understood, and with light places on the straps, where stars had been removed" (5). The shooter's combat jacket may have looked something like the one worn by Hemingway's friend Charles "Buck" Lanham. It is believed Hemingway may have used Lanham, or certain aspects of his character, as a model for the Colonel. It would be easy for most readers to pass lightly over the phrase "with a patch on the left shoulder that no one understood" without assigning it any particular significance. Again, Hemingway obscures a great deal of information in this one phrase, which turns out to be the essential clue to understanding the actions of the characters and broader meaning of the novel. "No one understood" the patch because the military provides a great variety of patches that are worn and understood mostly by fellow military personnel. Since the duck hunt is a nonmilitary, or civilian, activity, the guide would not be expected to understand the significance of such patches. The patch to which Hemingway refers is likely a combat patch, worn on the left shoulder and signifying a particular unit affiliation within the structure of the military, one involved in combat operations. "The light places on the straps, where the stars were removed" would most likely indicate that the shooter had perhaps once been a higher ranking officer, such as a brigadier general, possibly promoted to that rank during the war, then later demoted later. It is crucial to note here that to the observer who is familiar with military decorations, the jacket and insignias would identify the shooter as an officer of the Allied Forces with World War II combat experience.

What the shooter doesn't know and what the reader also doesn't know at this point in the story is how the boatman infers meaning from the jacket and how that relates to his personal history and the actions and attitudes he projects onto to shooter. What Hemingway slips in along with his description of the shooter's clothing is the submerged part of the iceberg, a style he discusses in *Death in the Afternoon*: "If a writer of prose knows enough about what he is writing about, he may omit things that he knows and the reader, if the writer is writing truly enough, will have a feeling of those things as strongly as though the writer had stated them. The dignity of movement of an iceberg is due to only one-eighth of it being above water" (192). In the latter chapters of *Across the River and into the Trees*, the decorated combat jacket, though seemingly insignificant initially, later becomes a material object crucial to understanding the boatman's motives and contrary actions.

While the narrator initially describes the patch as something that "no one understood," which may have been the shooter's point of view, the shooter fails to link the boatman's contrary actions to Italian military history. At least in a general sense, the shooter, as an Allied officer who served in the Italian campaign in World War II, would have likely been aware of the infamous war crimes that occurred there and their adverse effect on the civilian population (Bimberg). Perhaps preoccupied with his desire to enjoy one last shoot, the shooter fails to relate these events to the boatman's actions and thus fails to recognize the boatman as an enemy. Moroccan indigenous fighters supplemented Allied forces against Fascist forces in Italy. Extremely effective as fighters, the Moroccans were nonetheless notorious for committing war crimes. By some accounts, these fighters, whom the French called Goumiers, were responsible for committing more than seven thousand rapes of civilian men, women, and children (Bimberg). As readers learn later, it was precisely this event, the raping of Italian women by Moroccan soldiers, that laid the bedrock of the boatman's animosity toward Allied soldiers, as recounted by the Colonel's friend Alvarito: "It was the old battle-jacket. Allied uniform affects him that way. You see he was a bit over-liberated." "Go on." "When the Moroccans came through they raped both his wife and his daughter." Hemingway's use of the term *over-liberated* is an ironic twisting of *liberated*, used militarily to describe the dispersal of occupying forces. Here Hemingway delivers a sarcastic punch in the gut to members of certain liberating forces who committed atrocities as egregious as those perpetrated by the enemies they were attacking. Hemingway conveys all of this information only suggestively and succinctly with the material military patch, which holds the primary clues for understanding the boatman's actions.

The boatman's tactics have been used by subversive groups on both small and large scales, when an enemy of superior strength and power confronts a smaller or less technologically advanced opponent. These strategies, known variously as sabotage, resistance, or subversion, seem to be lost on the shooter, a military man, but a person whose preoccupation with self perhaps prevents him from recognizing the actions of the boatman. The shooter continues to express surprise and bewilderment at the boatman's actions right up until the end when he asks the Barone, "[W]hat was the matter with that game-keeper who poled my boat?" (277). Not surprisingly, then, readers similarly may experience doubt and perhaps confusion over the enigma that Hemingway creates in crafting the interplay between the two oppositional characters.

To some students, too, the boatman's actions may not seem unusual, except when compared to the usual expectations for a boatman-guide. Upon reflection and discussion prompts from the instructor, however, the reader can discover that the boatman's actions constitute a form of resistance. As analysis of the material clues proceed, the boatman's motives, initially obscure, can then be discussed. It is doubtful that the boatman intends to physically harm the shooter. The boatman is unaware of the shooter's medical condition. That the shooter has been recently examined by a doctor who ordered "rest and light exercise" is unbeknownst to the boatman. Perhaps the boatman is just negligent but has no contrary motive, which would explain why he tosses out the decoys haphazardly but would not account for this key phrase, "as though he were ridding himself of something obscene" (14). This phrase changes the dynamics of the meaning by assigning the boatman a perverse attitude while still leaving doubt in the reader's mind as to the boatman's exact motive. The reader must wait until the final pages for the meaning of "something obscene" to be revealed.

The action of the duck hunt picks up again in chapter 41, near the end of the novel. After the shooter has killed four ducks, a flock begins to fly toward him. Before the shooter has a chance to take aim and fire, the boatman does the unpardonable thing for a guide: he raises his gun and fires twice in the direction of the incoming ducks, causing them to flare off in another direction, a blatant act of sabotage. For the shooter, this action constituted "as bad a thing as one man can do to another" (258). Filled with anger, the shooter retaliates by firing twice in the boatman's direction. The two shots are more symbolic than purposeful. The shooter knows that the shotgun pellets will drop off before reaching the distant boatman, but they send a message of shooter's uncontainable disgust.

The exchanges of shots between the boatman and Cantwell metaphorically end the war between the two. When Cantwell signals the boatman to come get him, the "boatman's anger seemed to be gone and to be replaced by a solid satisfaction" (271). This response certainly begs the question, why was the boatman satisfied? Here is where the story beneath the story begins to unfold. After sharing a drink, Cantwell asks the boatman, "Why did you shoot?" and for the first time, the boatman expresses contrition, admitting, "I'm sorry that I shot. I shot in anger" (273). Cantwell accepts this response tacitly, without asking what the anger was about. He doesn't learn the answer to this until he returns to the lodge and asks his friend, "Look, Alvarito, what was the matter with that game-keeper who poled my boat?" (277). The Colonel's reaction to Alvarito's explanation is nonjudgmental, and he merely says, "I think I'd better have a drink" (277). At the end of the day, the boatman was satisfied because he had succeeded in disrupting Cantwell's duck hunt, causing him unnecessary aggravation, and limiting him to shooting just four ducks. The Barone, while shooting from another blind, took more than ten times as many: "The Barone killed forty-two" (275).

At this point, teachers may want to ask their twenty-first-century students if the low number of ducks shot may constitute injury to Cantwell's pride. Additionally, they may ask students to consider if the difference in numbers of ducks shot by the two men demonstrates the success of the boatman's subversive actions. Furthering the discussion, we can ask whether the boatman feels the satisfaction of revenge by successfully ruining the Colonel's hunt. In fact, the boatman becomes apologetic, saying "I'm sorry I shot" and acknowledging his ire, "I shot in anger" (273). These are two critical points for teachers to bring out: the boatman expresses contrition, which represents a significant change from the beginning of the hunt, and acknowledges his anger. And Cantwell accepts the apology. Both of these character developments run counter to the other critics' interpretation that Cantwell is a static character, and our understanding of his character's evolution rests on our knowledge of concrete particulars.

The more extreme effects of the boatman's resistance become evident in the final three chapters. His tactics may have had a far more adverse effect on the shooter than merely causing him to miss out on some good duck shooting. They also may have weakened the Colonel physically and psychologically: physically weakening him through the unexpected and unnecessary exertion, the lack of water, and excessive sweating, and psychologically damaging him by causing anger, annoyance, and frustration, outcomes his physician advised him to avoid.

The quiet "war" between the Colonel and the boatman somehow settles old scores for both characters. The boatman gets revenge but then becomes contrite, "I'm sorry that I shot." Finally, the boatman appears to accept Cantwell for who he is, as is indicated in these parting words, "'I'll see you later,' he said to the boatman. 'Yes, my Colonel,' the boatman said" (276). The boatman's use of the possessive, *my*, indicates familiarity and respect, a major change in attitude for someone who has previously presented himself antagonistically. So too has the Colonel experienced a transformation. After the blatant conflict between the two had ended, Cantwell seems more accepting of the insignificance of his persona than he was at the beginning of the hunt, as indicated in this passage: "Now take it easy, the Colonel said to himself. Any further concern you may have is about yourself and that is just a luxury" (281). For perhaps the first time in the novel, Cantwell recognizes that he has held himself as the center of his own universe and gently chides himself for the shallowness of this attitude. At the twilight of his life, he tries to change his ways and think about others, following the example of Stonewall Jackson, who, considering the welfare of his troops above his own deteriorating condition, suggested, "'[L]et us cross over the river and rest under the shade of the trees."

When teaching Hemingway to students in the digital age, teachers should consider focusing on this small frame section of one novel, which provides students illuminating connections to the prose's "concrete particulars." As in the examples presented in this essay, the methods used in teaching the story beneath the story in *Across the River and into the Trees* provide instances of intrigue, sustaining interest, inferential thinking, and problem solving. The themes of revenge, reconciliation, humility, and acceptance are just as relevant to our digital-age students as they were for readers in Hemingway's era. Our students' lives have been greatly affected by terrifying events such as domestic and foreign terror attacks and the subsequent retaliatory actions of by governments and individuals.

War and its consequences are themes as present and as relevant today as they were when Hemingway wrote about them. The lessons that can be drawn from the novel are that reconciliation is possible and necessary in order for an individual or, by extension, a country to move forward. The consequential damaging effects are compounded by various mental and physical war injuries, which move Cantwell's final thoughts to the welfare of others: "What I would like to give her is security, which does not exist anymore; all my love, which is worthless" (253). This and other important lessons relevant to our digital-age students may be lost if we as educators fail to impart the knowledge of the role that the physical activities and the physical environment played in the works of the meticulous and observant writer that Hemingway is. That knowledge of these activities and environments are both in decline in the twenty-first century adds even more importance to the role of the educator in effectively communicating those messages to our students.

Putting the Medium and the Message in Perspective
Teaching *The Sun Also Rises* in the Digital Age

Nicole J. Camastra

> In introducing the personal computer to the classroom, we shall be breaking a four-hundred-year-old truce between the gregariousness and openness fostered by orality and the introspection and isolation fostered by the printed word.
> —Neil Postman

After fifteen years in higher education, I recently left to teach English at an independent school. Regardless of where or what I teach, one question persists: what *is* an education for? I used to believe it was only to help students acquire a particular skill set, which sounded so practical. "It seemed like a fine philosophy," Jake Barnes would say (*The Sun Also Rises* 152). However, students need more than proficiency in subject areas, especially those who cling to a business or pre-med major as a means of joining the work force in as financially viable a way as possible. We do not need more people with "skills," since we increasingly outsource many skills-dependent jobs to computers. Moreover, viewing an education from this perspective suggests America is "not a culture but merely an economy," to cite media theorist Neil Postman, who believes this thinking is "the last refuge of an exhausted philosophy of education" (*Technopoly* 174). No, we need people who can solve problems creatively, an educated electorate that can think analytically.

One reason critical thinking grows increasingly more difficult is that our devices relate information to us in a way that prioritizes "what is sensational over what is nuanced, appealing to emotion, anger and outrage" (Lewis). In 2017,

James Williams, a former tech engineer for Google, who left after becoming disillusioned by the virtual world he helped create, cogently observed, "[W]e've habituated ourselves into a perpetual cognitive style of outrage, by internalizing the dynamics of the medium" (Lewis).[1] In 1986, Postman argued that the new media ecology, led by television, was directing "not only our knowledge of the world, but our knowledge of *ways of knowing* as well" (*Amusing Ourselves* 79); finally, more than half a century ago, in 1964, Marshall McLuhan presciently proclaimed "The medium is the message" (7). The trajectory outlined here poses no surprise to those who have been paying attention. In rushing to add technology to our classrooms, we might overlook ways it undermines a different outgrowth of thought, one that demands slow, careful consideration over quick, results-driven processes and emotionally charged responses.[2]

Instead of carefully selecting how and when we use technology in the classroom, we are seduced by its ostensible promise to make learning more efficient. Efficiency, however, produces only a "technocrat's ideal," according to Postman, a "person with no commitment and no point of view but with plenty of marketable skills" (*Technopoly* 186). In the last decade, developing a "point of view" has become exponentially harder for students. This may stem from the advent of Facebook, Instagram, and Snapchat, online platforms that allow users to essentially craft their life stories and that, in turn, mirror back only the world they want to see since they are its curators.[3] McLuhan predicts this phenomenon when he writes that "all media are active metaphors in their power to translate experience into new forms" (57). Today, highlights of a digitally lived life surpass those of a real one, but studies repeatedly articulate the damaging psychological effects of hitching one's self-esteem to the number of electronic "likes" a single post can garner. Addicted to feedback from the virtual world, we have become, according to Williams, "less rational and more impulsive" (Lewis). Our digital selves offer up different ways of seeing our lives, and we mistake this vision for insight, but there are other, better ways of seeing.

Thematically focused, in large part, on vision and the lack thereof, Ernest Hemingway's *The Sun Also Rises* (1926) employs several literary devices that illustrate blindness and sight, including the opening characterization of Robert Cohn, the antagonist, who lacks the ability to see many things clearly throughout the story. The conversation among Cohn, "his lady" Frances, and Jake that ends chapter 1, other than being emblematic of Hemingway's signature dialogic ambiguity, prefigures the thematic focus on clarity and a lack thereof, both of which precipitate subsequent misunderstandings and revelations. When Jake suggests a trip to Strasbourg because he knows a girl "who can show" Robert and Jake "the town," someone kicks him "under the table" (14). The kicker remains unclear, but Cohn tells Jake "he wanted to buy a paper," which grants him an opportunity to explain, apart from Frances, her disapproval of Robert's vacationing with "any girl." This does not mean Frances kicked Jake, however; it could very well have been Robert. After their private discussion, Jake reminds him that he "forgot to get [his] paper" (15). Having gotten it, Robert grasps it, and Jake watches him "walk back to the café holding his paper." This type of triangulation, of eliding information for some characters while making it explicit for others, develops tension throughout the novel because it subordinates information to its context and characters' subsequent ability to interpret it.

Over the course of the novel, Jake acquires vision, but Robert never does. Initially described by Jake as his "tennis friend," Cohn later becomes the antagonist—after his fleeting affair with Brett, whom Jake has been in love with "off and on for a hell of a long time" (13, 128). Though the novel takes place in Paris, Burguete, Pamplona, and Madrid and follows characters who drink, dance, and have sex, it illustrates existential, even religious, concepts far from the ostensible wasteland narrative for which it is often mistaken. Instead, Jake's quest suggests a metaphorical pilgrimage that, though it remains "unfinished" at the end, nonetheless delivers the essence of a knowledge he seeks. Writing implicitly helps afford this perspective (244).[4]

As a wordsmith, Jake Barnes actually *composes* his story, which helps to translate his experience, to render it in such a way that he understands what was previously unclear to him. Jake gains much-needed perspective to finally demonstrate control in his damaging relationship with Brett. Whether this results from the composition of his narrative or the narrative stems from his self-assurance might well be a chicken and egg scenario, a moot point for our purposes. Nevertheless, the only reason we have Jake's story is that he wrote it. By the end of the book, Jake begins to learn "how to live in it," but that knowledge is not predicated on skills alone. Rather, it grows from, among other things, the ability to scrutinize, process, analyze, and understand his surroundings. Hemingway's first novel serves a meta-pedagogical role in the context of teaching writing and critical thinking because it is foremost a story told by a writer who desires to know "how to live" in a world driven by a new media ecology (152).

Foregrounding this ecology, newspapers, letters, and telegrams punctuate almost every chapter of the novel, including the first one, which ends with repeated reference to Cohn's "newspaper" (15). A newspaperman by trade but distracted by Brett, Jake composes letters that are not "very good" (48). Brett admits she never "write[s] letters" (69). Mike "can't read letters" but writes "damned good ones," and Cohn writes "a damned amusing," one in which he refers to Brett as Circe (69, 148, 89). Different from missives, which typically provide context to their purpose, telegrams contain no such context. Subsequently, telegraphy changed public discourse by "introducing . . . irrelevance, impotence, and incoherence" (Postman, *Amusing Ourselves* 65). Divorced from context, it was the original soundbite, often cryptic in its meaning but valuable nonetheless to whomever reads it since these readers often provide the missing context. From such hodgepodge meaning-making, misunderstandings will typically arise. Being "blind, unforgivingly jealous," Jake decides to "devil" Cohn about Brett and puts a telegram from Brett and Mike in his "pocket. Ordinarily, [he] should have handed it over" (105, 104). When Cohn sends one to Jake, explaining his travel plans for Burguete, Jake complains that it is a "lousy telegram. . . . He could send ten words for the same price." Instead, "Vengo Jueves Cohn" offers no "dope," as Jake puts it (133). Bill even asks what "the word Cohn" means (132).[5] Finally, Brett, via telegram, urgently asks for Jake's help in a nondescript emergency, to which he replies "with love" (242–43). The speed at which characters receive their news, rather than its content, assumes primary importance, for despite all this communication, much remains vaguely intimated.

Different from the other characters, Jake searches for missing context. He scrutinizes isolated news fragments such as the one about Cohn having been "middleweight boxing champion" at Princeton. Though it comes from Cohn himself, Jake "mistrust[s] all frank and simple people, especially when their stories hold together" (12). As a newspaperman in the foreign press service, Jake depends on getting "dirt." Referring to information in this way suggests that though he acknowledges it as a kind of professional currency, Jake simultaneously recognizes its ability to stain, discolor, and otherwise mottle life or circumstances. Its value is therefore relative to the context in which it is placed. Getting the "dirt" is different from composing his narrative, the novel. Jake immerses himself in language and communication. He reads "the French morning papers" and can "talk Spanish" (18). Many of his friends are "writers and artists," and, unlike Robert who is discouraged by writer's block, Jake anticipates his job, feeling it "pleasant to be going to work" (25, 43). He is cordial with his colleagues, some of whom are in very different life situations, with "a wife and kids" (44). For work, he goes to a news conference with "about a dozen correspondents." There, Jake's ability to distinguish between those who "asked questions to hear themselves talk" and the "news service men who wanted to know the answers" signals his acute analytic ability, which allows him to conclude "there was no news." Jake excels when it comes to prioritizing, analyzing, and synthesizing data, whereas Robert resists risky interpretations and clings to static ideas; for example, continues to believe that Brett cares for him, even though her behavior and all other evidence suggests that their affair "didn't mean anything" (185).

Cohn's writerly point of view is quite different from Jake's. With some of his inheritance, Cohn "backs a review of the Arts" (12). He serves "as a member of the advisory board" but soon after becomes "sole editor" (13). Though he "liked the authority of editing," he "had discovered writing [and] he wrote a novel" that was "very poor" (13). One reason Cohn's writing does not succeed might stem from his attitude toward it. Visiting Jake at work, Robert, "gets sleepy while reading the trade journal of his ostensible profession" (Stoneback, *Reading* 29). According to H. R. Stoneback, the "Editor and the Publisher" in chapter 2 is a publication, not two people, as the punctuation, mistakenly inserted by Hemingway and reprinted by Scribner's, suggests (20). Surrounded by words and language, Robert is ironically inept at communicating. He consumes a lot of information, but he cannot necessarily understand it. Jake knows this as he explains Cohn's rereading of W. H. Hudson's *The Purple Land*, a "sinister book if read too late in life" (17). In Jake's estimation, Cohn takes the romantic world Hudson illustrates as a "guide-book for what life holds," much the same way an R. G. Dun Report might be interpreted (17). Because Cohn cannot differentiate between fantasy and reality, because he cannot prioritize and analyze information, the ideas in all the books he reads provide plausible alternatives to his own (20). The modern equivalent would be the person for whom following someone's Instagram account provides elusive satisfaction, elusive because the unquestioning viewer tends to believe that all lives look "just like the moving pictures" (18). Cohn's quasi-biography as a magazine editor–turned–novelist provides an alternative view to Jake, the newspaperman, even though both men deal with typographic systems of information.

Robert and Jake are two different kinds of writers. Needless to say, of the two, Jake is more successful. Jake surrounds himself with "writers and artists" (25). He knows, as Nick Adams does, that "the only writing that was any good was what . . . you imagined" ("On Writing" 237) thereby rendering as "dirt" the material he puts together for the newspaper. Jake also maintains a compositional perspective that Cohn lacks. Early in the book, he emphasizes his compunction over not showing "Robert Cohn clearly"; later, he describes the archivist and his office in Pamplona only to point out that the information "has nothing to do with the story" (52, 102). These obvious references to his craft, to the choices he makes, indicate that he knows how and why he writes. Jake enjoys the composition process, whereas Cohn likes the "authority of editing," of controlling and manipulating words (13). After the somewhat accidental luck of his first novel, he can't get the "second book going" (45). Cohn lacks a confident point of view. He seeks to emulate the actions of characters in the books he reads, but he writes books in order to, presumably, understand his actions. Instead of wanting to know "how to live in it," Robert merely wants to live like other people do (152). As a medium, writing offers both men a metaphor for translation, but only Jake demonstrates a genuine ability to transform, interpret, and convert experience.

There are many such writers in Hemingway's oeuvre. Before Jake, there was Nick Adams, who knows that writing must come "from inside yourself" ("On Writing" 239). Following Jake, there are the protagonists of *Winner Take Nothing*, Hemingway's 1933 collection of short stories. In "The Gambler, the Nun, and the Radio," Mr. Frazier tries to hold off his writer's imagination while he struggles in physical pain from an injury; there is also the narrator at the heart of "A Natural History of the Dead," who operates from the perspective not of a fiction writer but of a naturalist scribe, of one who records the events around him, namely death. Decades later, there is David Bourne, from Hemingway's posthumously published novel *The Garden of Eden* (1986), whose efforts to write are challenged by his wife's, and his own, psychological demons. These are only a few examples, but they stress that, throughout his career, Hemingway's writers consistently struggle with the tension between the desire for community and the isolation requisite for creative production. It is a struggle because writing, as Hemingway famously put it in his Nobel Prize acceptance speech, is "a lonely life." It is also, as Walter Ong tells us, a "solitary" activity that "throw[s] the psyche back on itself" (68). The rewards are great, however, because the "very reflectiveness of writing—enforced by the slowness of the writing process as compared to oral delivery as well as by the isolation of the writer as compared to the oral performer—encourages growth of consciousness out of the unconscious" (147). The writing process is anything but efficient, because we only know what we want to say after we try saying (or writing) it many times over. Writing is a recursive act, and most people, including me, resist that truth.

In a writing course particularly, it "is not what you say to people that counts; it is what you have them *do*" (Postman and Weingartner 19). If we want students to realize the truth of Jake's quest through telling his story, why not have them engage in a similar activity? Ken Macrorie's I-Search Paper project outlines the search for a particular truth. It begins with identifying a question, something that students want "intensely to know or possess" (62). The search for answers produces more of a narrative than a cold academic treatise, and it outlines what the student knew about the topic, identifies the need to research it, articulates the search, and summarizes what was learned (64). Macrorie refers to the Moebius strip as an analog for the process, which is supposed to help students understand others by first understanding themselves. Moreover, he directs them to living sources first, promoting interviews with "experts," before consulting books.

When I first encountered it, the I-Search Paper felt reminiscent of Ralph Waldo Emerson, especially his famous exhortation to "insist on yourself; never imitate" (60). This is, of course, easier to do if one has a fairly solid level of self-awareness, which grants a point of view. More and more of my students complain of not knowing what matters to them, which might be a byproduct of an age in which we constantly aspire, through narratives presented on Facebook and Instagram, to live like other people do. This longing dissociates us from ourselves, and students suffer a particular disadvantage, since they typically lack the kind of experience that grants enough aplomb to distinguish between who they are and who they want to be. Emerson guarded against this when he suggested that "envy is ignorance; that imitation is suicide" (32). The correction? To "do that which is assigned thee and thou canst not hope too much or dare too much" (61). Emerson was not original in this suggestion. Ben Franklin advises us to "be encouraged to diligence in thy calling, and distrust not Providence" (56). It seems naturally fitting to discuss Ernest Hemingway in this tradition. Indeed, if students are reluctant to read Emerson and Franklin, they typically show more enthusiasm for Papa. The work of these authors suggests that the American ethos is the "lengthened shadow" of self-reliance, but our deep-rooted sense of individualism has given rise to social schisms that become increasingly more volatile (44). Hence, I adapted Macrorie's I-Search Paper for a collaborative setting.

In addition to helping students work better together, my adaptation of Macrorie's paper helps achieve what Postman calls a "kind of peace" between "two forms of learning." On one side stands "orality," which "stresses group learning, cooperation, and a sense of social responsibility" and on the other, print, which "stresses individualized learning, competition, and personal autonomy" (*Technopoly* 17). Working in groups of three, students choose a subject from among a list of topics related to the novel's historical and cultural contexts. Their project involves library research, an oral presentation, and a typed, two- to three-page paper that details their findings. They must first discover, from talking with each other, what they already know about their topic, for only then can they start to prioritize their search. I usually direct them not just to primary and secondary print sources but also to mixed media ones such as *Films on Demand*, a database that students can mine for snippets of films and documentaries that illustrate their subject. Since they are responsible for turning their research into a fifteen-minute presentation, I stress the multimodal aspect.[6]

One of the assignment's many challenges lies in not only selecting and prioritizing information but also presenting it. They must aim to teach their audience something we did not already know, which works to their benefit, since we learn a topic best when we instruct others about it.[7] A multimodal approach will engage their audience most effectively, not least of all because students' peers are accustomed to receiving their information as quick and often visually stimulating data points. PowerPoint and Prezi typically provide the best platforms for organizing and displaying information, and they fill it with text but also images and film excerpts. To encourage their classmates' interest, and depending on their specific topics, some students have dressed up in period clothing, decorated the classroom, and brought in sparkling cider as a stand-in for champagne and the booming excesses of the 1920s. Finally, they must pose a discussion question, which helps synthesize and contextualize the material for their audience, classmates who invariably want to know why they should care about something that lies so far removed from their lived experience.

After reading *The Sun Also Rises*, one group of young women researched dating and marriage trends in the 1920s. Their findings fascinated them, because they discovered a social milieu comparable to their own. Instead of swiping left or right on Tinder, young men and women in the early twentieth century were getting in and out of automobiles. Moreover, when the group juxtaposed marriage and divorce statistics from the 1920s and the early 2000s, it identified social forces that prompted men and women to make choices that they themselves were contemplating. Ultimately, the presentation challenged the class's widely held beliefs about gender and ambition in the 1920s. Articulating cultural and social trends in front of their peers tends to put what Postman calls the "information-action ratio" into a better relationship with the student. If data "derives its importance from the possibilities of action," then students learn what, if anything, they can do about a given topic (*Amusing Ourselves* 68). This student-centered, interdisciplinary approach satisfies those curricular objectives that prioritize project-based learning and Essential Questions.[8] It also aids those determined to challenge or dissolve the categorical boundaries their educational experience might erect. What we do in the classroom has relevance outside of it.

Despite fifteen years in the classroom, I have taught *The Sun Also Rises* only a handful of times. This is the first time I have written about it. I am selfish with it because, since I initially read it as a student in H. R. Stoneback's class twenty years ago, Hemingway's first novel remains my favorite. Stoneback's emphasis on close reading and bringing outside knowledge to the text in order to know it more intimately appealed to my predilection for the causal relationship between order and discovery. I wanted to know stuff, mostly because, in my very early twenties, I was painfully aware of how much I did not know. It provided answers to this undergraduate on an existential quest. Looking back on that first encounter with the book, I'm reminded of how the character Black in Cormac McCarthy's *The Sunset Limited* (2006) refers to the Bible as "a guide for . . . the sick at heart. A whole man wouldnt [sic] need it at all" (68). Though I may not be "sick," I am still not "whole," like the "unfinished church on the edge of the cliff" at the end of Jake's story (244), and Hemingway's book continues to guide me. Among other things, it helps me understand what an education is for: perspective.

Notes

1. James Williams, who built the "metrics system" for Google's "global search advertising business," left the company recently and spoke with Paul Lewis for his online article in *The Guardian*, "'Our Minds Can Be Hijacked': The Tech Insiders Who Fear a Smartphone Dystopia." That "eighty-seven percent of people wake up and go to sleep with their smartphones" prompted Williams to worry about the consequences of the twenty-first-century media ecology, and he tells Lewis, "[T]he same forces that led tech firms to hook users with design tricks . . . also encourage those companies to depict the world in a way that makes for compulsive, irresistible viewing." From Williams's perspective, the implications here reach far beyond the confines of an individual's device. Indeed, he believes they will ultimately undermine democracy. This scary assumption resonates with what Postman describes in his criticism of our TV culture. Postman writes that "after television, the United States was not America plus television." Rather, to understand any media ecology, we have to realize that the "effect of our technology is not just additive but cumulative, all consuming, in a way that we can't predict" (*Technopoly* 18).

2. A few years ago, the phrase *digital natives* aptly described my students. I am no longer sure it is not an oxymoron. New research from psychologist Jean Twenge suggests that iGen, the generation that came into adolescence simultaneously with the advent of the smart phone, around 2007, is suffering with one of the worst mental health epidemics in recent history. At the same time, there are people who rebut Twenge's doomsday thesis—among them Alexandra Samuel, who points out that it is not teenagers who need to disconnect from their phones but adults. The data, accord-

ing to Samuel, shows that it was the eighteen to forty-nine demographic whose use of smart phones increased dramatically after 2007. Therefore, it is reasonable to "consider another possible explanation for why our kids are increasingly disengaged. It's because we've disengaged ourselves; we're too busy looking down at our screens to look up at our kids." As an educator, I try to remain cognizant of my personal technology use in the classroom and what it models for my students.

3. The type of public performances extant on platforms such as Instagram and Snapchat eerily resembles that of Jay Gatsby, the persona of James Gatz, whose wildly successful narrative is predicated upon an audience. Without one, it dissipates almost immediately. Fitzgerald's novel was published in 1925, one year before *The Sun Also Rises*. The new media ecology of the early twentieth century, composed largely by print news, was hastened by telegraphy in the nineteenth century. The two mediums have an intimate relationship, for "the fortunes of newspapers came to depend not on the quality or utility of the news they provided, but on how much, from what distances, and at what speeds" (Postman, *Amusing Ourselves* 67). Newspapers challenged not only the ways people saw themselves but also the ways people perceived *other people* watching them. Not incidentally, Baz Luhrmann's 2013 film adaptation of *Gatsby* emphasizes the role of newspapers and media in the social rise of its eponymous hero. The I-Search Paper described in this chapter works extremely well with Fitzgerald's novel.

4. There exists no shortage of critical essays that examine *The Sun Also Rises* and ways to teach it. My purpose here is not to provide an exegetical lens but, rather, to build on one that is already firmly in place in order to consider Jake and Cohn as two different kinds of writers whose craft helps or hinders the ways they know "how to live in" the world (152). My view of the book as quest or pilgrimage novel derives from H. R. Stoneback's reading, initially articulated in his essay "From the Rue St. Jacques to the Pass of Roland to the 'Unfinished Church on the Edge of the Cliff.'" Along similar lines, I also suggest Larry E. Grimes's "Even the Darkness Is Light?" in Peter Hays's *Teaching Hemingway's* The Sun Also Rises. Also useful for the point of view I hold in teaching the novel, Albert J. DeFazio's piece, in the same volume, on the "Skillful Teaching" of *The Sun Also Rises* claims that teaching the novel helps us instruct "the time-honored skills . . . at the heart of a liberal arts education" (69).

5. In his book *Our America: Nativism, Modernism, and Pluralism,* Walter Benn Michaels cites this same telegram, arguing that it demonstrates Cohn's efforts to be more like Jake, the imitation of the real thing. Michaels asserts that by writing the telegram in Spanish but inserting his name, which is untranslatable, Cohn unapologetically endeavors, in vain of course, to fit into Jake's crowd. Cohn's Spanish is not as strong as Jake's; Cohn does not have real *aficion* as does Jake; and Cohn is not "one of us," as Jake, Bill, and Brett note. Bill's response to the telegram, according to Michaels, underscores it "as if it were an effort of assimilation" (74). Michaels focuses on language, translatability in particular, to draw out the semiotic differences between the two men; from that difference, he creates a lens through which to examine the race consciousness that develops certain tension in the novel. While Michaels's argument is compelling, it ultimately serves a purpose different from my concern with the contrasting writerly ethos typified by both men (74).

6. Some students have expressed confusion about the assignment, since they are used to book reports and other assessments that indicate they have read and understood a text in a cursory way. This project is *not* such an assessment. I stress that students' presentations should *not* be concerned with discussing the novel; we do that in class. While they may make passing references to it, they are primarily supposed to teach their audience about a historically or culturally relevant topic, separate from the novel, that helps us understand the context that produced it. To keep perennially popular topics like "Prohibition" from getting stale, I encourage students to examine them alongside contemporary attitudes and/or data that illustrate shifting (or static) thinking about such topics.

7. Donald Daiker makes a similar point about *The Sun Also Rises*. He argues that because Jake teaches Brett about *torero*, he is ultimately able to understand it well enough to acquire a sense of control over his own circumstances, much the same way Romero acts in the ring.

8. Essential Questions are used to help guide the course of study in a given class or curriculum. They are designed to promote students' metacognition, a way of knowing how their education helps them be in the world. Subsequently, what students learn serves a larger purpose, one that ties to a community or collective identity.

Digital Resources for Teaching Hemingway

Using Digital Mapping to Locate Students in Hemingway's World

Richard Hancuff

Ernest Hemingway's body of work often reads as inseparable from the locations in which he either produced or set those works. His prominent associations with the places he lived (Oak Park, Paris, Key West, Cuba, and Idaho) or wrote extensively about (Spain and Africa, most notably) inform both the serious criticism of his work and the cultural tourism that has sprung up around the writer, from Robert Gajdusek's *Hemingway's Paris* (1978) to the "Hemingway Look-Alike Contest" held annually at Sloppy Joe's bar in Key West. As Laura Godfrey pointed out in 2006, "critical discussion of Hemingway's sense of place is no new enterprise, and what we may call 'place-centered' criticism of his work continues to be an active field of discussion" (48). As one of those places, Paris stands out perhaps most in Hemingway lore in large part because of his posthumously published *A Moveable Feast,* which brought back for an audience immersed in the latter day "Papa" Hemingway the Hemingway of youthful struggle and the era of expatriate American Modernism. As George Wickes asserts, "Paris always remained his favorite city," and through *The Sun Also Rises* (1925) and *A Moveable Feast* (1964) Hemingway crafted an image of the city as it was in the years following the First World War (167). Certainly, Hemingway's first successes as a writer occur in Paris, and if we are to believe some criticism, the "best relationship of his life was with Hadley," his first wife, and so Paris was not simply the city, but also the space of his memory so important to the aging writer's sense of both his literary and romantic accomplishments (Dearborn 590). In his mean-spirited reminiscence of friend and rival F. Scott Fitzgerald in *A Moveable Feast,* Hemingway lauded the city as "the town best organized for a writer to write in that there is" (156). Hemingway does not elaborate on what that organization entails or how it works.

Regardless of Ernest Hemingway's late 1950s reminiscences, Paris had seen another massive war and a midcentury rebuilding that changed its streets and cafes as well as its commercial life far from the sketches Hemingway conjured in *A Moveable Feast*. While Robert Gajdusek's 1978 declaration that "the Paris of Hemingway's youth is considerably transformed" speaks to the physical changes in the city, more recently critics have pointed out that Hemingway's places are bound up not only in their physical features, but also in the individual's experience and memory (9). In their edited collection *Ernest Hemingway and the Geography of Memory* (2010), Mark Cirino and Mark Ott note that "Hemingway's work reverberates with a continual blend of memory, geography, and lessons of life revealed through the trauma of experience" (xiv). Similarly, Laura Godfrey elaborates in *Hemingway's Geographies* (2016) that "any of the geographical, physical locations that he spends time describing in the text of the memoir, are for Hemingway all constructs built by memory and experience, places built out of the feelings evoked from those memories and experiences" (109). Given these considerations of memory, the continued presence of some of the most famous of Hemingway's haunts, such as The Select or The Dôme, would do very little to evoke the actual meaning of these locations in Hemingway's writing. As Godfrey argues, "Hemingway's exacting aesthetic for writing place moves beyond a faithful mimesis of what the eye can see, attempting in addition to capture the aesthetics of memory" ("Hemingway and Cultural Geography" 54). It is, she says, much more than a catalog of names and places: Hemingway performs the work of a cultural geographer (49). As she convincingly demonstrates in her analysis of "The End of Something," Hemingway's interest in geography concerns association; it is a highly personal transformation of objects into sites of memory.

In the early twenty-first century, nearly a hundred years removed from the events portrayed in *A Moveable Feast*, we are faced with the loss of both physical spaces and bearers of memory—not only of Hemingway's Paris, but also of Paris in general of the 1920s. Such, of course, is the challenge of literary historians, who attempt as best they can to recreate the milieu of movements and individual writers. One challenge of the literature professor, whether a literary historian or not, is to present a complex picture of a text's meaning that opens the text to generations of students for whom the writer, the text, and the setting are all remote, abstract entities. The number of undergraduate or even graduate students at many institutions who have visited Paris would be a small one, and those who have most likely have not journeyed there with an eye to the artistic haunts of the 1920s. The geography therefore, to say nothing of the social memory of the 1920s, presents itself as *terra incognita* in texts such as *A Moveable Feast*. Our jobs as teachers, I would argue, involve bringing students into texts that they may perceive as alien worlds and to see how the writer shaped that world and how, in turn, they may shape it through their readings. Fortunately, we have numerous tools at our disposal to develop geographic representations that can open spatial understanding to our students; simple tools such as Google Maps provide a basic understanding of location and movement for fictional and nonfictional people in Hemingway's work. Other tools, such as ArcGIS StoryMaps, provide a more curated narrative flow that students can both create and consume to put textual geographies into conversation with thematic concerns. Far from a mere exercise in tagging text locations to web-based representations of the city map, digital mapping tools can provide entry points for more complex approaches to the questions of access, privilege, and memory.

Mapping the Streets of Paris

In several sketches from *A Moveable Feast*, including the opening sketch, "A Good Café on the Place St.-Michel," Hemingway is very specific in detailing his movements. That first sketch begins, oddly enough, with a description of a bad café, the Café des Amateurs, "a sad, evilly run café where the drunkards of the quarter crowded together" (15). However, he nevertheless tells his readers about its location, as he labels it the "cesspool of the rue Mouffetard, that wonderful narrow crowded market street that led into the Place Contrascarpe," a location that would allow astute readers to know that this undesirable café was in close proximity to both his writing studio on the rue Descartes and the apartment he and Hadley lived in on the rue Cardinal Lemoine (15). In one passage, he notes the path he walks from his writing studio to a more preferable café: "I walked down past the Lycée Henri Quatre and the ancient church of St.-Étienne-du-Mont and the windswept Place du Panthéon and cut in for shelter to the right and finally came out on the lee side of the Boulevard St.-Michel and worked on down it past the Cluny and the Boulevard St.-Germain until I came to a good café that I knew on the Place St.-Michel" (16–17).

To the untraveled reader, these directions are meaningless, and many readers simply follow Hemingway into the café, where they can vicariously enjoy the drinking of a café au lait and a rum St. James. In doing so, however, they miss the importance of these details as Hemingway casually moves from the heights of the Panthéon toward the Seine. This "good café" would have taken Hemingway roughly a quarter hour to reach, underlining the disdain he felt for the Café des

Amateurs. A reader who mapped Hemingway's path would note that he had passed by or near the Sorbonne as he avoided the wind. The landmarks he does name evoke a cultural history of Paris: the Cluny, whose foundations literally consist of medieval Paris and whose contents impress on the visitor the long history of the city in which he or she now stands; the Panthéon, originally a church, whose construction coincides with the French Revolution and whose purpose now is to honor French luminaries and, not coincidentally, to provide outstanding views of the city; the Lycée Henri Quatre, which had originally been an abbey but, like the Panthéon, became secularized during the French Revolution; and the "ancient church of St.-Étienne-du-Mont," whose present building was completed in 1624 and which had also seen a brief secularization during the French Revolution.

These specific locations and buildings evoke much more than a simple position within the city, although that positioning is also important, as it places Hemingway within the heart of the Latin Quarter and reestablishes to his midcentury readers his central cultural position in the development of modernism and the expatriate American community following the Great War. Within one very short paragraph in this opening vignette of *A Moveable Feast*, Hemingway conveys the historical weight of the spaces through which he moved in his young adulthood. While it may not have been his intention, his attention to space and his remembrance of 1920s Paris have managed to place Hemingway within the tour books alongside the streets, institutions, and cafés that he names. Even the most basic internet search engine query for "Hemingway in Paris" will return countless blog posts and travel sites dedicated to following in the writer's footsteps, while one guidebook reposts an excerpt from *Michael Palin's Hemingway Adventure* (1999), in which Palin speculates that "perhaps the spirit of occupants such as Voltaire, Rousseau, Victor Hugo and Zola spurred Ernest on as he hurried across the windswept Place du Panthéon" (Palin). While Palin has clearly taken note of Hemingway's use of cultural capital, he is simultaneously suggesting to his readers that they may add a further luminary to the list of Panthéon occupants, if not the building, the intellectual spirits of Paris who may inspire their own journey: Ernest Hemingway himself.

(Re)Producing Space

Hemingway's double move of writing his history and writing Hemingway into history undergirds both the difficulty and necessity (or perhaps the usefulness) of bringing students into a spatial understanding of the text. Laura Godfrey recounts a 1952 exchange between Hemingway and Charles Fenton, who was writing on Hemingway's Oak Park, in which Hemingway castigated Fenton for his insensitivity to the difference between the surface geography of a place and the lived experience of the place across time: "Hemingway attempts to correct Fenton's misunderstanding of Oak Park as place . . . by creating . . . a miniature cultural geography that cites the varying forces that made Oak Park, Illinois, what it once was—the social forces, the natural forces, the economic development" ("Hemingway and Cultural Geography" 54). This attempted correction, though, is necessarily fraught with the impossibility of conveying for another a very personal experience: Hemingway "also emphasizes the way Fenton's mind and eye would be fooled into great misunderstanding by looking at Oak Park as it would have appeared to him, an outsider to this cultural geography, an observer who would be entirely ignorant of any personal or local history or meaning." The difficulty does indeed seem insurmountable, as Hemingway states in his letter, "[W]hen you come into something thirty-five years late, you do not get the true gen. You get Survivors' gen. You can get statistics and badly remembered memories and much slanted stuff. But it is a long way from the true gen and I do not see what makes it scholarship" (quoted in Godfrey 54). We do not have to agree with Hemingway's dismissive attitude toward this scholarly practice of examining space to accept the validity of his objections.

Similarly to Hemingway, Michel de Certeau, in *The Practice of Everyday Life*, questions the translatability of space. For de Certeau, the act of walking in the city is a highly personal one that cannot be separated from memory: "Places are fragmentary and inward-turning histories, pasts that others are not allowed to read, accumulated times that can be unfolded but like stories held in reserve, remaining in an enigmatic state, symbolizations encysted in the pain or pleasure of the body" (108). These "inward-turning histories" may be difficult or even impossible to read completely, yet they are nevertheless details in which we seek greater knowledge of an author or text; Hemingway's attempts at an introduction to *A Moveable Feast*, drafted over and over again and collected at the John F. Kennedy library in Boston (*A Moveable Feast: The Restored Edition* 229), reveal both the impossibility of "true gen," as he put it in his letter to Fenton, and the urgency, one might say the compulsion, to recreate the history: "This book is fiction. I have left out much and changed and eliminated and I hope Hadley understands. A book of fiction may eliminate and distort but it tries to give a fictional picture of a time and the people in it. No one can write true fact in reminiscences," and "This book is fiction and many things have been changed in fact to try to make it a picture of a true time" (229, 231). Hemingway translates his experience to the page, as he claims, fictionally to provide a "true" picture of the past, or as true a picture of the past as can be managed. His conflation of fiction, fact, and memory, therefore, doesn't speak to a cavalier attitude in his treatment of the past so much as it denotes the very condition of invoking the past.

If we accept the impossibility of recovering the past, even by a direct participant such as Hemingway, why continue with our spatial excavation? For the answer, I turn to two of de Certeau's contemporaries, Jacques Derrida and Henri Lefebvre. Derrida, according to Federica Frabetti, "makes references to technology and to the importance of technicity for the definition of the human throughout his whole work," which is why Derrida's critique of the writing and the tools used to create and disseminate knowledge—digital or otherwise—provides proper caution for the project of mapping Hemingway's Paris (8). Derrida's examination of the ultimate undecidability of language and therefore the failure of pure communication illuminates both Hemingway's own urge to recreate his past and our desire as scholars and teachers to drag that history out as best we can. In *Of Grammatology*, Derrida insists that we are drawn to these histories because they lie at the heart of writing, and writing—or to substitute a term that for Derrida is of course both the same and different, *language*—is the only opening we have to the experience of the other, imperfect though it may be. Far from caricatures of his thought, Derrida insists that the impossibility of the closure of meaning should not lead to the end of the production of meaning. Arguing that a "signifying structure" of interpretation must be built on "a certain relationship, unperceived by the writer, between what he commands and what he does not command of the patterns of the language that he uses," Derrida warns that "without this recognition and this respect, critical production would risk developing in any direction at all and authorize itself to say almost anything" (158). In effect, critics and readers produce meaning in engagement with the text, built on the material given in the text, in full knowledge of the limitations of our entry into that text. The implication for our re-creation of Hemingway's Paris is that it will necessarily be imperfect, but within what Derrida elsewhere calls an "economy of violence," the only opportunity we have to gain a deeper understanding of the other—and here we can read the "understanding of the other" as any attempt to reconstruct the milieu of a writer's memoir and life—is through an engagement with that impossible past ("Violence and Metaphysics" 117). We cannot possibly recapture the "true gen" of Hemingway's Paris of the 1920s, but to fail to attempt to do so leaves us without the hope of understanding.

While Derrida's exhortation that the impossibility of certainty does not preclude the gesture toward interpretation may seem rather abstract in the application of assigning spaces in *A Moveable Feast* to defined coordinates on a map, I find it a necessary reminder that my students and I are producing readings within the structures of available tools and understandings of space. For that reason, I provide students with readings from Henri Lefebvre, whose writings on the production of urban space foreground our discussions of Hemingway's re-creation of Paris. We read excerpts from Lefebvre's *The Production of Space* and *Writings on Cities,* which allow us to consider Lefebvre's analysis of space as socially constructed and consumed in relation to Hemingway's Parisian neighborhood and social life both in and out of the cafés. For instance, Hemingway's insistence in the "Secret Pleasures" chapter of *A Moveable Feast* that "it was necessary to have one presentable suit, go to the barber, and to have one pair of respectable shoes" to go to the Right Bank may be immediately understandable to students in terms of proper social etiquette, but the larger distinctions between the Rive Droite and the Rive Gauche in Hemingway's time would almost certainly be lost without further examination (183). In *The Production of Space,* Lefebvre states that "social space 'incorporates' social actions, the actions of subjects both individual and collective who are born and who die, who suffer and who act. . . . From the point of view of knowing (*connaissance*), social space works (along with its concept) as a tool for the analysis of society" (33–34). Hemingway's observation opens up questions about what he values in rejecting social restrictions on "presentable" or "respectable" appearances as well as the types of social spaces on either bank of the Seine. While students gain a better sense of neighborhood and community embedded in Hemingway's quick comments through extending their reading to the wealth of scholarship on the Left Bank in the 1920s, such as Sheri Benstock's *Women of the Left Bank, Paris 1900–1940* (1986) or Mary McAuliffe's *When Paris Sizzled: The 1920s Paris of Hemingway, Chanel, Cocteau, Cole Porter, Josephine Baker, and Their Friends* (2016), many introductory courses do not have the syllabus space for the commitment to extensive secondary readings. Questioning why Hemingway would need to go to the Right Bank to begin with allows students to understand the way he separated—both geographically and mentally—his artistic life from his employment life. Exploring Lefebvre's notion that our associations with physical space shape our concepts of the city—that social space is constructed through these relations that are material and geographical—provides students with a deeper understanding of their own negotiations with the spaces through which they move.

Classroom Application: Google Maps and *A Moveable Feast*

For most students, Google Maps is a readily accessible and easily understood tool. While other mapping tools, such as StoryMap (https://storymap.knightlab.com/), may provide more narrative coherence, Google Maps has the advantage of being readily deployed for short projects, and many institutions use the Google Suite for Education, which conveniently allows users to share maps with groups. Maps of Hemingway's Paris, including publicly available versions in Google Maps, abound on the internet, so it's important to keep in mind that the pedagogical goal is to familiarize students with the way Hemingway remembered Paris and to use the spatial representations to ask questions of what forces—individual, institutional, historical, et cetera—shape, construct, and consume the space of the city. Importantly, I ask them to avoid the "tour guide" aspect of mapmaking and to situate the places within Hemingway's world, keeping in mind the associations that Hemingway may have had with these spaces.

I begin by creating a shared map of Paris, which is as easy as searching for "Paris" in Google Maps and saving the map. I then place students in small groups and assign each group a separate chapter from *A Moveable Feast*. I instruct them to highlight and annotate every single place name that appears in their chapter. I assign myself to the aforementioned first chapter, "A Good Café on the Place St.-Michel," because I have found that results are much more to my liking if I model the process for the students and there are fifteen named places in that chapter. I will only briefly mention here that the places allow us to think of the movement from the heights of the Panthéon to the bank of the Seine and the evocation of French cultural history embodied in these spaces. For its application on the map, I create a separate layer for my chapter, showing students how to create the layer for their own chapters. Using my list of highlighted place names from the text, I mark each space with a pin using the "drop pin" function of the application; for movements from one point to another, I show students how to connect points on the map (a particularly useful feature for both this chapter and "The People of the Seine"). Pins are not limited to marking location; they can be expanded to include text and images. The project's next step is to assign context to the points on the map, and I demonstrate for students how to add these materials while at the same time I am modeling the sort of research they will need to do to complete their projects.

The groups then complete work on their chapters, preparing not only a layer of the map for each chapter but also an oral presentation to demonstrate the significance of their work to the class. This presentation becomes the basis for the class discussion of the corresponding section of the text, effectively placing the students in charge of the direction of our exploration of the text. I request that as much as possible, students use both direct quotation from the text and analysis from our critical theory readings to contextualize the pin points they have placed on the map. As we move through the project, we also reflect on the research we are doing as a class, as we compare map layers, noting the Paris familiar to Hemingway and the Paris on which Hemingway is silent and evaluating those differences.

The culmination of the project is a side-by-side comparison of all map layers, as Google Maps allows you to toggle on or off each layer, providing us with both isolated views of each particular chapter and a summative overview of Hemingway's Paris. Along the way, students have created historical snapshots of places such as Shakespeare & Company (and woe to the group that puts up a picture of the current shop along the Seine without appropriate commentary), delved into the culture of horse- and bicycle racing, and composed brief biographical sketches of Hemingway's artistic circle of friends.

For closure, the students submit an online survey evaluation of the project, which is a step I highly recommend to anyone seeking to do a similar project. Through this survey I not only discovered that students were mostly meeting my goals for learning but also that some elements could be improved; for instance, students asked for more time to present their materials in class as well as more technical guidance on the use of Google Maps. Using the feedback from the first round of students, I reorganized the project to provide more modeling of the process by recreating some of the work in class, rather than showing it to them as a finished product, and to recenter the presentation days around the student presentations rather than make them just one part of that day's activities.

Conclusion

Hemingway's map of Paris is a personalized one, created from his memory and by necessity inscribed with the weight of his own prominence as an elder statesman of modernism and with the preeminence of modernism in the canon of twentieth-century literature, as well as the dominance of New Criticism, modernism's enforcer in the academy. The Hemingway myth looms large over popular culture notions of Hemingway's Paris, and it's important to recognize the myth-making Hemingway participates in as he fashions *A Moveable Feast* (details of which can be found in Jacqueline Tavernier-Courbin's *Ernest Hemingway's* A Moveable Feast: *The Making of Myth* and Ronald Weber's *Hemingway's*

Art of Non-Fiction). One way of engaging students with this myth, while at the same time promoting their spatial awareness of the text, is through researching and recreating the Paris of the 1920s through visual tools such as Google Maps. If done carefully, with proper attention to the historic specificity of 1920s Paris, the use of these tools brings Hemingway's world closer to today's readers.

Stories in the Land
Digital "Deep Maps" of Hemingway Country

Laura Godfrey and Bruce R. Godfrey

Hemingway rarely saw himself as a visitor to any place. He was a skilled and sensitive reader of any landscape, whether natural or human, and when in the company of friends, he valued his role as "the professor of place" by seeking out the full and experienced insider's perspective. Always compelled, according to Scott Donaldson, "to be the knower and conveyor of expert information," nowhere was Hemingway's compulsion more manifest than when he sought immediate immersion in an environment through research, conversation, and direct experience (*By Force of Will* 91). He was single-minded in his desire to get the "true gen" of any particular place, studying terrain "the way some men study the stock market" (Reynolds, *Final Years* 34). Through the copious information that he collected and recorded in his work, Hemingway's representations of place embodied the intensive documentation of an environment now often called "deep mapping."

Deep mapping is both practice and product: it can be seen as a physical manifestation of the cultural geography of a place, a way of recording the social, historical, sensory, ecological, or intensely personal histories that become entwined within, and thus part of, any given physical location. It is what Rebecca Solnit means when she writes that any "place is a story, and stories are geography, and empathy is first of all an act of imagination, a storyteller's art, and then a way of traveling from here to there" (*Faraway Nearby*). It is an engagement in the "mutual dynamic of place and self," and it involves an intensive study, awareness, and sometimes, ultimately, a recording of the bricolage of entanglements that make up a place (Flannery 158). According to Kent

Ryden (*Mapping the Invisible Landscape*), "deep mapping" is a way to capture "the depth that characterizes a place," which "is human as well and physical and sensory, a thick layer of history, memory, association, and attachment that builds up in a location as a result of our experiences in it.... [It] brings places to life more than 'cartographic coordinates' can ever do" (38). "Deep maps" often surface as narratives, in stories about people's lives, the places they know, and their memories of those places. Through the practice of deep mapping, places become more than mere locations or settings or backgrounds. They emerge as complex totalities of composite experiences, and they materialize through layered "sedimentation of impressions" (Roorda).

There are deep maps everywhere in Hemingway's fiction, nonfiction, and letters, depictions of places that blend natural and cultural histories with personal place memories. There are many examples: in "The End of Something," Marjorie comments "there's our old ruin, Nick," demonstrating the careful weaving together of Hemingway's human characters with their communities and their landscapes, just as the abandoned lumber mill in the story is an echoic reminder of many other similar "endings" (personal, ecological, economic) in that northern Michigan landscape. Remembered, multitextured terrain takes up significant space in most of Hemingway's novels: think of Frederic Henry's luminous memories of a green oak forest, destroyed by battle, in *A Farewell to Arms*, or Robert Jordan in *For Whom the Bell Tolls*, drinking absinthe in Spain and unlocking sensuous place-memories of Paris. Even the smallest moments in lesser-studied stories contain deep maps; the posthumously published, unfinished story "The Last Good Country" repeatedly incorporates the characters' "sedimentation of impressions" of northern Michigan, as when Nick Adams's sister Littless "came out to the fence at the far corner where Nick was making up his pack beyond the big hemlock that had been struck by lightning the summer before and had fallen in a storm that autumn" (*Collected Short Stories* 511). Hemingway places these memories casually and directly in front of readers—summer lightning, autumn storms, the fallen hemlock tree—making accessible Nick and Littless's intimate relationship with the landscape. A lightning-scarred hemlock tree is not a place coordinate that would make sense, or ever likely appear, on a traditional map. Nevertheless, it is a point in space that resonates with dense personal detail. Place, through Hemingway's observant narrative voice, is built out of private "fragments that all but force us to imagine the larger context" of Nick and Littless's emotional connections to their physical environment (Turchi 46).

In this sense, Hemingway was always deep mapping terrain, and his writing invites readers inside those maps precisely because of the suggestive power of the place-coordinates he allows us to see. When teaching Hemingway to twenty-first-century students, as instructors work to connect readers more intimately to his writing, identifying the existence of these narrative deep maps in Hemingway's body of work is a good place to begin. Once students understand that a faithful attention to (and love for) *places* was one of the enduring aesthetic interests that runs throughout Hemingway's oeuvre, they can see both the man and his work with greater clarity and—usually—with more sensitivity. Places, indeed, are some of the great and constant loves in Hemingway's life, a fact that becomes even more evident if we read his writing as a form of mapping in itself.

But the question of *creating* a Hemingway-esque deep map, in digital form, is a more difficult one, given the quiet and intimate nature of many of the Hemingway sites that would exist on such a narrative map. Beyond simply highlighting where Hemingway traveled or the routes his characters followed within different literary works, how can a digital deep map convey Hemingway's geographical aesthetic to twenty-first-century students? Can new digital visualizations of "Hemingway country" help illuminate his love of place, as well as his appreciation for the stories hidden within the landscapes he visited and in which he lived? And in what ways is a digital deep map of just one Hemingway region—central Idaho—useful for twenty-first-century students? These are the questions we sought to answer with the project which we describe below, an interactive digital ArcGIS Story Map, which ultimately came to be titled *Mapping Hemingway in Idaho*.

In Hemingway-focused classes, we begin the discussion of Hemingway cartography by noting that the impulse to map Hemingway's fictional worlds has been around for decades. *For Whom The Bell Tolls*, Hemingway's Spanish Civil War novel, is a book almost obsessively rooted in spatial locations and place coordinates—to such an extent that, upon the novel's acceptance in the Book-of-the-Month Club (in August of 1940), one of the club's judges "suggested including a map of the novel's setting as the end papers" (Trogdon 212). Many other examples demonstrate this desire to map Hemingway: these include Michael Palin's well-known travelogue documentary video series, Aaron Silverman and Molly Maguire's paper map titled *Ernest Hemingway Adventure Map of the World*, or literary guide books such as Noel Fitch's *Walks in Hemingway's Paris: A Guide for the Literary Traveler*.

Recently, this interest in the cartography of Hemingway country—fictional and real—has begun to take a digital turn. The website for Palin's documentary series—*Michael Palin's Hemingway Adventure*—includes an ancillary digital tool, a spinning globe with points across it marking the various stages of Hemingway's travels. Freelance journalist David Frey's blog *Papa's Planet* guides users through the different geographical locations that inspired Hemingway throughout his life. And digital mapping tools such as *Neatline* (created by the Scholar's Lab at the University of Virginia) are being tested as ways to examine the spatiality of Hemingway's stories: students in a 2015 Digital Humanities Summer Institute class in Victoria, Canada, titled "Text Mapping as Modelling," used *Neatline* to map "The Killers" in an "attempt to faithfully adapt the short story's linear plot time and detailed descriptions of the characters' movements in space" (Kotecki). In part, such efforts become a form of deep mapping in and of themselves, a way of weaving Hemingway's stories into the global cartography. In another sense, they represent a new digital shift in the longstanding desire to visualize the terrain of Hemingway's fiction and nonfiction.

Teachers can situate these newer digital forms of interest in the cartography of Hemingway's life and writing within broader theoretical frameworks. "In recent years," Rita Barnard writes, "a concern with spatiality (as opposed to temporality) has come to be regarded as the defining trait of postmodernism (as opposed to modernism)," signaling a shift from an interest in *when* to an obsession with *where* (46). But why would such a shift occur in the twenty-first century? Robert Tally argues that the digital age brings unique, often technologically driven alterations to humans' sense of spatiality: as he explains it, these shifts have much to do with the economic and social forces associated with globalization, which "has brought home to many the degree to which disparate places are crucially interconnected" (qtd. in Darici). Those of us who are equipped with digital devices and internet connectivity are enabled to see the world as simultaneously vast and minute, a disorienting and paradoxical subjectivity. Even further, "our cartographic anxiety," Tally argues, "expands exponentially in a world in which electronic transactions executed largely by computers using mathematical trading formulae can have more dramatic and lasting effects on a given socioeconomic order than entire national industries once did." The result of this "cartographic anxiety" or confusion can be that space becomes both compressed and expanded, or as Tally frames it, both "less real and more urgent in such a world."[1]

Hemingway's writing was always rooted in the *where*. Sparking students' interest in Hemingway's near-obsession with place, however, can be a difficult task. In a recent in-class writing about "Big Two-Hearted River," one student commented that at first he found Hemingway's story unimaginably boring for the way it tracked one man's detailed movements through a physical landscape. After reading and discussing it, though, the student admitted that he found himself enjoying the way the story was an exterior and interior map, both a physical and mental cartography; he jokingly wondered whether he, like Nick Adams, could make his way through unmarked terrain without the help of his smartphone's GPS capability. This students' response is representative, and it is a refrain heard weekly (if not daily) when we discuss Hemingway's writing. It can be difficult to engage many students with the exhaustive, concrete detail with which Hemingway maps his fictional worlds: as one brave student recently put it, she had to "fight the urge to skim" all of the landscape, café, and place details while reading *The Sun Also Rises.*

This frustration with the concrete physicality of Hemingway's geographies is not unique to digital-age readers; in fact, over the decades, critics have both lambasted and celebrated this characteristic of his writing. Dwight Macdonald, for example, complained about it in his 1962 essay for *Encounter*, calling Hemingway's detailed depiction of geography "peculiar"; he singled out for criticism the first paragraph of "In Another Country," asking: "*Why* must we be told about the two ways of walking to the hospital and the three bridges and the chestnut seller? The aim is probably to create tension by lingering over the prosaic . . . just as the purpose of stating that it is warm in front of a fire and that newly roasted chestnuts feel warm in one's pocket is to suggest the coldness of Milan that fall. But these effects didn't 'carry' me, I just felt impatient" (120). If, however, we look at Hemingway's writing another way, it becomes possible to see that the opening of "In Another Country" contains yet another deep map, the prose charting the route of the narrator in Milan with specific mention of meaningful, personal points along the way (the "three bridges," the "roasted chestnuts," the warmth of the woman's "charcoal fire" and the chestnuts that "were warm afterward in your pocket").

Thus, in no way are we suggesting that our twenty-first-century students are the first readers to need better help connecting to Hemingway's geographies, nor that they are all suffering from environmental or sensory impoverishment. Nor are we arguing that these students are all disoriented without the help of their digital navigation devices; nor do we mean to suggest that all students have the same level of access to digital technologies, since of course they do not. But it is also evident that part of life in the twenty-first century, for an ever-increasing number of people, involves the ownership of a digital device, and the habits we may form with those devices are inevitably going to shift some of the ways we encounter literary texts.

Thus, in this digital age, Hemingway's writing—always rooted in the physical and sensory details of the *where*—can become simultaneously more difficult and more important to teach. Digital maps emerge as one tool to help connect twenty-first-century students to the "where" in Hemingway's life and writing. There is considerable evidence of growing pedagogical interest in creating interactive digital maps, using basic geographic information systems technology, that identify literature which was produced within—and about—particular geographical locations. There are now interactive web maps of places as far-flung and diverse as Brontë country in England and literary locations like Alabama's Monroe County Courthouse from *To Kill a Mockingbird;* there are digital maps of literary sites from San Francisco to Manhattan. These creations have several important outcomes: one, these maps complicate and enrich our understanding of these regions and their long, rich literary histories; two, the maps show the physical locations in which authors created some of their most well-known works, grounding the literary art in a specific place of origin; three, the maps often align discrete locations with literary passages describing those particular places, showing us how real places become imaginative spaces and how the terrains of the material world and of the imagination influence each other.

As an extension of our regular class discussions on Hemingway's deep mapping, we created the digital pedagogical tool *Mapping Hemingway in Idaho,* an interactive digital story map that is being used in several Idaho high school, college, and university classrooms. The story map is an ongoing collaboration between the University of Idaho Library and the North Idaho College English department, and the idea for it began at the 2015 Hemingway Festival in Ketchum, Idaho. At that event, we attended a presentation by the Ketchum Community Library's regional history department of a video called *Remembering Hemingway in Central Idaho.* This video—available for anyone to access both on the Ketchum Community Library's website as well as on YouTube—includes a compilation of historical photographs and accompanying audio clips from the Ketchum Community Library's collection of oral history interviews with people who spent time with Hemingway in Idaho. The video is intimate and revealing.

Sitting in the audience that bright, warm September day (fitting, since fall was one of Hemingway's favorite times of year to visit Idaho), we listened to stories of Hemingway's Idaho years told through multiple perspectives of the people who knew him. We heard audio clips from Bill Brohan, a longtime maître d' for the Sun Valley Lodge and a Hemingway acquaintance, who remembered how Hemingway and Gary Cooper hung the ducks they shot from the rafters out at Trail Creek Cabin. (Brohan was mildly disgusted and surprised that Hemingway liked to age ducks this way for two weeks). We heard about smaller, more intimate moments from Hemingway's good friend Anita Gray, who would take long walks with Hemingway up to Proctor Mountain after a drink at the Sun Valley Lodge's Duchin Room. We heard George Saviers, Hemingway's Ketchum physician and friend, describe—still with sorrow and exhaustion in his voice, it seemed, in the 1990 interview—the difficult decision to remove Hemingway from Ketchum for treatment at the Mayo Clinic in Rochester, Minnesota. The author's life surfaced in refracted perspective, and bit by bit Hemingway emerged in a way simultaneously conflicting, complicated, familiar, and compelling. Taken together, these reminiscences built a deep map of their own, imposing new layers of meaning on the lovely central Idaho landscapes that surrounded us. Strikingly, but perhaps not surprisingly, most of these friends' memories of Hemingway centered on places, on specific geographical locations in which they spent time hunting, fishing, hiking, drinking, talking, or exploring with him.

We took a long walk after the presentations were over for the day, passing the sagebrush-covered foothills and the quaking aspens, their leaves just beginning to turn gold. The landscape of central Idaho is, we realized, chock-full of concealed Hemingway stories. How, we asked ourselves, could we bring those stories to the surface in a new kind of digital literary cartography—how could we create a tool that would enable users to "read" these landscapes with a greater literary and cultural literacy? How could we make a digitized deep map that could include historical images and audio clips from the Hemingway oral histories gathered by the community library? How useful or compelling would it be to geolocate portions of the audio files, enabling users to listen to specific Hemingway stories embedded in disparate geographic locations?

As faculty members at two different Idaho institutions of higher education, too, we thought it was remarkable that so much about Hemingway's Idaho years remained unknown by the students who attended school in the state, and we immediately began to envision this digital map as a tool for literature instructors in Idaho classrooms. And, finally, we hoped that georeferencing these figures' memories of Hemingway—in addition to placing events from more traditional Hemingway biographies as points on the map—would give users access to an "invisible" Idaho landscape made up of Hemingway stories, passing along a different kind of deep map with a unique "insider's sense of place" in the very spirit of place lore that Hemingway fiercely valued (Ryden 58). Unearthing the hidden stories in the land by creating an accessible digital map, we anticipated, could be a project in keeping with Hemingway's own philosophies on art and storytelling.

Mapping Hemingway in Idaho

By combining digital 2D and 3D maps, audio clips from the Ketchum Community Library's oral history collection, historic images from the University of Idaho Library and the Ketchum Community Library's Union Pacific photograph collection, flyover videos that move users up and over the countryside (following Hemingway's own travel routes), and biographical research, we created a multimedia map that not only traces Hemingway's movements throughout his many trips to central Idaho but also conveys his love for Idaho landscapes and the diversity and range of his travels within the region. Our map also marks the locations of important Hemingway legacy sites, such as his grave and the Hemingway Memorial. This map helps illuminate for students more about how Idaho's landscapes inspired Hemingway, but it is also a digital tool that populates Idaho's landscapes with stories of Hemingway's time spent there. Because it is easily accessible on any mobile device, it can travel anywhere with each individual user. Each time a Hemingway student, fan, or scholar stands at the top of Trail Creek Summit, or along the banks of the Big Wood River, or at the entrance to Silver Creek Preserve, this digital tool allows them to be better able to visualize the Hemingway stories that exist in the land all around them.

The ArcGIS Story Map application was the instrument that appealed to us as we explored ways to communicate Hemingway's sense of place and the stories of his time spent in Idaho. We searched for a tool that would allow us to create an interactive map that would not only enrich students' sense of Hemingway's time in central Idaho but also allow us to create a kind of living map, digitized and accessible from any type of device—from desktop computer to laptop to smartphone—letting users explore the hidden Hemingway stories in the landscapes. Hemingway was consistently drawn toward these hidden stories, toward the buried tales that lay waiting to be uncovered in the landscapes he loved to study. In this sense he was always participating in a tradition of "spoken cartographies, describing landscapes and the events that took place in them" (McFarlane 140). His philosophy regarding all geography seems to have been to look closely, to study, and to watch carefully: this attitude, revealed in his writing, clearly applies to both built and natural environments. He constantly sounded the depths of any landscape's visible, physical features for buried narratives, for meaning, and for import. This is, after all, the very same standard (often called the "iceberg principle") that he demanded of his readers—to look beyond the simple surface of his prose to find the stories underneath. In this way, the Esri Story Map application became a digital means to mirror Hemingway's ideas about reading any landscape.

Story Maps are part of an increasing attentiveness to the many possibilities opened up by the concept of narrative mapping: "'Story maps,' 'fictional cartography,' 'narrative atlas' and 'geospatial storytelling' are some of the terms that characterize the growing interest in the relationship between maps and narratives" (Caquard 135). Maps, of course, in a sense have always created narratives about the land they represented, but the concept of a "story map" that "describe[s] forms of spatial expressions that embody our personal experiences of the environment and contribute[s] to creating a deep understanding of places" is a more recent development (136). Story maps and history frames have been used for some time in the humanities and other disciplines to aid in the understanding of events or characters within texts. Esri Story Maps build on this idea by providing the ability to combine numerous types of digital content such as maps, images, text, audio, and video to represent a place. Of the various ways to organize information—alphabetically, chronologically, taxonomically, hierarchically—organizing information spatially provides "unique insights and the potential to visualize information" (Carroll and Essinger). Since 2012, when the Story Maps application was first released, more than 250,000 story maps have been created. Instead of conceiving a map as containing untold *potential* stories, a story map becomes a tool to help tell a highly *personalized* story about a particular place or region.

Such a perspective on place—place as formed by layers of individual memory—both echoes Hemingway's sentiments on geography and matches up with many twenty-first-century-student perspectives on the very meaning of place. Many of our students, so often accustomed to a highly personalized and individualized (perhaps *customized* is the proper word) views of the world, often instantly relate to the basic principles behind the story map. If students have grown up with technology, they have, often from a very young age, been trained to customize their virtual spaces, curating a digital identity with the photos and captions they post, turning generic templates of social media pages into something unique to them and their personalities. This comforting customization of digital spaces seems, in part, to translate directly to the way some students interpret physical places—as one student remarked in a recent interdisciplinary seminar titled "Physical and Virtual Environments," the entry screen on her smartphone felt as viscerally real and comfortable and beloved to her as her childhood bedroom. She had adorned that entry screen, digitally, the way many children and teenagers decorate their bedroom walls with posters and pictures and other personal artifacts.

According to the story map philosophy, a place comes to life because of the way a person moves through it, because of the experiences people have within it. This is a decidedly humanistic view, but the practice of story mapping or deep mapping does not exclude the world of the nonhuman. Indeed, as some of the audio clips on *Mapping Hemingway in Idaho* show, Hemingway loved to tell stories about the land that included the human and nonhuman narratives alike. Hemingway wished, always, to possess a "folkloric sense of place," sometimes pretending that kind of "insider's sense of place" even when he did not possess it (Ryden 58). For him, it was the narratives and stories of places—both human, personal stories and nonhuman narratives—that brought them to life.

Digital Intimacy: Hemingway's Idaho Stories

Although Hemingway's Idaho connection is well established and well known among the Hemingway scholarly community, his Idaho stories often appear parenthetically in the major biographies, and Idaho usually emerges as a place Hemingway stopped while waiting for another trip elsewhere (and, of course, as the place where he ultimately took his own life). It is a surprise to many people, including lifelong Idaho citizens, that this author had such a long history in, and connection to, the state. And yet Idaho is an important part of the Hemingway story, making up one small geographical component of the global range of places in which Hemingway lived and wrote and through which he traveled. There is very little out there—beyond two small pamphlets, published locally, in Ketchum, Idaho—that provides a comprehensive sense of how, and where, Hemingway spent his time in Idaho. There is no definitive scholarly book on Hemingway's Idaho years. There is no formal compendium of the smaller memories and moments Hemingway experienced during his time spent in the region, including his favorite route out of town (Trail Creek Road, according to his friend Lloyd Arnold) or the paths he regularly walked with friends. There are hundreds of rich and evocative stories from those Idaho visits that illuminate Hemingway's complex personality, lasting friendships, and love for immersing himself in the places he stayed. Hemingway stories are thus part of Idaho's "regional consciousness," his meanderings in the state woven into the fabric of the landscape itself (Ryden 58). And yet many of these stories remain invisible to a broad swath of the public or to the students who study Hemingway's writing in Idaho state high schools, colleges and universities.

Some of the most vivid memories of Hemingway in Idaho are the quietest ones, including the recollections from interviews with Hemingway's friend Anita Gray. Gray was a longtime resident of Sun Valley, and in one audio clip from the Ketchum Community Library's collection she describes meeting Hemingway at a party in Trail Creek Cabin, shyly introducing herself as someone who shared his bond with Michigan: "I came from Illinois, where he was born . . . and he used to go up to Michigan . . . around Little Traverse Bay. Well I spent my entire childhood there, every summer. So I was familiar with every inch of what he was describing in those Nick Adams stories . . . all those stories are places one could recognize" (*Remembering Hemingway*). Gray also recalls Hemingway, at this first meeting, eventually asking her if she liked to hunt. When she replied that she did not, but had always wanted to learn, he replied, "Well, get a license"—and that was, according to Gray, the beginning of their long friendship.

This memory is one of many that occurred at Trail Creek Cabin, an important Hemingway site located northeast of the Hemingway Memorial. Originally built as Sun Valley founder Averell Harriman's hunting cabin, Trail Creek Cabin became a regular haunt for Hemingway and his Idaho friends. Photos in Lloyd Arnold's book *High on the Wild* show a New Year's Eve 1947 gathering there: the guests include Hemingway; his wife, Mary; Gary Cooper; and Ingrid Bergman. The Hemingways often used Trail Creek Cabin for their parties, and after Hemingway's death in 1961, Mary continued to hold birthday parties for him at Trail Creek Cabin each July, using the gatherings as an "annual reunion of Ernest's Idaho friends" (*How It Was* 523). The cabin is still open for visitors to see if they travel to the region, although the property is often reserved for private parties. It rests on a hill overlooking Trail Creek, and inside, there are comfortable sitting areas, walls decorated with photographs of Hemingway and his Idaho friends, a small, wood-paneled bar not surprisingly named Papa's Place and an upscale yet rustic restaurant that is open only in the winter season. Because so many of Hemingway's central Idaho friends remembered events that took place at Trail Creek Cabin, we added the cabin as a point on the digital map, including, in a multimedia pastiche, photographs, biographical information, and an audio clip—to build, for students, a layered impression of the place as Hemingway experienced it. Students can click on the Trail Creek Cabin map point, which then zooms in on that location on the main map. The accompanying audio clips, biographical information, and photographs are available on the left-side panel of the map interface.

Other highlights of Hemingway's travels in Idaho were his trips to Silver Creek, near the town of Picabo. "Located in a broad, pastoral valley with little incline," Hemingway's oldest son, Jack, describes, and

> surrounded by high, humpbacked, sagebrush-covered hills on both north and south, with the north hills backed by great mountain ranges, Silver Creek is formed by the confluence of a number of small tributary spring feeders into three prime tributary creeks, all of which join together on a property which belonged [in 1939] to the Union Pacific Railroad—owners, at the time, of Sun Valley. It was called the Sun Valley Ranch and was composed of about 780 acres. (44–45)

At Silver Creek, Hemingway liked to fish and hunt ducks; Mary Hemingway, his fourth wife, who accompanied him on many of his visits to Idaho, describes those duck hunts with "the satin river reflecting the sky, the rust, crimson, carmine stalks of willows stretching up to their clusters of tawny leaves and a surprise around every turn" (*How It Was* 211). In an earlier letter to his son Jack, Hemingway also evoked the loveliness of the place—and his fondness for it—when he wrote: "You'll love it here Schatz. . . . [T]here's a stream here called Silver Creek where we shoot ducks from a canoe. . . . Saw more big trout rising than have ever seen. . . . Just like English chalk stream. . . . We'll fish it together next year" (qtd. in J. Hemingway 36).

Silver Creek marks another important point on *Mapping Hemingway in Idaho,* largely because of the many memories Hemingway, his friends, and his family built up over their repeated trips to the place. For this geographical location—a portion of the creek and surrounding land now under care of The Nature Conservancy and called Silver Creek Preserve—we added in photographs, quotes from Jack Hemingway's and Mary Welsh Hemingway's memoirs, and a three-minute audio clip of Anita Gray recalling her trips with Hemingway to Silver Creek. As they listen to Gray's audio file while simultaneously seeing the digital map of the area, users experience the odd digital intimacy that this map format allows. In the clip we selected, Gray remembers how, on one winter trip to Silver Creek, Hemingway taught her how to "read" the story told by bobcat tracks in the snow: "I'm going to give you a little nature lesson," Gray recalls Hemingway telling her. She goes on to remember, "All from these tracks, he taught me [to see] how the bobcat had taught her cub to kill a bird. All of this was out in the snow. And he could read it. . . . It was a beautiful setting. I can still see it in my mind's eye" (*Remembering Hemingway*). Students who have used the *Mapping Hemingway in Idaho* tool report that these *smaller* moments are some of their favorite Hemingway stories embedded as points on the map. Anita Gray's memories are nostalgic, to be sure, but it is also clear how much she loved Hemingway for the way he helped her see the stories in the land. When they listen to her memories of Silver Creek while simultaneously examining the map, we want students to see those stories in their "mind's eye" just as she did.

In another sense, we designed this digital Story Map to bring students closer to understanding the paradoxical complexity that marked Hemingway's experiences in Idaho. His life was often a study in jarring contradictions, and one particular point on the map provides a small but telling example. For one fall 1941 excursion, Hemingway took his brand new, sage-green Lincoln Continental convertible (undeniably a luxury car) up Trail Creek Road, ultimately to explore the Bitterroot country of western Montana and Idaho. Trail Creek Road runs northeast out of Sun Valley, and it is less of a road and more of a narrow, gravel trail clinging to the side of a canyon wall. The drop to the bottom becomes heart-stoppingly steep as you climb (worse, though, is the descent *into* Sun Valley, when your car is on the canyon side of the road). The road runs through stunning country of unimaginable scale, and the vastness of the land is both awesome and intimidating. Hemingway's good friend Lloyd Arnold reports that, probably for those reasons, this road became one of Hemingway's favorite routes to take on their hunting and exploring excursions—Arnold describes it as a "rough, dusty, teeth-rattling road . . . a hair-raiser, to put it mildly, and the very thing that appealed to Ernest when we started clawing our way up the canyon wall" on their first trip up in 1939 (16).

On this 1941 trip, there were five men packed into the convertible. As Arnold remembers it, "as we were winding up the Trail Creek Summit road . . . a rolling rock knocked a hole in the exhaust pipe. We yelled ourselves hoarse for forty miles to Challis and a mechanic with a welding torch for repairs" (62). The image of burly, bulky Hemingway packed tightly into a brand-new convertible, driving a luxury car in the midst of the rugged and remote terrain, struck us as the exact kind of paradoxical moment we sought to highlight for students. The event would never register as a major moment in the life story of the author, but it is nevertheless a telling one, a hilariously revealing demonstration of the way Hemingway enjoyed the places in which he lived and wrote.

How, though, to communicate this paradoxical Hemingway to students in this digital format? We wanted to not only to pinpoint the general geographical location of this trip and this event (although we had no way of knowing the specific section of Trail Creek Road where the rock rolled down from the mountainside) but also give users a *virtual* sense of how it felt to drive up the road. As closely as we could, we sought a way to give students a feel for the remoteness of the countryside and to digitally immerse them in the place, placing them in the same perspective as Hemingway as he traveled northeast out of the valley. Both of us have traveled up and down Trail Creek a number of times, and we wanted to convey the sheer lunacy of taking a new luxury vehicle "off-roading" into the wilderness of central Idaho—which we both saw as a classic example of Hemingway's zest for intense and memorable experiences. The link we created allows users to "fly" up Trail Creek Road, following one of Hemingway's regular routes out of Sun Valley with a bird's-eye perspective. While the visualization, produced using Google Earth Pro, provides users with a sense of the area's landscape and the steepness of the climb up Trail Creek Road, the video is merely the starting point for where this technology may allow users to go. In five years' time, as virtual, mixed, and augmented technologies advance and become more mainstream, our "flyover" app will probably seem laughably rudimentary.

"Bodily Transporting" Readers

Taken together, Hemingway's Idaho stories mix with the landscape, and this digital map weaves a discrete physical geography with memories of Hemingway (some nostalgic, some loving, some bitter, some angry, some sad). We wanted the result to be a familiarizing and immersive digital experience. Thus far, *Mapping Hemingway in Idaho* has only been used in high school, college, and university classroom settings, with students researching Hemingway's sense of place by selecting locations and exploring the multimedia options available to describe how he spent time in each place—where he walked, what his favorite routes out of town were, where he went to escape "town life," such as it was (the wilderness of the Middle Fork of the Salmon River was one escape). Though students are experiencing only a digital version of this "Hemingway country," they nevertheless report that the map allows them to feel, as one student put it, "immersed in Hemingway's Idaho stories." Another student, after exploring the points on the map, commented that the digital tool gave her a strange awareness of one person's love for a physical place, perhaps the highest compliment that we could receive for the tool. In the end, it is a digital deep map that attempts to highlight (and celebrate) both an author and a geography.[2]

For Hemingway, traditional maps clearly had a beauty and allure all their own—purely and simply, it appears, because (like his fiction) they seem at once empty and deeply evocative. Traditional maps tell only part of a story, omitting all but the most suggestive details. The reader of any map must do the interpretive work to fill in the rest of the narratives embedded within the place-names, the landmarks, and the topographical features. It is in the perceived emptinesses that map readers invent meaning, like Joseph Conrad's Marlow, recalling (near the beginning of *Heart of Darkness*), "Now when I was a little chap I had a passion for maps.... At that time there were many blank spaces on the earth, and when I saw one that looked particularly inviting on a map (but they all look that) I would put my finger on it and say, When I grow up I will go there" (22). Like Harold Krebs in "Soldier's Home," who reads World War I history books but wishes for "more maps," looking "forward with a good feeling to reading all the really good histories when they would come out with good detail maps" (*Collected Short Stories* 113), Hemingway seems to have understood the evocative power of compressed experience that maps communicate. In the oft-quoted interior monologue of Frederic Henry, Hemingway's protagonist in *A Farewell to Arms*, "[t]here were many words that you could not stand to hear and finally only the names of places had dignity.... Abstract words such as glory, honor, courage, or hallow were obscene beside the concrete names of villages, the numbers of roads, the names of rivers, the numbers of regiments and the dates" (185).

Stylistically, then, Hemingway's aesthetic attention to concrete images—partly an influence of modernist writers like Sherwood Anderson, Ezra Pound, and Gertrude Stein, who helped him gain entrance to the literary world—can also be seen as a form of what Robert Tally names "literary cartography," of writing as mapping. Describing the art and science of cartography, Kent Ryden could very well be detailing Hemingway's prose aesthetic when he writes that "through the precise graphic shorthand of modern cartography, [mapmakers] have been able to summarize in a very small space a wealth of topographical and cultural information that would otherwise have taken pages and pages of verbal description and mathematical figures to contain" (20). Maps, Hemingway understood, were suggestive for both what they plotted and what they left out of the picture. Often, what is left out can only be brought back again in memory, and "Hemingway was always concerned with the utilization of memory, trying to understand how it can be used as an aesthetically satisfying component of his fiction" (Cirino and Ott xiii). Thus emerges a writer for whom places are made from memories and memories are, quite often, made up of places.

On our digital map, Hemingway's movements throughout these Idaho years appear as intimate and meandering wanderings: they are nonlinear and often unpredictable, suggesting instead what common sense already tells us, that a body in space will always violate inflexible grids or binaries. This new visualization, then, serves to inform us that Hemingway's experiences within Idaho can be seen in the context of "a . . . cartography of folded, relational, 'transformational' space where an 'interplay of roots and routes' disrupts any monological representation of this region" or this writer (Maher xvi). Future digital-visual renderings of Hemingway's fictional and biographical spaces may enable fresh readings of long-studied texts in Hemingway's oeuvre; questions about how Hemingway defines concepts like *belonging, home, migration, dislocation,* or *expatriation* could all be partially answered through digital-spatial renderings of the ways he and his characters move through the spaces and places of their lives. And, finally, such projects would help complicate the broad notion that an interest in spatiality is "the defining trait of postmodernism (as opposed to modernism)," a broad distinction that Hemingway's life—and his body of work—belies (Barnard 46).

So far, digital visualizations primarily exist to illuminate Hemingway's travel patterns or his gyrations within a particular locale, like Paris or Idaho. Future opportunities exist, however, to create digital maps for the movements of characters in his short fiction and novels, visualizations that could provide scholars and their students new ways of seeing his writing as a form of mapping in itself. Students and instructors could map Hemingway's fishing trips around northern Michigan, or chart the frenetic movements of the characters in *The Sun Also Rises,* or digitally visualize his African safari routes to record and communicate those travels in new ways. And what would Hemingway's early (and spatially insular) stories like "The End of Something" or "The Three-Day Blow" look like if we created digital maps for them? How could a digital cartography show us how much wider Hemingway's spatial sense of the world became just a few short years later, as he composed *The Sun Also Rises?* In that book alone, there is a nearly constant stream of place references, places of the heart and imagination that exist just out of reach. In the spring of 2018, Hemingway students at North Idaho College counted the novel's place references during one class discussion, coming up with this meandering list of cities, countries, rivers, and mountain ranges: New Jersey, Paris, South America, New York, London, Cannes, San Sebastian, Bayonne, Monte Carlo, the Pyrenees, Madrid, Tafalla, Pamplona, the Irati River, Burguete, Biarritz, Montana, Kansas City, Chicago, Vienna, Budapest. This is not a complete list, but in making it, we saw just how far Hemingway's characters had come from the time when going "into town" Saturday night or "fishing the 'Voix" were the furthest extensions of their imaginary horizons.

Perhaps some of the best pedagogical methods for teaching Hemingway in the digital age are those that use technology to remind students that everywhere in his work are celebrations of embodiment, of humans' existence in and movement through the physical world. We built *Mapping Hemingway in Idaho* to remind students that Hemingway's work helps us see that we all carry deep maps of physical places inside of us, holding close our most beloved place memories in a shifting cartography that changes with each new story that unfolds in a particular location.

Notes

1. Still, it is also of course true that "the dialectics of subjectivity and space" have long been of interest to writers preceding the postmodern and digital ages (Barnard 46–47). While our digital-age experiences with technology and globalization may bring on some simultaneously compressed or expanded conceptions of the physical world, the modernists were also acutely interested in spatiality: think of Willa Cather's explorations of indigenous, masculine, feminine, and urban domestic spaces in *The Professor's House,* or of Virginia Woolf's examinations in *Mrs. Dalloway* of how subjectivity influences spatial perceptions.

2. For instructors interested in using this particular tool in their own Hemingway classes, access is free, and navigating through the map is similar to navigating the basic links on any website or digital map. By clicking on the *Mapping Hemingway in Idaho* URL, teachers can take students through the points on the map in class, or they can assign students to explore the map's different points on their own. In our own Hemingway-focused classes, we usually introduce students to the map in the midpoint of the semester, after the class has had a chance to read many different narrative examples of Hemingway's love for creating deep maps. Rachel Lyon, an English teacher at Moscow High School, notes that she "likes to have kids pick a location on the map and read a piece directly related to the location (if one is available), like the 1952 piece Hemingway wrote, 'The Shot,' so they can see a connection between the geography and Hemingway."

Using Digital Tools to Immerse the iGeneration in Hemingway's Geographies

Rebecca Johnston

Nearly without fail, when I speak with students about Ernest Hemingway, the question of whether his works were autobiographical arises. This is often worded as "His works are autobiographical, right?" since students, and much of society, frequently have the preconceived idea that Hemingway wrote solely from the script of his own experiences. The vision of Ernest Hemingway as Lieutenant Henry or Robert Jordan is the one that will remain in the minds of many students when they study Hemingway online. This association has a great impact on students' interpretative habits: when they search the internet to follow Hemingway's adventures, they further equate the author with his characters. However, by taking a solely autobiographical approach, students miss the complexity Hemingway's geographical and historical settings add to his fiction. Furthermore, by not moving students' focus from Hemingway as the internet presents him, instructors may fail to bring a deeper and more accurate understanding of Hemingway's fiction to their classes.

Hemingway did incorporate autobiographical details in each of his works. He was a father of three boys and hunted German U-boats during World War II, like Thomas Hudson in *Islands in the Stream*. He did serve in the Red Cross in Italy during World War I, just as Lieutenant Henry did in *A Farewell to Arms*. However, his works are not entirely autobiographical, and interpreting them as such can lead to misinterpretations and misunderstandings. While there is often merely the thinnest layer of invention between Hemingway's life and his fiction, the information about Hemingway's life and travels available on the internet can distract students from the novels he left behind. According to many of the images of Hemingway online, in Cuba he is Santiago, and in Italy he is Lieutenant Henry. By avoiding internet sources with such a heavily biographical focus and instead using sites that allow a more historical and geographical focus in an effective manner, instructors can separate the man from his works: this will allow students to learn more about Hemingway, and his writing process.

Instructors are often under pressure to turn to the internet to find sources that will digitally illuminate the literature that they teach. However, many web sources perpetuate images of Hemingway as the Most Interesting Man in the World, pushing a specific brand of beer, or as an alcoholic, frequenting Paris pubs and moodily discussing hunting in Africa.[1] The issue facing professionals is how to best present Hemingway in their classrooms to bring a deeper understanding of his works without perpetuating false ideas or images. Hemingway's novels are very geographically specific and historically rooted. Used wisely, the digital realm, allows students to visualize both of these aspects of his settings. Redirecting students away from sites that present the more distracting images of Hemingway and toward sites that help them understand Hemingway's complex geographical and historically situated settings will allow students to understand Hemingway's novels more intimately and thoughtfully.

Numerous websites allow instructors to shed light on Hemingway's geographies, but not all websites are created equal, and some perpetuate false or distracting images. Unfortunately, many of these sites are the easier ones to locate and use. It is, for instance, easy to find Michael Palin's pages on the Public Broadcasting Service's website, *Michael Palin's Hemingway Adventure*. The information Palin gathered from his 1999 trip, which followed Hemingway's travels, allows instructors and students to explore the areas of the world that influenced Hemingway (and that Hemingway subsequently influenced). Palin's site has its merits. Hemingway aficionados will find interesting pictures of Hemingway as a child and a Red Cross volunteer, recipes for foods he enjoyed (such as Trout au Bleu and Hunter's Safari Steak) and interesting information on the places that affected his life and influenced his writing. Palin gives an overall image of Hemingway as an adventurer, which many students will undoubtedly find appealing. However, Palin's site is not the best option for instructors, as it is not without flaws and inaccuracies. For example, Palin claims that after the First World War Hemingway did not visit Italy again until the 1940s. However, Hemingway visited Italy with Hadley in July 1922, a trip he documented in the *Toronto Star* in "A Veteran Visits the Old Front"; the pair returned in 1923; and Hemingway traveled through Italy on his own in 1922 on his return from Turkey (*Dateline* 176; Meyers, *Hemingway* 91; *Letters* 2:33–34).

Hemingway also visited Italy with Guy Hickock in 1927, a trip he wrote about in "Che Ti Dice la Patria" (Baker, *A Life Story* 183; *Complete Short Stories* 223). A biographical mistake of this nature gives one cause to question other material on Palin's website. When I am preparing lessons on Hemingway, I do not have time to sort through sites that may or may not contain false information, and I can only assume others are in a similar time crunch.

While the locations Palin visited did influence Hemingway, Hemingway's works also need to be understood within their own historical and geographical contexts, not as part of the many skewed or exaggerated images of Hemingway's life. My twenty-first-century students often come into the classroom with preconceived ideas of who Hemingway was and how his works should be interpreted based on those ideas. Hemingway's life and travels have appeared just as interesting to subsequent generations, as they do to readers during his lifetime. Instructors may struggle to separate students from their established ideas of Hemingway, and if they use internet sources that merely highlight Hemingway the adventurer, these students will continue to miss the rich and complex geographies and histories Hemingway presented in his fiction.

Most of my students, for example, assume that Hemingway used his travel destinations as the exact settings for his works, and that is not consistently true. Frederic Henry served on the frontline of World War I in an area Hemingway could not have accessed until after the war, as the front lines shifted into Italy before his arrival in the war. Hemingway served alongside a military defending its home country; Lieutenant Henry served in a military trying to take land from its neighboring country, and thus the futility of the war in *A Farewell to Arms* is more vivid when the geography of the novel is studied separately from Hemingway's life. As Michael Reynolds explains, "Hemingway went back to someone else's front and recreated the experience from books, maps, and firsthand sources" (*Hemingway's First War* 15). Paul Smith has also confirmed Hemingway's focus on exact topography of place ("The Trying-out of *A Farewell to Arms*" 42). Hemingway worked diligently to create the historical and geographical contexts of his works, and websites—ones focused on the mythology of his personality more than his geographical fidelity—can perpetuate a misunderstanding of *A Farewell to Arms* and of Hemingway's other works.

Another such site is the one advertising the Ernest Hemingway Collection, laid out to follow Hemingway on his travels. This site presents viewers with an assortment of glossy, inviting links for eight of the locations central to Hemingway's life: Oak Park, Illinois; Italy; Paris; Key West; Africa; Spain; Cuba; Idaho. The website also contains a collection of links to items, available for purchase, that represent Hemingway's "lifestyle." Links lead, for example to the websites of companies selling furniture "inspired by his work, travels, and appetite for life," and promise that "while your days might not be as exotic as his, you can rest easy and recharge on the Ernest Hemingway Collection of luxury mattresses." The Ernest Hemingway Collection site even labels hotels around the world as Hemingway-like, branding them as places Hemingway may have chosen to stay if he had the chance. This webpage seeks to profit from a specific interpretation of Hemingway's life: Hemingway as the rugged and glamorous celebrity. While Hemingway did at times encourage this image of himself, he also focused intently on creating works of fiction with accurate and immersive depictions of geography and history, and as educators we must decide whether we would like our students to focus on Hemingway, "the man, the myth, the legend," or on the accurate and detailed literary worlds he created. By accessing this website, instructors wishing to understand Hemingway's geographical contexts or present them to their students will instead be led to various locations that others have, for financial reasons touted as "like Hemingway," and students will be led to items supposed to represent him. Thus, students will focus on the mythical, rugged, explorer Hemingway instead of on the places Hemingway wanted his works to bring to life. Palin's site and the Ernest Hemingway Collection website are similar in that both lead students toward a version of Hemingway that takes us further from his writing.

Immersive Digital Maps

Rather than sort through those sorts of prepared websites that "follow" Hemingway, in my own classes I use digital tools like Google Maps and Google Earth to teach my students about the dense sense of place and history within any of Hemingway's works. These tools are readily available and free: Google Maps is a site many instructors probably already use as an app on their phones. If an instructor is teaching *A Farewell to Arms*, for instance, she can type the location "Gorizia" into Google Maps and receive directions from Gorizia to Plava, Kuk, and the Bainsizza Plateau, immediately giving students an idea of how far Lieutenant Frederic Henry traveled to the front lines. Google Maps' view of Gorizia can be further expanded to include the area "on the Isonze [sic] north of Plava . . . north of Gorizia" where Lieutenant Henry was injured (75). Similarly, one can also bring up Via Manzoni in Milan, where he wanted to walk "in the hot evening and turn off along the canal" and where he later met up with "old Meyers and his wife" at the Gran Hotel (32, 103). Instructors can enable Google Maps' Ground View in Milan, allowing them to virtually walk their students around the Scala, which Henry and Rinaldi both mention, as well as some buildings on the street nearby that users can virtually enter (66, 104). While their classes are reading about Lieutenant Henry's part in the Italian retreat after the Battle of Caporetto, instructors can type the locations of Gorizia and Udine into Google Maps to see possible areas through which Henry would have traveled. From there, the map can help students envision him in the Tagliamento River, then traveling on to Milan and Stresa as he retreats into Switzerland. Students can also search for Kobarid (Caporetto) on Google Earth. Where possible, while looking for each city instructors should use the ground view feature, to give a view of the area. In Kobarid, they should take the time to view the mausoleum outside of town, which houses the remains of thousands of Italian soldiers who died in the Battle of Caporetto. This type of virtual immersion will allow students to explore the locations actually mentioned in or used for Hemingway's novel, an immersion that will add to their understanding of *A Farewell to Arms* by highlighting Frederic Henry's sometimes desperate, sometimes deliberate and plodding movements.

When he wrote, Hemingway spent time poring over maps and history books, as well. He was so sure of detail that the roads, streams, rivers, and houses he describes in his novels and short stories are often portrayed surprisingly accurately. These accuracies were aspects of craft that he wanted seen in his writing, so he made them painstakingly detailed. We can bring these aspects of place to life for our digital-age iGeneration or Generation Z students—while also making the written material more accessible for them—by using virtual maps to highlight the geographies and histories of Hemingway's works. In doing so, we will help our students see the depth of suffering Lieutenant Henry went through just in *getting* to Milan while he was injured, or when he was retreating from the Tagliamento. Furthermore, by adopting these digital tools instructors can help their students visualize the distances Hemingway's characters pass through, thus bringing to light, for example, Lieutenant Henry's nomadic movements and his suffering. We can help students better connect to remote places they have likely never heard of before—such as Segovia or Plava—and help them to see these as real locations that had a deep impact on the characters about whom they are reading.

This technique is widely translatable to other Hemingway works, as well. Instructors can also pull up locations like Fox River, Black River, and Seney, Michigan, on Google Earth and Google Maps to give clear visuals of these important Hemingway geographies. While ground views are typically not available for wilderness areas, directing students' attention to the woods around the rivers and their general locations in Michigan is still instructive. We can add depth to students' interpretations of Hemingway's writing by helping them see the areas Hemingway is describing in such spare, sparse detail. Google Maps, for instance, will give students an idea of how long "Big Two Hearted River"'s protagonist, Nick Adams, had to walk in the woods to reach the Fox River. If a class is reading *For Whom the Bell Tolls* or *The Sun Also Rises*, Google Earth can pull up Segovia, Madrid, and Pamplona. (However, ground level images are typically only available in cities, while only aerial images are available of wilderness areas). Robert Jordan's movements in *For Whom the Bell Tolls* can be tracked on Google Maps, as well. Cuba has fewer ground views available; however, many images have been attached to Google Earth, so students can view Harry Morgan's "Morro" and see how vast is the sea around Cuba in which Santiago fished, and yet, when considering Morgan's trips across the Florida Straits, how close Cuba is to Key West. My own students are able to more fully understand Hemingway's works associated with World War I when they can see that the Soča Front is a beautiful area filled with small cities and villages, much like the small cities around the college they are attending. This ability to relate to Hemingway's fictional geographies gives students a better idea of the disillusionment he—and his characters—so powerfully felt after seeing these areas needlessly destroyed by war.

I used this technique of accessing Google Maps recently, when teaching my undergraduate students to analyze "Now I Lay Me." Many of our twenty-first-century students live in a very visual world, and their textual understanding is enhanced when they can see where the story is happening. While this enhancement may not have been necessary in the past, our digital world has created different pedagogical expectations and demands. We would, of course, like to have students enter the classroom already knowing how to fully comprehend and analyze the literature in front of them. However, just as many undergraduate students must be taught how to use citations and quotation marks, many also must be walked through analyzing literature at the challenging level that Hemingway's writings demand. One way to gently do so is to provide them with images and maps that help them to begin to understand aspects of the stories important to Hemingway. It would be wonderful if my students came to my class able to dive into literary interpretation without digital aids, but it would also be wonderful if they all came to my class fully understanding what a sentence fragment is. This is not the case, so I must meet students where they are so I can bring them further along as writers and literary scholars.

In this particular lesson, I chose a pre–World War I picture of Hemingway from the John F. Kennedy digital archives ("Ernest Hemingway Photograph Collection"). I mentioned that he was in the war as an ambulance driver but concentrated on the story's geography and history. I also added images from World War I to help my students understand the dire situation Nick was in as he tried to heal, physically and mentally, from the trauma of war. The closest image many of them have of that is from video games such as Battlefield I, which is of course not entirely accurate or representative. By looking at images of men not much older than themselves fighting in muddy trenches next to their dead or dying friends, my students began to understand just why Nick Adams could not sleep at night. They no longer viewed the war as the context for entertaining digital conquests but instead saw it more clearly as the deadly conflict that cost nearly 8 million lives and led many survivors to post-traumatic stress disorder and alcoholism (Howard 146). Further underscoring this lesson, the British Imperial War Museum has thousands of digital images from World War I online, including seventy-two images from the Soča (Isonzo) Front. The Library of Congress also has some useful digital images online ("Italian Forces"). On these sites instructors can easily download verified images into PowerPoint presentations, giving nuance and pathos to Hemingway's works without focusing on Hemingway.[2] The Imperial War Museum even has an image of Italian soldiers gathered in Gorizia wearing their helmets, just as Lieutenant Henry mentions "[W]e were supposed to wear steel helmets even in Gorizia but they were uncomfortable and too bloody theatrical in a town where civilian inhabitants had not been evacuated" (Barbour; *A Farewell to Arms,* 24). The British Imperial War Museum also includes several propaganda images from the war, images that underscore the disillusionment expressed in *The Sun Also Rises* and *A Farewell to Arms.*

Digital Videos and Hemingway's Sense of Place

Videos are another excellent source for bringing the settings of Hemingway's works to life. YouTube videos produced by groups such as CrashCourse can add understanding to the historical contexts of *A Farewell to Arms* and *The Sun Also Rises,* as can videos by The Great War or Hemingway's own creation, *The Spanish Earth.* Historical videos provide students with helpful context for details Hemingway may only barely mention in his fiction, and these accompanying digital images will allow the students to visualize the places Hemingway memorializes, rather than focusing on the glossy and often hypermasculine digital images of the rugged, mythical Hemingway.

For example, in *The Sun Also Rises,* Jake mentions

> a big religious procession. San Fermin was translated from one church to another. In the procession were all the dignitaries, civil and religious. We could not see them because the crowd was too great. Ahead of the formal procession and behind it danced the riau-riau dancers. . . . All we could see of the procession through the closely pressed people that crowded all the side streets and curbs were the great giants, cigar-store Indians, thirty feet high, Moors, a King and Queen, whirling and waltzing solemnly to the riau-riau. (134)

Jake also mentions "the giants, with the men who danced in them" (134). The San Fermin procession itself can easily be seen in YouTube videos, and a 1920s video of this same procession is even available ("Giants"; Ray). Viewing videos such as these will bring the written text to life and emphasize the rich local history of the festival at San Fermin.

The Library of Congress is also a useful source for videos when teaching *The Sun Also Rises.* It has acquired the Prelinger Collection, which is a collection of historical motion pictures ("Library Acquires"). Among the motion pictures in this collection is a series of videos taken in Paris in the 1920s which have been made available for viewing and downloading on a separate site (Holmes). In the motion picture *Seeing Paris: Part One: On the Boulevards,* viewers can see Elias Burton Holmes looking over the Avenue de l'Opera, an avenue Jake mentions in *The Sun Also Rises* (Burton; *The Sun Also Rises* 13). Café du Dôme and Champs Élysées are also visible. This motion picture will give students an idea of life in Paris as *Jake* saw it. Because our students often come to the classroom with Hollywood images of Paris—or with little sense of Paris at all—as instructors we are competing with those preconceived images, as well as with the ubiquitous images of larger-than-life Hemingway that proliferate online. By providing videos of Jake's Paris, instructors give their students a clearer geographical and historical context for *The Sun Also Rises.*

Also located in the Library of Congress is the Carol M. Highsmith Archive. Highsmith's photography is particularly useful when teaching *The Old Man and the Sea* or *To Have and Have Not.* Instructors can download images of Cuba from this collection and show them to classes, giving students a visual image of the settings in parts of each of these works. Included in Highsmith's collection is even a picture titled *Cuba Capitol on the Prado*. According to Kirk Curnutt, when Harry Morgan is sailing away from Cuba and states that he can see the "dome of the Capitol," he is speaking of the Capitol located on the Passeo de Prado (*Reading Hemingway's* To Have and Have Not 41). Helen mentions this same boulevard when she recalls getting her hair done "in that beauty parlor on the Prado" (258). Use of Highsmith's pictures as accompaniments to their reading will help give students an image of a location that Hemingway chose to highlight, helping students to focus on *places* as deliberately as Hemingway did when he wrote.[3]

The Hemingway App in the Twenty-First-Century Classroom

No matter the age of the students, our undergraduate students love games to challenge their knowledge. The Hemingway Trails and Quizzes App is one available game for studying Hemingway's works. The app opens with a picture of Hemingway inside of what appears to be a life preserver. Once the life preserver logo is tapped, a list of Hemingway trails appears. "Traveling" virtually to each location costs ninety-nine cents, and once users buy the map, they will have the opportunity to virtually "walk" through locations in which Hemingway lived or worked. (The instructor can download this phone app in advance as a supplement to the digital material already loaded into the classroom computer.)

Each page of the tour ends in a question that relates to that portion of Hemingway's life, and students can compete for correct answers while testing their knowledge of Hemingway's life. This tool is a real asset for those who happen to be teaching in one of these geographical areas; however, the app does not require users to be in a specific location. An excellent way to use this tool is to stay consistent with a focus on the setting Hemingway used. A good example of the trails one can follow is "Hemingway in Valencia," a trail that consists of eighteen questions that range from questions about the facade of a local train station to a specific hotel that is mentioned in "The Night before Battle" and a statue of Belmonte, mentioned thirty times in *The Sun Also Rises*. Instructors can queue each of these locations in Google Earth and then challenge the students to find each of these details in the digital image. Thus, this digital application can be useful in showing students more about Hemingway's characters and his places in an informal (and informative) digital environment, while helping them gain a deeper understanding of the fiction they are studying.

Application

Practicality is always important for instructors. Our time is limited and valuable. Digital tools are an important asset to our teaching, but they need to be organized in such a way as to make them easily accessible, or they will not be useful. To this end, I build a document in my computer with all of the links I will need for teaching a particular book. Thus, for *A Farewell to Arms* I will have a document labeled "*FTA* Links," and on that document I will put a link to Google Maps under a labeled header for the site with a list of the cities I wish to digitally bring my students to, such as Kobarid, Gorizia, and Milan. I will do the same for the John F. Kennedy Library Hemingway Archives, the Library of Congress, YouTube, and the British Imperial War Museum. I have also, for example, loaded all of the images into a PowerPoint labeled "*FTA* Lecture." Screen shots from Google Maps can be put into the PowerPoint, and images can be downloaded and placed into the presentation. However, to give students a ground view of a particular location including a direct link for Google Maps is still helpful. With either method, the digital document or PowerPoint presentation can be prepared once and used in the classroom for years.

Using these digital tools to immerse students in actual locations in Hemingway's stories and novels allows students to gain a better understanding of the geographies and histories behind Hemingway's fiction. Those who are just being introduced to Hemingway's works may not have the ability to easily separate Hemingway from his characters, and so in their lectures and presentations instructors must be careful to separate Hemingway the man from Hemingway's works. According to Carlos Baker, Hemingway once said that "his job was not to think about himself but to concentrate on his work, his family, and his daily problems. The only way to achieve his goal of living forever 'in his work' was to enter wholeheartedly into every book he wrote. If he began thinking and talking about himself, it might, he feared, choke out everything else" (Baker, *A Life Story* 487). There is a related danger of "choking out" the life and depth in Hemingway's works by merely concentrating on Hemingway's own life and travels.

While the internet does offer easy access to Hemingway's life and travels, a focus on Hemingway's life is too often a distraction for students at the high school and undergraduate level. He was—and is—as Suzanne del Gizzo phrases it, a "glow-in-the-dark author," a writer whose enormous celebrity was a constant source of conflict and struggle. Before going on to study his life and travels in more depth, students need first to understand his works. For those teaching at the undergraduate level and below, the focus must remain heavily on his works; Hemingway himself encouraged this separation between the man and the writing.

When Carlos Baker was trying to convince Hemingway to allow him to write a full-length study of his life, Hemingway initially turned Baker down. He was "resolved to impede in every way, including the legal, the publication of anything biographical" during his lifetime (*A Life Story* 491). When Baker assured Hemingway his work would be focused on Hemingway's works and not his life, Hemingway responded that "he would gladly help with information about his writings. As for his life, it was 'no more important than my body will be when I am dead'" (491). Hemingway knew that a concentration on his life could take away from and distract readers from his works: thus, in spite of the celebrity status he at times directly courted, he wanted his legacy to focus on his art. If instructors separate Hemingway from Jake Barnes, Frederic Henry, Santiago, and Robert Jordan, we will give our students a clearer distinction between Hemingway and his protagonists. To immerse students in digital images, videos, and maps that clarify the works' historical and geographical settings—geographies into which Hemingway poured so much time and thought—allows them to look beyond the "glow-in-the-dark" author to more fully appreciate the realism and complexity of his writing.

Notes

1. See Kirk Curnutt's essay "A Meme-able Feast: Teaching Modernist Citationality and Hemingway Iconography through the Internet's Most Infectious Replicator," in this volume.

2. In its story "Remembering the 1918 Influenza Pandemic," the Center for Disease Control offers good information on the influenza, which would be valuable to class construction of the historical background of 1918.

3. See Richard Hancuff's essay, "Using Digital Mapping to Locate Students in Hemingway's World," in this volume.

Teaching Hemingway through the Digital Archive

Michelle E. Moore

When I teach Hemingway in the second half of an American literature survey or in a more focused class on American modernism, my students inevitably respond to the writer's name and yet know very little about him. Students' curiosity about Hemingway has provided a wonderful opportunity to teach about how literary knowledge is created: through archival research. Students in this digital generation seem to understand literary letters and archival material as no others have, perhaps because of their own experiences with texting, Snapchat, and email. Teaching students how to read through Hemingway's prolific socializing in his letters, showing them how to examine his crafted image in newspaper interviews and pictures, and encouraging them to find new historical contexts for his work all reveal a different kind of Hemingway through which they may now approach his novels and stories. This Hemingway tends to be one the students can relate to quite well. As a result, because they are less bogged down with his carefully created "Papa" persona and the literary caricature he became, they see a more "real" Hemingway than the students in previous generations did.

My chapter offers strategies for teaching Hemingway through digital archival sources, his letters, photographs, and other contextual material. The first part shows the wealth of archival material available to students through newly published and online digital sources. The second part gives a blueprint for teaching how to use archival sources and incorporating assignments that require the use of these sources. An instructor who has extensive experience in research can easily forget how complicated, overwhelming, and confusing it is to approach archival material for the first time as an undergraduate student. Teachers of Hemingway will find my approach useful, because it allows the general and theoretical concept of intertextuality to be discussed through concrete found documents. Finally, this chapter provides an alternative way to teach Hemingway, by embracing the approaches to modernist studies that have been emerging in the last fifteen years.

The Hemingway Society's Hemingway Letters Project is publishing scholarly editions of over six thousand Hemingway letters. While these are not currently a digital source, the project makes available resources that can be held up against online digital sources. Instructors can make the collections available to students through library reserves or, at upper levels, by adding the bound volumes to their reading lists. They can also use Google image searches to find the copious amount of scans of Hemingway's letters available as digitized images. Many of these letters accompanied press releases, but auction houses also publish digitized images to accompany the sales of many of Hemingway's letters. Instructors should make these letters available to students before allowing work in the scholarly editions, so that students have a sense of Hemingway's handwriting and what has been typed and transcribed into an easily read page in a bound book. Instructors could also choose several batches of letters from the vast array available as digitized images and limit the class work to those carefully chosen letters.

When working with archival documents, students need to be led step by step. When looking at a document directly, it is easy for them to think that everything about this source is obvious, but when they walk away from the document, they need to have good notes that explain thoroughly what it is, what it was at the time it was created, and what it meant when it was created and means today. I suggest that instructors create a worksheet that asks students to answer a series of questions. First ask: What is it? Is it handwritten? On letterhead? Are there drawings? Second, have students record who wrote the document, who received it, from where it was sent, and where it was received. Third, ask the question that leads to the difficult part of summarizing the document: what is the document talking about? Have the students paraphrase and quote parts of the document to explain and summarize it. Fourth, ask questions to prompt further analysis. Why might the author have written it? Sometimes the author states the reason outright, but sometimes the students need to be pushed to interpret carefully. Be sure to have the students record evidence for their interpretations. Fifth, have them consider what was happening in Hemingway's life at the time the document was created. Sixth, consider what was happening historically at local, national, and international levels. Finally, have the students answer these questions: Does the document reveal anything new about Hemingway, his life, the texts? What are the new directions for research that you may now have as a result of having come across the document and reading it thoroughly?

Photographs are another kind of artifact with which the Hemingway world is replete. Boston's John F. Kennedy Presidential Museum and Library has an extensive online media gallery. The Oak Park Public Library has digitized more than three hundred artifacts, including a large number of early family photographs from Oak Park Public Library's Special Collections and The Ernest Hemingway Foundation of Oak Park ("Early Years"). Also of interest would be publicity photographs and newspaper photographic spreads that aided in creating the celebrity image of Hemingway. These are easily found through newspaper databases and are quite extensive.

Before giving an assignment that includes photographs, project a photograph and after a few minutes, remove it and have students write down everything that they remember having seen. Put the image back on the projector and lead a discussion in what each student recalled, left out, or simply got wrong. Then show students how to examine each quadrant of the photograph by going through, with them, the same worksheet created for document sources. Divide the students into small groups, or, in the case of a small seminar, let each student work on an individual project with a single photograph. Develop a second worksheet, one that asks students to identify the kind of photo it is, noting stock, size, and color. Then have them look at the subject matter and consider what kind of picture is it. Is it a family portrait? An event? A landscape? Consider the way the picture is framed. Who or what is in the center? Who is at the sides? Who or what is obscured or visible? Are people smiling? Have them list everything they see, including objects and scenery. Then ask the student to try and place the photograph as you would a document and stamp it with time, place, and historical context of Hemingway's life and around it. Ultimately, have them tell why the photograph was taken and perhaps by whom. Again, ask what new information the photograph offers about Hemingway's life and works, and consider any new directions for research.

In addition to the Oak Park Public Library's collection of artifacts, the JFK library created a press kit from their recently acquired scans of materials housed at Hemingway's former Cuban estate, Finca Vigía ("New Hemingway Materials"). The JFK library has also digitized renditions of the scrapbooks Grace Hall Hemingway made and annotated documenting Hemingway's first eighteen years.

The artifacts available range from Hemingway's birth certificate to telegrams to stamped envelopes with writing on the back. It's important that students know what to do with these kinds of materials because, especially if they are English majors, they are used to having a linguistic or visually based text to decipher. Just as with the photographs and letters, create a worksheet that asks students to explain what the artifact is: the age, what it is made out of or looks like and if anything is visibly written on it. Then have them figure out what the object is, who created it and for what reason, who used it and how; and ask the students to provide evidence for their ideas. The students may be very unfamiliar with the technology of telegrams or early photography norms, and they may need to do some research to learn about the technology standards at the time the artifact was created. Finally, ask questions that prompt the students to place the artifact within the context of a larger timeframe in which it was created. For example, was Grace unique in creating scrapbooks? Was her focus unique or of the time? What does this, then, tell us about Hemingway's upbringing?

The Hemingway archive consists of more than letters, photographs, and artifacts. Hemingway benefited from the emergence of the little magazine culture of the 1920s and his friendship with Ezra Pound, the editor and consultant on many of these small publishing venues. Students in the new millennium have no knowledge of the long-term importance of print culture and understand Hemingway and other modernist writers only through well-curated book and short-story collections. As a result, students don't see Hemingway as a writer who constantly navigated between popular culture and a more serious European literary modernism. Having students read Hemingway in the little magazines or against the little magazine culture of his time, available in digitized format, will give them a picture of Hemingway that strays far from the masterful writer "Papa" presented himself as.

The Blue Mountain Project at Princeton has made available, among other little magazines, the complete *Broom: An International Magazine of the Arts*. *The Little Review* is available in full at the *Modernist Journals Project*. *The Dial* is available through the online books library (Ockerbloom). *Esquire* has digitized full issues. The Poetry Foundation has a complete archive of *Poetry* online as well as a history of the magazine ("Magazine Archive"). The *Index of Modernist Magazines* provides overviews of the little magazines not yet available on online, most importantly to Hemingway studies, *The Transatlantic Review* (Bowman and Churchill). Finally, *The Toronto Star* has reproduced digitally more than seventy articles by Ernest Hemingway and several about his time spent at the paper as well ("Hemingway Papers").

Multiple editions of Hemingway's novels are easily available for viewing through Google image searches. Looking at specific Hemingway manuscripts (if possible), then early-twentieth-century editions, late-twentieth-century editions, and finally new millennial editions provides a concrete sense of the cultural forces and conventions that have shaped the publishing history of Hemingway's novels. It is useful to have students compare the ways Hemingway's work was packaged over time, and research projects could be easily developed that ask students to examine how cover art changes and provide a cultural explanation as to why it would change.

Students have often not considered a writer's reading lists and library and have not heard an author reading his works: two more valuable sources for new interpretations through archival research. The JFK library has made available a record of Hemingway's library and an inventory of his reading available for download (Brasch and Sigman). His reading lists, beginning with high school curriculum lists are also available; see Michael Reynolds's *Hemingway's Reading 1910–1940: An Inventory.* In addition, The JFK library has made public a recording of Hemingway reading his remarks for the Nobel prize banquet in 1954, after the fact, since he did not attend nor read his remarks himself at the banquet. Hemingway's album, "Ernest Hemingway, Reading," is available on YouTube, including the tracks "In Harry's Bar in Venice" and "Saturday Night at the Whorehouse in Billings Montana." The entire album is available on Spotify and available in short excerpts at *Openculture* (Jones, "Hear Hemingway"). Students can have difficulty taking in information aurally so it's important to have them take notes on how, if at all, the reading changes their perception of Hemingway and how it adds to or changes the work he is reading.

Scholarly discussions surrounding the uses and interpretations of archival sources should be part of upper-level seminars, or at the beginnings of large units on the archive in lower-level classes. Randal Bass's article "Story and Archive in the Twenty-First Century" and Francis X. Blouin Jr.'s "History and Memory the Problem of the Archives" can be useful in generating discussion. Bass explains the profound change in relationship between the story and archive that has happened as the result of the proliferation of technology and the new access to the archive. He argues that the result of the change is that the "Story of English" is no longer one of periods and hierarchy. Blouin raises the question of history and the archives and shows that the historian and archivist are no longer the same figure. Each has developed its own methodology and in doing so have raised the question of what the relationship between the two fields actually is. Both articles introduce students to the complexity of archival work, and a discussion about each article's arguments will introduce students to the problems of the archive in literary studies.

Instructors can construct small assignments that ask students to think across archival materials and in some cases connect that material to Hemingway's writing life. These assignments would be appropriate in a lower-level survey class, where Hemingway is not the sole focus. Students can choose or be assigned a year of Hemingway's life and then work through all of the archival sources available digitally to construct a picture of Hemingway's life during that year. In lower level classes, it is useful to pick a few photographs, letters, and archival sources that the instructor thinks are particularly noteworthy and have student groups or individual students write short essays or give presentations that work through the significance of a particular group of archival objects. For example, it would be interesting to pull out some mementoes from Grace Hall Hemingway's scrapbooks and cross-reference those with the Hemingway Foundation's records of Hemingway's reading and activities in school that year ("Hemingway's Oak Park Roots"). Students could also trace the publishing history of a single short story through the letters, artifacts, and into print in one of the journals. Hemingway's difficulties in getting published, as well as the process of modernist publication, would become immediately apparent to students. Essays about the significance of the research could be assigned.

Instructors can also design more guided assignments for students that make use of the online archives. Students can research one concrete element of a novel or story, such as a fashion, architectural, gastronomic, or landscape detail. They can also research a linguistic anomaly, a key word that keeps appearing across a particular work. Students can search newspaper databases to find articles on historical events or individuals mentioned in the novels or stories. Instructors might have students locate a Hemingway story published in a little magazine and have students look around the publication. Then, they could ask them to consider what other work was published along with Hemingway's, as well as the publication's reputation, cover art, and any advertising. All of these assignments demand that students consider how the new information illuminates and affects their interpretation of Hemingway's individual work.

In a research-based class or upper-level seminar, students can be assigned a large research project that asks them to investigate a Hemingway novel or short story, through situating and explaining the work against the historical backdrop and insights provided by the archive. I instruct students to think of their own work as adding to the literary knowledge about Hemingway. The assignment requires that students explore and work through the online archives mentioned above as well as their library's databases, which provide access to newspapers and magazines not listed above. At the end of the semester, students turn in a portfolio containing evidence of their research over the course of the semester as well as at least three of the following items: a research journal or research narrative documenting the process of investigation; transcriptions of at least five items; an annotated bibliography of primary and secondary sources; an introduction to the Hemingway novel or story; a longer essay in which they position Hemingway either stylistically or culturally; and/or an explication of Hemingway's novel or story based on the research. Students present their research formally to the class at the end of the semester, when they turn in their portfolios. The assignment could easily be modified from a portfolio to a more supervised project by assigning due dates for each component. The class would then end with the final paper, an explication of Hemingway's novel or short story, and a research presentation.

Teaching Hemingway through the digital archive always stimulates students to think actively about literature and history and prompts meaningful discussions about literary personas, the interpretation of texts through historical research, and the idea of a "real" Hemingway. My methods of teaching Hemingway through the archives embrace the ideas that make studying Hemingway so complicated and complex for scholars and break them down for students in an understandable way. Students walk away from class with a palpable sense of what intertextuality is and an understanding of the labyrinthine structure of the archive, literary history, and Hemingway's life.

Teaching Materials

Appendix A

English 482, Hemingway

End-of-Term Writing Prompts and Student Responses

Laura Godfrey with Kelly Owens, Ricky Baldridge, Lee J. Brainard, Marshall J. Palmer, and Allison Gneckow

While Hemingway's literary reputation and legacy remain strong, the manner in which many twenty-first-century readers encounter his work is obviously shifting. At the end of each Hemingway-focused class that I teach, I ask students to consider those shifts as we close out our discussions. I don't grade these writings; they are simply intended to get students thinking about whether aspects of digital life in the twenty-first century somehow alter Hemingway's relevance or importance. After collecting these writings from my fall 2017 Hemingway seminar (University of Idaho's English 482 course), I asked several students for their permission to include their responses in the appendix to this *Digital Age* collection. Below I've included the writing prompts, followed by five provocative student responses, which will hopefully give instructors ideas about how digital-age students encounter Hemingway's writing

Prompt 1: Some readers might argue that an appreciation of Hemingway's work depends in large part on an understanding of the physical world he recreates. In his 1935 *Esquire* piece "Monologue to the Maestro," Hemingway stated that aspiring writers must "be able to go into a room and when you come out know everything that you saw there and not only that. If that room gave you any feeling you should know exactly what it was that gave you that feeling" (*By-Line* 219–20). The generative power of *things* is an important principle in Hemingway's entire body of work. Can twenty-first-century readers effectively glean the intensity and fidelity of Hemingway's literary environments if, as Glenn Adamson has argued, our twenty-first-century "collective material intelligence has steadily plummeted"? (4) If today's average readers are more often immersed in *virtual* environments, if they have not been trained to pay attention to the places—and the things-in-their-places—that surround them, how then do we encounter Hemingway's object-oriented prose? Or does training one's eye more toward virtual environments, paradoxically, somehow give us better (or different) skills for reading Hemingway?

Prompt 2: Does digital-age life—so often focused on connection and collective, minute-by-minute updates of our thoughts and all our daily "data"—prevent readers from engaging with some of the core traits of Hemingway's characters, who are often solitary observers or introspective outsiders? How do we, for instance, read Hemingway texts such as "Big Two-Hearted River," a narrative of an entirely solitary fishing trip, if we are rarely or never alone? Or on the contrary, in what sense can readers inhabiting a highly connective digital universe possess new or illuminated understanding of Hemingway's writing—can they somehow *better* understand the relationships between Hemingway's individual characters and their communities?

Kelly Owens (English major, theater minor)

Many of us live in an age where the world is at our fingertips and in our pockets. If I have even the slightest desire to know what the landscape of Nepal looks like, I do not need to dig out an encyclopedia or a fifteen-year-old *National Geographic*, let alone go there myself. I can easily gain knowledge of Nepal from Wikipedia or by visiting the official "Nepal" page on Facebook—all in less than fifteen seconds. Through breathtaking photos taken on the average iPhone, and now even more with 360-degree view videos, I can feel as though I am immersed in the action happening on the opposite side of the world. Mount Everest is no longer an experience reserved for those brave few who are willing to endure its extreme conditions; I am allowed to share in climbers' experiences by following their Instagram or subscribing to their blogs. Google Earth has the capability to take me even further, and can show me my cousin's house in Santa Barbara or what standing on the edge of the Grand Canyon would look like—once again, usually in less than thirty seconds with access to a computer and a few clicks.

According to the Pew Research Center, 77 percent of Americans own a smartphone. 92 percent of American students, ages eighteen to twenty-nine, who are currently in college and with an income of less than $30,000, own a smartphone—clearly, ownership of digital devices now extends beyond social and racial demographics ("Mobile"). In our digital age, capturing numerous images of life and contributing them to the collective image of Earth has never been easier. We no longer even need to type a text message to a friend to describe what's occurring around us, because we can just as easily snap a photo or video so they can see for themselves—for better or for worse. No words are required, and those we might choose are often brief, quippy, and ironic: "Here we are," we say over and over again with our images, #LivingLifeAlltheWayUp.

But my friends and I also constantly complain that we have lost the ability to be present. We may hike to the top of a mountain simply for the likes on our Instagram rather than to sit in the stillness of nature at the top of the world. We may film a musician's concert to share afterward—so often finding ourselves watching our favorite artists through a screen, even while they stand in front of us. While I increasingly experience the world through a lens and a screen, I worry that I begin to miss the small observations and the depth of my senses that comes with immersion. Often I live with half-attention: seeing something and immediately wondering how to convert it to the digital world. Perhaps one of the major reasons why so many members of my generation—the iGen, so named by Jean Twenge in her 2017 book by that title—Snapchat and Facebook Live is because we hunger to be there with those who are experiencing something we cannot, or because we hunger to share our own experiences with others. It's a hunger that humans have always had.

Ernest Hemingway's characters do just that for us. Think of Jake and Bill fishing the Irati River in *The Sun Also Rises*, the rocks Robert Jordan hides behind and the pine needles he lies upon in *For Whom the Bell Tolls*, or the serene, green views seen through Nick Adams's eyes in "Big Two-Hearted River" as he hikes "beyond the fire line" and into the country of "jack pine" and "sweet fern." These are moments when we forget that we are reading, and instead, encounter the landscape with these characters, *feel* the ice-cold river water or the crunch of the dry pine needles. Hemingway always takes us beyond the visual and into the sensual. We know what the salty pretzels would taste like with that dark beer Frederic Henry is drinking in the Swiss lodge in *A Farewell to Arms* because Hemingway recalls the sensation, not the picture, for us. His writing calls us to be fully present with his characters.

In my Hemingway seminar, I sometimes heard students voice the frustration that Hemingway's readers get left *out* of the picture. I wonder if the widespread digital-age cultural desire for constant personal interconnectivity and moment-sharing made some students feel that Hemingway too often ignored the precious interiority of a character. And it is true that many Hemingway characters do not readily reveal their inmost thoughts, especially in his earlier body of work, like *In Our Time, The Sun Also Rises,* and *A Farewell to Arms.* When we are not allowed to see inside a character's mind, when we must settle for only the limited range of what the narrative focalizer gives us, connecting to Hemingway's work seemed to become difficult for some students who were used to constant invitations directly inside others' lives and minds. (I doubt Hemingway's early characters—if they lived in our day—would ever answer Facebook's persistent question, "What's on your mind? " to update their status.) Nick Adams's reticence can either intrigue us and encourage us to read his story further, or it might shut some readers out altogether. We as readers must often figure these characters out for ourselves. The question for me always comes back to how I can appreciate working with what I am given in a Hemingway text and how I can be trained to let his landscapes and images speak for themselves.

Hemingway's emphasis on "presence" and attention and awareness always inspires me to look at myself and wonder how I rate in this area. Over fifty years after his death, Hemingway is still idolized for living life on the edge, or for #LivingLifeAlltheWayUp. He believed that writers must go out into the world and do things for themselves if they want good material. However, much like our Instagram captions, he also believed you may express ideas in fewer words than you initially think—as long as you choose the right ones. In a generation where so many of my peers hunger to know the world, to experience everything they see others experiencing, I was inspired to learn about Hemingway; he emerges for me as a figure who lived life in the present (possibly even to a fault sometimes), who actually went to the action or places he desired to learn about, and really *did it* all himself.

Ricky Baldridge (MA candidate in English)

When I was seventeen years old, one of my favorite bands, Streetlight Manifesto, had a song titled "Here's to Life," which heavily referenced the authors Ernest Hemingway, Albert Camus, and J. D. Salinger. The Hemingway lyric goes like this:

> Hemingway never seemed to mind the banalities of a normal life
> And I find, it gets harder every time
> So, he aimed the shotgun into the blue
> Placed his face in between the two
> And sighed, "Here's to Life"

Having a great deal of respect for this band, I decided that I should read those same authors, and I soon found myself neck-deep in all their works. Hemingway's prose stood out immediately compared to what I had previously read (mostly, at that point, Oscar Wilde, F. Scott Fitzgerald, and a bulk of philosophers). I quickly became infatuated with his style, simplicity, and attention to detail.

At this time in my life I was on constant journeys around the country while touring in various punk rock bands, and what really bonded me with Hemingway was the approach and exploration of what were, to me, foreign surroundings. The way that Jake Barnes and Fredric Henry dove into foreign contexts, instantly forging further understandings of wherever they were, reminded me of myself whenever I would enter a new city. I never wanted to see the exposed, prepackaged tourist side of the cities I visited. Instead, I always wanted to get straight to the show we were playing, speak to the local punks in the city, and find out just what it was that they loved about their area. I wanted to eat the food that they ate, drink the drinks that they drank, and walk the same streets that they knew so well. By the end of my brief stay in any city, I wanted to further understand what made the people of the city who they were and what made their cities *what* they were. With this understanding, I felt, I gained more insight into myself as a body in space, as a person moving through these cities at lightning speed. The other impulse driving my explorations was simply a need to understand what it is that makes people *who* they are. For all the places I have yet to go and all the people I have yet to meet, I believe that my studies in Hemingway's prose have helped to forge this drive just to try and understand.

I see a lot students around me—myself included—also striving to connect, belong, and understand, although these days, many connections we forge often become virtual, rather than viscerally physical. For a lot of us, the term *connection* itself brings up images from the digital world, and we might think first of connections with others on social media platforms like Facebook, Twitter, Instagram, blogs, or vlogs. Many of us turn to our devices for connections, for ways to get a glimpse into the lives of others, to see what they do and how they live. And sometimes, we virtually seek out others as a replication for experience, since so many social media posts focus on where a person is traveling, what they are seeing, or what they are eating and drinking. People post about the soufflé in a fine French restaurant or the IPA in a Portland bar. They post photos of their journeys in the Alaskan wilderness, of their train trip in Italy, or show themselves wandering down some hidden side street of their own city. In so doing, they are opening a portal for others to walk through so that we may all get a chance to experience what they have already experienced (or are currently experiencing).

Hemingway understood those desires—the desire to share, the desire to experience—perfectly well. That same urge to share experiences (and to share the feeling of those experiences) was always a fundamental part of Hemingway's prose. Whether it be Nick Adams facedown on a picnic blanket after a break up, Jake Barnes floating on his back in the sea at San Sebastian, or Robert Jordan smelling pine-scented Spanish night air, readers of Hemingway's work are always bodily transported to other times and places. Like all good writers, Hemingway's writings, fictional or nonfictional (or the fictional that is almost certainly nonfictional), forge connections that violate geographical and temporal boundaries. This, I think, can help us feel more connected to Hemingway's writing, even though the times and places he lived in were in other ways so different.

And Hemingway shares some of the same interest in *belonging* that we see everywhere in twenty-first-century social media platforms. *Green Hills of Africa,* Hemingway's nonfiction work about a hunting expedition in Africa, or his prose in *Esquire* about his deep-sea fishing, or his classic "lost generation" bullfighting novel *The Sun Also Rises:* all these works give his readers invitations to travel and belong somewhere they had never been before or may never get the chance to see. His war correspondence was a personal insight into conflict zones many would never see or ever get close to. In so many ways, Hemingway's prose precedes, and echoes, the twenty-first-century infatuation with social media. We often look to social media posts to take us somewhere that we have not been, to give us feelings of intimate knowledge and connection. We look to fictional prose to create worlds which we may never know. The real difference is the choice of medium.

Lee J. Brainard (professional writing major)

As a new student of Hemingway, I learned very quickly that, in order to understand his words, his readers are also challenged to understand the man. Enrolled in English 482 at the University of Idaho, a course in which we studied this single author and his life, I fully immersed myself in another man's life and body of work to the point where my understanding and knowledge began to feel saturated and voyeuristic. I read and presented on the biography *Writer, Sailor, Soldier, Spy,* by Nicholas Reynolds and listened to other students report on the biographies (and "micro-biographies") of Hemingway that they all chose to read. I read multiple letters from the Cambridge *Selected Letters* volumes, I read (in part or whole) selections from most of Hemingway's impressive body of work, and I listened to scholarly article presentations each week on a variety of topics—from the possible symbolism of pine needles in *For Whom the Bell Tolls* to the "dysenteric" narrative structure of *Green Hills of Africa* (still not sure what to make of that latter essay). And in the midst of it all, I kept imagining that I was sitting down to have a conversation with Hemingway himself. Did I know so much about this person that I thought I could converse easily with him? Was I impressed by his writing but angered at his personal failings? I'm not sure, but the scenario kept playing over and over in my mind.

I also discovered, along the way, that there are a distractingly large number of digital resources devoted to Hemingway's personal life, some factual and some not, that are readily available online. I became so fascinated and horrified by the various stages of Hemingway's conflicted life—or the fragmented, fractured picture of his life that I built from internet, biographical, and scholarly research—that my personal judgments for a time clouded my literary analysis. Who was this figure, this macho bully, this "badass pimp" (as one YouTube commenter labeled him)? Before studying his work, I didn't know the man or much about the man; I only knew *of* him. I knew he wrote for a living and had a reputation for being good at his job. I knew he hunted, he liked to fish, that he had lived for a time in Cuba; Key West, Florida; and southeastern Idaho and that he had spent some time in Spain.

But as my semester of studying Hemingway progressed, I kept repeatedly imagining that he and I sat down and talked. I entered into this conversation enthusiastic but apprehensive. I am always intimidated by individuals who demonstrate superior perception, intellect, insight, and influence and who have the ability to capture their perceptions with words in a manner that few have or can. I am not so intimidated by the person but by the fear of not belonging in the conversation. This is a fear with which Ernest Hemingway was intimately familiar, and it is this fear—I was to learn—that compelled him throughout his life.

Initially, in my imaginary conversations with Ernest, we navigated the awkward orientation phase common to new relationships: that period when you don't know enough to ask educated questions and you fear sounding like an inarticulate, inept boob. But even more, you fear the impression you make when you can't think of a thing to say. That was how we got started: I, devoted to sounding intellectual and bookish, trying to project intellectual observations of substance, and Ernest speaking plain language and saying things that were disorienting. I assumed much, and he revealed much more. I had the idea that Hemingway was the Hemingway of Woody Allen's *Midnight in Paris*, that strange, hybrid writer/he-man that emerges from the hundreds of internet memes inspired by him. Everything I studied about him was incompatible with everything I had presumed. The collective voice of the internet seemed to ask me to mythologize Hemingway. But I needed real answers.

I initially presumed many things about Mr. Hemingway, but by researching his life through multiple lenses, I discovered more. I have yet to reconcile all of this, but I have concluded that Ernest Hemingway simply lived the best life he knew how to. I have learned that he was a brilliant, luminous, singularly gifted, freakishly talented individual. I learned that he possessed an unprecedented ability to paint landscapes of color, light, line, tone, texture, movement, scent, sound, and form, that he could conjure instantaneously vivid images packed with motives, memory, emotion, tension, tragedy, triumph, honor, selfishness, sacrifice, fear, physical courage, moral courage, cowardice, valor, fortitude, gallantry, and indomitability. And despite the darker aspects of his life story that glare out at us in every corner of the digital realm—from YouTube to Google searches to Facebook memes to Wikipedia pages—I reconciled the conflicts by returning to the writing.

At the close of my semester, I had another conversation with Hemingway and shared with him what I had learned in my research. I imagined Hemingway sounding the way Kirk Curnutt writes his voice, in *Coffee with Hemingway*, where Hemingway closes out the interview by saying:

> [I]f we could have made this enough of a dialogue, it would've had everything in it that matters—everything about the writing, that is. It would have the clicking oarlocks of the canoes in "Indian Camp" and the limestone foundation of the deserted sawmill in "The End of Something" and the whap of the blackjack on Ad Francis's skull in "The Battler." It would have the acetylene flares on the avenue des Gobelins that Jake and Brett notice in *The Sun*. . . . It would include the ants trying to escape the burning log in *A Farewell To Arms* and the old man's stack of brandy saucers in "A Clean, Well-Lighted Place." . . . It would have every detail that I worked hard to pack into every sentence, and *work*'s the word I want you to walk away with—not personality, not fame, not reputation, not Paris nor Papa nor *Papa dobles* at the Floridita nor a shotgun barrel on a summer Ketchum morning when there was finally peace after so much pain. The only thing that matters is the work. (131, 132–33)

Marshall J. Palmer (English major)

How does Ernest Hemingway's writing translate for people in the twenty-first century? There are obvious parallels between his generation and my own. My world is not a world of hopeful optimism; nor was that the world that Hemingway, or many of Hemingway's earliest readers, lived in. People of my own Millennial generation are prone to share morbid jokes among themselves about social anxiety, economic and political anxiety, depression, and suicide, hoping that the humor will offset insecurity; characters in Hemingway works, like *In Our Time* and *The Sun Also Rises*, similarly exchange ironic barbs reflecting the darkness of their times (I am thinking of Jake Barnes's remark in *The Sun Also Rises* to Georgette the prostitute, where he says "We would probably have gone on and discussed the war and agreed that it was in reality a calamity for civilization. . . . I was bored enough" [25]).

The increasingly restricted wallets and the current unstable intensity of international politics in the twenty-first century have reshaped the ways in which human minds digest literature itself. My world is a world which is uneasily creaking and groaning, where we stand under the shadow of an ominous and uncertain future that might have either suffering or success in store. What I long for is a world of emotional, financial, social, and political stability; I think Hemingway understood just that same sense of unease.

Still, for some reason, Hemingway's world often seems to me more legend than reality. When I picture the world of Hemingway, it appears with almost magical dimensions. Hemingway caroused with his friends in faraway pubs and cafés. He harbored a Tennyson-like affinity for the glory of combat, and he willingly participated in wars that were not his to fight. When he saw matadors slicing up live bulls, the crowd roared with him. Things feel *different* now. I'm not as willing to partake in the belligerence of war, the lion hunts, the raucous drinking, or the horrors of watching a drugged bull being eviscerated for sport; those things represent a completely foreign culture to me. Lion or rhinoceros hunts are now reserved for the rich and heartless. I don't ever get the urge to charge through Cuba's blue waters looking for nonexistent Nazi submarines.

But this isn't to say that I have nothing to glean anything from Ernest Hemingway. His stories are legendary in more than one sense of the word. The classical Greeks might have imagined a time in history when they could have witnessed all the events of Mount Olympus, that they could have stood as subjects of the gods and seen all the legends for themselves if they had only lived a few hundred years earlier. That's where I'm at with Hemingway. The stories of Hemingway and stories of Greek legends are equal parts interesting and alien to me, and I can only vaguely imagine what it would be like to live in those times. The appeal of Hemingway to modern, twenty-first-century readers might not be *faded* so much as it is *changed*.

Allison Gneckow (English major)

Ernest Hemingway and his writing are arguably more relatable in the twenty-first-century digital age than ever before. While some people might assert that a "digital divide" separates my generation (and I'm grouped in the Millennial category) or even younger generations (sometimes referred to as iGen or Generation Z) from understanding Hemingway's prose, or that digital technologies and social media distract too many of us from reading at all, I see things differently. Instead, these platforms like Instagram, Facebook, or Twitter (no matter what we name them, since the names will change as the years pass) reveal things about Hemingway's work and his aesthetic that we may not have otherwise been able to see.

In every way, Hemingway's writing—and this is an impulse I think most writers share—marked an attempt to break through the impossible boundaries of time and space to convey the real and the authentic. In one of the letters we read this semester—Hemingway's 1926 reaction to Dos Passos's *New Masses* review of *The Sun Also Rises*—Hemingway complained to Max Perkins that the review "was fine about his [Dos Passos's] not liking the book and wanting it to be better but a poor criticism that Pamplona in the book wasn't as good as Pamplona in real life—because I think it was maybe pretty exciting to people who'd never been there—and that was who it was written for" (*Letters* 3:183). Ernest Hemingway wrote to bring *outsiders* a sense of what it was like to be *insiders* to places, and his ability to transcend those boundaries is the mark of a man who has a deeper understanding of the weight of having a large audience hanging on your every word. Hemingway has a way of writing that makes a reader comfortable in a strange place.

When I think about my social media pages or the pages of all the people I know and with whom I'm friends, I see that exact same impulse, and this connection helped me better relate to Hemingway's work. In large part, those of us who participate in any form of connection online are doing what Hemingway tried, always, to do: to bring outsiders an insider's perspective. In our own twenty-first-century era, the connections established through just about any social media outlet allow for this same boundary-transcendence. As just one example, think of the social media platform Instagram, which through its many filters allows individuals to create their own narrative of their experiences through pictures. Each picture encapsulates an experience, and when viewing one profile, all the pictures or experiences come together to create a scrolling, seamless narrative of that individual's life, or at least the manufactured illusion they have created of their life. I scroll through my friends' pages and see them on ski lifts, at the ocean, drinking wine with their fiancées, traveling back home to Russia. I am not *in* any of these places, but for a brief moment, there I am, nonetheless.

Of course, a lot of the time/space boundary spanning we see these days is accomplished mostly with pictures, not words. While communication has burst open in the digital age, it has also been irreparably altered—not necessarily for the worse or better—but altered just the same.

Hemingway spans boundaries the harder way, in his novels and short stories and journalism: with words. A. E. Hotchner recalled Hemingway remarking on that difference between writers and painters, and remembers Hemingway lamenting that "artists have all those great colors, while I have to do it on the typewriter or with my pencil in black and white" (*Papa Hemingway* 187). But it is important to acknowledge that Hemingway's places are manufactured illusions too, just like my most recent, filtered Instagram photo. I can easily manufacture beauty from something that is average in appearance. So could Hemingway.

In what must be the universal frustration—and inspiration—of all writers, Hemingway keenly understood that when he narrated an experience, the ability to adequately manufacture that same experience was not technically possible. That was the whole point. Experience is unique and can only be held by the individual. Through any manufactured illusion, whether it is a novel or memoir or a digital photograph on Instagram, there is an immediate removal from the experience the very moment when it is "captured." There is no capturing an experience. Our attempts are incomplete and flawed for the very reason that all experiences are unique to the individual. We cannot become each other, and we cannot capture experiences from one another, though we like to try.

And Hemingway never stopped trying. I think of his author's note at the beginning of *Green Hills of Africa* as the embodiment of this effort. There, he wrote:

> Unlike many novels, none of the characters or incidents in this book is imaginary. Any one not finding sufficient love interest is at liberty, while reading, to insert

whatever love interest he or she may have at the time. The writer has attempted to write an absolutely true book to see whether the shape of a country and the pattern of a month's action can, if truly presented, compete with a work of the imagination.

Though critics and readers have debated now for decades on how successful Hemingway was in that attempt, none of us can deny that he always tried to reach out, grab readers' hands, and pull them into whatever world he was sharing. And that constant striving and reaching for connection, in essence, makes up one of the biggest currents in the stream of digital-age life.

Appendix B

The Sun Also Rises I-Search Project

Nicole J. Camastra

> Do that which is assigned thee, and thou canst not hope too much or dare too much.
> —Ralph Waldo Emerson

As you, hopefully, will learn this semester, historical and cultural contexts figure prominently in understanding a literary work. However, what's not always so clear is the way our own unique perspective of such contexts underlies our comprehension of the same work(s). In the tradition of Ralph Waldo Emerson and Benjamin Franklin, I'd like you to follow what you feel called to show interest in and apply it to your understanding of Ernest Hemingway's *The Sun Also Rises*.

Ideally, you would use a personal interest as a starting point for such critical inquiry. Are you planning on pursuing an accounting, finance, or business major? Why not research political trends, presidents, or the financial excesses of the roaring twenties (with or without the stock market crash of 1929)—conditions that prompted many writers and artists to live and work abroad, especially in Paris, during this time. Alternately, if you have an interest in music, why not research popular artists of the day such as Django Reinhardt, a musician Hemingway would have heard in some of the Paris bal-musettes he frequented during the 1920s. You could also research Jazz, particularly its reputation and reach in Europe. You get the idea. There's a way to make it work, no matter how irrelevant you feel your interests to be in reference to the novel, or vice versa. If you plan to go into forestry or landscape design, you could still do a lot with the use of geography, topography, and/or industrialization in the novel. See the list of possible topics below for some ideas and feel free to propose your own if you don't like what's on there.

The Assignment (15 percent)

Working in groups of three (3), you will report your findings to the class in a fifteen-minute presentation. Each person *must* contribute and speak for at least a few minutes. You may use props or not, including Prezi, PowerPoint, posters, handouts, or anything else you believe will help disseminate and elucidate the information you want to present. At the end of your presentation, you must turn in a two-to-three-page report that details and sums up your research and findings. This report must include a works cited page not only for the sources you cite but also those that you consult. A solid presentation will go beyond the ostensible topic and ask difficult questions of its relation to the primary text and, hopefully, demonstrate the presenters' understanding of them. A mediocre presentation will regurgitate facts and rely on lists or bullet points to highlight what most of us will already know in regard to the given topic. A fancy PowerPoint presentation does not equal a good one. This assignment demands critical thinking more than technological savvy.

The Option

Since you will be spending a decent amount of time on this project, I will allow you to use some of your findings toward your third essay, which is worth 20 percent of your final grade and will require outside research anyway. You don't have to do this, by the way, especially if you'd like to focus on another idea for your third paper. But you may find it useful to extend what you learn here to a more comprehensive critical analysis of the novel.

Important Dates

September 12: Library day. We will attend an informational session, which will help you locate and use resources in the Main Library. Meet in the Main Library Computer Lab.

November 3–12: Presentations in class. Your one-to-two-page (hard copy) report is due as soon as your group is finished presenting. The report must follow the standard formatting used for the other assignments in this class. This means a twelve-point type, Times New Roman font, double-spaced document that also uses MLA format to document *all* sources.

Possible Topics

You are also *free* to come up with your own. (Remember: a more specific topic yields a more interesting and manageable presentation!)
- Stock market/finance of the 1920s, including the crash in 1929
- Catholicism/pilgrimage
- Expatriation in the early twentieth century
- Industrialization and/or urban versus rural landscapes
- Music—this includes music of the 1920s, especially (European) jazz, or a focus on a particular performer such as Django Reinhardt or Louis Armstrong, who played in European cities frequently.
- Prohibition and current alcohol culture
- Alcoholism and treatment of it in the early twentieth century
- Shifting feminine roles and domestic expectations in the early twentieth century
- Feminine fashions and consumerism
- Dating and marriage trends of the 1920s
- Toreo, or the Spanish bullfight (*corrida*)
- Food and/or wine in the novel
- The Fiesta of San Fermin

Possible Websites and Databases to Begin Your Search

Media/Visuals:
American Memory Project
Digital Public Library of America
Films on Demand
Historical Statistics of the United States
TED-ed Lessons Worth Sharing

Databases:
Academic Search Complete
Historical Newspapers Online
Reader's Guide Retrospective: 1890–1982
History Reference Center
Humanities and Social Science Index

A lot has been written on this novel. A lot. You are not writing *on* the novel. You are instructing us on a contextual topic that extends *from* the novel and its historical production. Focus on what *you* respond to in this assignment, not what some scholar thinks is important.

> Be encouraged to Diligence in thy Calling, and distrust not Providence.
> —Benjamin Franklin

Appendix C

English 296
Major Figures (Hemingway) Midterm Presentations

Laura Godfrey

I created this midterm presentation project to allow students the freedom to explore the many different "virtual Hemingways" that exist online and also to get them to see how much art has been produced *in response to* Hemingway's art. It is deliberately a project that allows students to either be serious or playful or some mixture of both, but the general goal is to allow them to see the wide impact Hemingway's life and writing have had on others, and how the Internet acts as a collective repository for these cultural productions.

Midterm Presentation (20 percent of course grade). This fifteen-minute multimedia presentation is meant to give our class a sense of Hemingway's "ripple effect" on readers throughout the ages. Hemingway's life and writing have (negatively and positively) inspired all kinds of people to create their own art. And when I say *art,* I mean any creative products that someone makes directly in response to Hemingway's life or work—these could be long or short films, songs, vlogs or blogs, short stories, novels, memes, pictures, photographs, symphonies. (See our Blackboard "Inspired by Hemingway" folder for some examples to start with.) What I want you to do for your midterm presentation is to conduct research to collect and *compare some (at least two) artistic creations* that have been made in response to/in honor of/as a reaction against Hemingway's life or writing.

    1. Describe and show samples of the artistic creations you've found that were inspired—negatively or positively—by Hemingway. Use audiovisual aids to help us see them. Feel free to play clips, use the document camera, et cetera.

2. Compare the artistic creations you've located, noting interesting differences or similarities between them.

3. Last, analyze how Hemingway appears to have affected these artists (positively? negatively?) Why does that impact matter—what does it say about our own era's cultural aesthetics? How does it help us better understand Hemingway and/or his work?

4. Finally, I urge you to be creative and to have fun with this assignment. It's meant to provide a bright spot in the midterm fog and the gloom of north Idaho weather in early March! You will be graded on the depth and thoughtfulness of your research/analysis, and on the clarity, grace, and polish of your presentation. Please practice your presentations beforehand and make sure they do not run long, since we only have two class days to complete them all.

Appendix D

Interdisciplinary Studies 250 Syllabus

Laura Godfrey and Ed Kaitz

INTR 250: Physical and Virtual Environments Course Description

This course develops the student's ability to collaboratively inquire using at least two disciplinary perspectives or frames of reference on a chosen theme, issue, problem or concept to complete a learning product, project, or presentation. As part of the course, students will develop their capacity to critically reflect on their learning process and how values, ethical considerations, and noncognitive factors shape their learning. The course's specific content will vary depending on the term.

Course Materials

In addition to the required texts listed below, there will be a significant number of handouts that comprise an essential part of your INTR 250 reading list. *All INTR 250 students will need to purchase a three-ring binder and have access to a hole puncher to keep course handouts in order.* To save students book costs, we will either upload these readings into Blackboard (for printing) or we will provide you handouts of these materials.

Required Texts:
Ernest Hemingway, *The Sun Also Rises*
Henry David Thoreau, *Walden*
Willa Cather, *The Professor's House*
George Orwell, *1984*
Dave Eggers, *The Circle*

Outcomes

Students will
- Develop and demonstrate the ability to critically reflect on their learning process using the course theme of the physical and the virtual
- Engage in inquiry of physical and virtual environments (or place) using both a literary and a philosophical disciplinary frame
- Collaborate with others in developing an academic presentation on of physical and virtual environments (or place)
- Relate their learning about the physical and the virtual to affective, ethical, value-based, or moral perspective/reasoning
- Express how their learning is framed or shaped by affective, ethical, moral, or value-based perspectives

Assessment

Your grade in INTR 250 will comprise the following:
In-class writings, take-home exercises, and class discussion participation: 200 points
Two Literary Analysis Essays: 125 points each (250 points total)
Two Philosophy Essays: 125 points each (250 points total)
Semester-Long Group Project: 200 points
Final Self-Reflective Essay: 100 points
Total: 1000 points

1. *In-class writings, take-home exercises, and class discussions: 200 points*

INTR 250 is a seminar-style class that will involve significant amounts of reading, writing, and thoughtful discussion. Class discussions will take up a large portion of our time together. There will also be times where we write short essay responses during class, and times where your professors will assign take-home writing prompts or other exercises to bring back when you return to class the next day. *Your scores on these smaller writing prompts and take-home exercises will be averaged at the end of the semester, and put together with your overall discussion participation they will comprise your full participation grade.*

Discussions are always meant to be generative: new ideas and connections will constantly emerge as the semester progresses and as we work together to inquire how the digital age influences our perceptions of "being" in place. Every student is expected to attend class regularly and to actively participate in discussions. (Remember that part of good discussion habits also involves listening to others and taking good notes.) We know more collectively than we do individually, and so your comments and your in-class writings are essential for helping us make the kinds of discoveries these texts and ideas demand.

Finally, some brief words on empathy and respect: we will cover some difficult and controversial material throughout the semester. Your empathy skills (reading others' emotions and even understanding/feeling them yourself) will inevitably be called to action. It's your job to see that your comments in class are always made with respect, no matter what your opinion may be.

2. *Literary Analysis Essays: 3 pages each, 250 total points*

Essay 1: 3 pages, 125 points. Choose an assigned chapter from Thoreau's *Walden* and conduct a close reading of the author's *attention to place*. You might consider structuring your analysis around one (or more) of the following questions: How does the author present the physical world in this text? What kinds of attention are paid to physical environment, and to what effect? What role does the physical environment have in shaping the author's (or different characters') thoughts, feelings, worldview? Does the author's presentation of the physical world connect to overarching themes or ideas throughout the text as a whole?

Your essay should present a clear and sustained textual analysis throughout. Explicitly state a clear, central idea somewhere at or near the beginning of your paper and make sure to fill your essay paragraphs with support (this means textual evidence—quotes from the literature itself). Each quote you include in your paper, even the small ones, should be explicated and analyzed. In other words, after a quote you should first explain what the text is saying and then should follow with an analysis of how the idea is expressed: *what* the words mean and *how* that meaning is constructed by the language itself.

You do not need to consult secondary research materials for this paper, although you are welcome to use any of the *library literature databases* for support. If you include secondary sources, though, make sure they support—and do not distract from—your primary job of close reading the text itself.

Essay 2: 3 pages, 125 points. Choose either Hemingway's *The Sun Also Rises* or Cather's *The Professor's House* and address one of the following questions: How present and engaged are the characters in their environments and/or in their relationships—in other words, are they fully immersed in their environments, friendships, and in understanding themselves, or are they distanced and detached from places and people? Or you might consider whether full place-presence and engagement is shown in a positive or negative light throughout the text (in other words, is it better for these characters, in some instances, to be detached from place and people)?

Your essay should present a clear and sustained textual analysis throughout. Explicitly state a clear, central idea somewhere at or near the beginning of your paper and make sure to fill your essay paragraphs with support (this means textual evidence—quotes from the literature itself). Each quote you include in your paper, even the small ones, should be explicated and analyzed. In other words, after a quote you should first explain what the text is saying and then should follow with an analysis of how the idea is expressed: *what* the words mean and *how* that meaning is constructed by the language itself.

You do not need to consult secondary research materials for this paper, although you are welcome to use any of the *library literature databases* for support. If you include secondary sources, though, make sure they support—and do not distract from—your primary job of close reading the text itself.

3. *Philosophy Essays:* 250 total points.

Essay 1. 3 pages, 125 points. On page 75 of *The Shallows,* Nicholas Carr summarizes the conclusions of author Elizabeth Eisenstein:

> Like painters and composers, writers were able "to alter perception" in a way "that enriched rather than stunted sensuous response to external stimuli, expanded rather than contracted sympathetic response to the varieties of experience." The words in books didn't just strengthen people's ability to think abstractly; they enriched people's experience of the physical world, the world outside the book.

In other words, according to Carr and Eisenstein, the revolutionary Gutenberg Press ultimately served to *open* our access to our physical environment in a very *positive* way. With this argument in mind, think about our current situation with respect to the digital revolution. Are we in a similar type of healthy and exciting "Gutenberg moment," or will the digital revolution bring dark times ahead? Write an essay defending what you believe to be the positive and/or negative effects of these new technologies. Reflect on the essays and books we have read so far and construct an argument that defends a particular position on this issue. Make sure to utilize plenty of quotations from the material we have read so far in order to help support your claims.

Essay 2. 3 pages, 125 points. After considering all of the philosophical readings covered between 16 February and 10 March, explore the relationship between human nature, character, wisdom, ethics, and the new digital technologies. In other words, reflect on the issue of whether current and future generations will create, implement, and utilize these new technologies in healthy or unhealthy ways. Can we be confident that morally and intellectually sound individuals will be promoting products that benefit these current and future generations?

4. *Semester-Long Group Project: 200 points.*

For these integrative courses, collaborative and experiential learning are important student learning outcomes of the class as a whole. Semester-long collaborative intellectual and experiential work for students allows you to engage with one another to explore the concept of place/environment, being-in-place, and what it means to live a "present," fully flourishing life.

Using the ideas that have been presented to you in both literary and philosophical texts this semester, choose one of these central INTR 250 questions to use as your guiding inquiry question for the final presentations:

1. The authors we have covered from each academic tradition (the literary and the philosophical) all express different ideas on what it means to lead a fully present, engaged life in *all* of the different environments in which we dwell—the physical, the virtual, the imaginary. What meaningful connections can we—as twenty-first-century readers—make to these texts?
2. Your group can consider the different ways these authors express what it means to live a flourishing life. Are there patterns and commonalities among the literary and philosophical texts that we've covered? Are there differences and divergences? (What does it mean to flourish in Thoreau, Hemingway, Aristotle, C. S. Lewis, and Cather's texts?) Choose a balanced number of texts from each tradition to guide your presentation.

Guidelines for Group Project Work

Students will work in groups of four or five, depending on final enrollment numbers for the class. We expect students to meet every other week (once groups have been chosen), or more often than that, to discuss their ideas, select a presentation topic and then to start forming their presentation goals, content, and outline. *Group presentation proposals and outlines must be submitted by Saturday, 7 November, to Turnitin dropbox for approval.*

We expect all presentations to be twenty minutes long and to involve multimedia and/or multimodal elements. (You are encouraged to show images, clips from video games, videos taken of particular real-world sites, clips of interviews or to demonstrate products or creations you have made. As part of your presentations, you can also elect to lead the class through questions, discussions, or activities, et cetera.) Your presentations can involve experiential learning, too (short excursions, activities, et cetera), if you would like to have your audience experience your ideas in some unique or particular manner. *We expect all students to have active roles both in creating the presentation and in presenting the material.*

We expect all presentations to be guided by the central INTR 250 course inquiry questions (stated above). Presentations must also be fully and equally grounded in works of *both literature and philosophy* from our reading list this semester.

5. *Final Self-Reflective Essay: 100 points.*

In a personal essay, four pages long, chart the changes that have occurred in your thinking about being fully present in physical and virtual environments throughout the semester. Have your ideas shifted, altered, or simply deepened throughout the course of our discussions and readings? What new ideas have occurred as your studies progressed this semester?

As you describe the changes in your thinking about space, place, and what it means to lead a fully present, engaged life in all of the different environments in which we dwell, *ground your descriptions in works from both the literature and the philosophy that we have covered this term.*

Appendix E

INTR 250 Physical and Virtual Environments
Class Calendar

Laura Godfrey and Ed Kaitz

Week	Tuesday	Thursday
	Daily readings and assignments should be completed *before* you arrive in class.	Daily readings and assignments should be completed *before* you arrive in class.
1	12 January Introduction to the class; syllabus review	14 January Place Presence—(Godfrey) Crawford: introduction, *The World beyond Your Head* (Blackboard) Tim Cresswell: "Place: A Short Introduction" (handout)

2	19 January
	  Solitude and Place (Godfrey)
	
	Thoreau: *Walden*, "Where I Lived and What I Lived For" and "Solitude"
	Gitlin, "Nomadicity," (from *Digital Divide*, Blackboard)
		21 January
		  Solitude and Place (Godfrey)
		Thoreau: *Walden*, "Sounds," selected pages from "Spring," and "Conclusion"
		Deresiewicz, "The End of Solitude" (from *Digital Divide*—Blackboard)
		Literary Analysis Essay 1 due FRIDAY NIGHT, 22 January, in the Turnitin dropbox by 11:59 P.M.—see your syllabus for full assignment description.

3		26 January Attention Span (Kaitz)	28 January Attention Span (Kaitz)
		Carr, "The Juggler's Brain" (*The Shallows*)	Dreyfus, "Anonymity versus Commitment: The Dangers of Education on the Internet" (handout)
		Carr, "Search, Memory" (*The Shallows*)	Kierkegaard, *The Present Age* (handout)
		Carr, "The Deepening Page" (*The Shallows*)	Bauerlein, "Screen Time," from *The Dumbest Generation*
		Turkle, "The Nostalgia of the Young" (*Alone Together*)	Tolstoy, "Three Questions"
4		2 February Arguments for Technology (Kaitz)	4 February Belonging (Godfrey)
		Mesthene, "The Social Impact of Technological Change"	Hemingway: *The Sun Also Rises* (book 1)
		Tapscott, "The Eight Net Gen Norms" (*Digital Divide*)	
		Stein, "The Surprising Joy of Virtual Reality"	
		Turkle, "Identity Crisis" (*Digital Divide*)	
5		9 February	11 February
		Belonging (Godfrey)	Belonging (Godfrey)
		Hemingway: *The Sun Also Rises* (book 2)	Hemingway: *The Sun Also Rises* (book 3)
			McGonigal, "Collaboration Superpowers" (266–76 Blackboard)
		Form groups for semester group project: project discussion today.	*Philosophy essay 1 due in class.*
6		16 February	18 February
		Classical Sources on Character and Identity (Kaitz)	Classical Sources on Character and Identity (Kaitz)
		Plato, *Alcibiades I* (selections)	Aristotle, *Nicomachean Ethics* and "Friendship"
		Aristotle, *Nicomachean Ethics* and "Friendship"	Goerger, "Friendship and the Ethics of Social Technology"

7	2/23 Topophilia (Godfrey) Yi-Fu Tuan: Introduction (from *Topophilia*, handout) Cather, *The Professor's House*: 1–75	2/25 Topophilia (Godfrey) Cather, *The Professor's House*: 76–155
8	1 March Topophilia (Godfrey) Cather, *The Professor's House*: 159–258 (finish novel)	3 March The Question of Human Nature and Wisdom (Kaitz) C. S. Lewis, *The Abolition of Man* (selections) *Literary Analysis Essay 2 due FRIDAY NIGHT, 4 March in the Turnitin drop box by 11:59 P.M.—see your syllabus for full assignment description.*
9	8 March The Question of Human Nature and Wisdom (Kaitz) Jonas, "The Altered Nature of Human Action" (*The Imperative of Responsibility*) Pascal, *Pensees* Heraclitus, *Fragments* Johnson, "Self-Deception"	10 March Asian Philosophy and Presence (Kaitz) Hui Neng, "Stabilization and Insight" (*Platform Scripture*) Chuang Tzu and Taoism, *Chuang Tzu* (selections) Dogen, *Moon in a Dewdrop* (selections)
10	15 March The Protest Novel Tradition (Godfrey) Eggers: *The Circle* Turkle, "Anxiety," (from *Alone Together* Blackboard)	17 March Private and Public Places (Kaitz) Eggers: *The Circle* *Group project description and outlines due in Turnitin by Friday, 18 March, at 11:59 P.M.*
11	22 March Private and Public Places (Godfrey) Eggers: *The Circle* (complete novel) Philosophy essay 2 due in class.	24 March *GROUP MEETING DAY IN CLASS: Each presentation group will meet with the professors to receive feedback on their presentation outlines.*

12	29 March *Spring Break: no class*	31 March *Spring Break: no class*
13	5 April Dystopian Tradition (Kaitz) Huxley, *Brave New World* (selections) Orwell, *1984*	7 April *Advising Day: no class*
14	12 April Dystopian Tradition (Kaitz) Orwell, *1984* Bostrom, "The Future of Humanity" Sarewitz, "The Idea of Progress"	4/14 Catch-up day (Godfrey), TBA
15	19 April Final Group Presentations	21 April Final Group Presentations
16	26 April Final Group Presentations	28 April Final Group Presentations
17	3 May Final Group Presentations	5 May *Last Day of Class (to be used for final presentations if needed).*

Appendix F

Directing Students toward Hemingway's "Concrete Particulars" and Intergenerational Connections

Mark Ebel

To help students achieve intellectual growth, teachers may use directed instruction designed to unveil implied context and draw conclusions from concrete particulars within the reading context. As noted by Benfer and Shanahan, many twenty-first-century "students are accustomed to instantaneous answers that do not require deliberation or mental examination. As a result, they may not have developed the tools to extract the depth of information necessary to develop critical thinking" (131). Rather than asking students to report what they read, educators might encourage them to search for material objects that infer subtle or symbolic meanings—examples of Hemingway's iceberg theory in action, or what T. S. Eliot called the "objective correlative."

A sample assignment related to this topic of seeing the importance of material objects and details in Hemingway's writing might be to ask students to make a list of objects referred to in the text that infer, suggest, or even symbolize meaning. In other columns, they would identify the reference passage and state the meaning that might be associated with the object. An example from *Across the River and into the Trees* is provided below.

Object	Reference passage	Meaning
Flask of Grappa	"English grappa" (258)	the two former antagonists dismiss their animosities by sharing an alcoholic drink. Flask of Grappa thus suggests forgiveness and friendship.

A useful method for joining together students with older, more experienced persons is to invite guest speakers to the classroom. The students could be asked to provide names or invite directly persons of particular interest who might be willing to visit the classroom and make presentations. I have given this option along with the promise of extra points and have been amazed at the human resources lying hidden in the fabric of the community, unknown to me but familiar to my students. Teachers should encourage students to speak about their own experiences or invite family members or friends with military background or knowledge of such themes as the meaning of military insignia, military uniforms, military ranks, and military history, all of which may help to elucidate meaning in the novel's duck hunting frame. With the number of military service personnel now returning to populate classrooms across the country, students with military backgrounds may be found right in the classroom. Such students may be willing and able to present relevant topics based on their own experiences.

Methodologies such as these may serve the students well, both as a means of developing their listening and observational skills and as serving as a bridge to unite generational gaps and create a sense of shared experience. This, in turn, helps build community in the classroom. Hemingway was well aware of the importance of developing good listening skills. He provides aspiring writers with this advice, applicable to classroom learning experiences such as the ones previously mentioned: "When people talk listen completely. Don't be thinking what you're going to say. Most people never listen. Nor do they observe. You should be able to go into a room an when you come out know everything that you saw there and not only that. If that room gave you any feeling you should know exactly what it was that gave you that feeling" (*By-Line* 219–20).

This passage may be useful to teachers for designing writing activities following the appearance of a guest speaker. Teachers may assign students to write a summary of the speaker's presentation, including quoted remarks, which will utilize their listening and note-taking skills, and conclude by identifying their reactions to the speaker on an emotional level, which will help them identify and express their feelings in written form.

Appendix G

How to *Not* Read Hemingway

Brian Croxall

For the full semester-long set of assignments and blog posts, please see Croxall, *Introduction to Digital Humanities*.

Rationale

As we've explored in a number of assignments throughout the semester, you can get a different sense of texts if you do pattern recognition at a slightly different angle. So far, this has meant that we've considered a novel via its geography, a poetry collection at the macro level, and films that we summed. But in each case, we did the "normal" humanities thing by reading or watching the text and discussing it. Only then did we look at it through a computational lens.

But what if we decided to try pattern recognition and interpretation on something so large that a class could never read it in a single semester, let alone the last two weeks? Consider this one last crazy digital humanities experiment!

Part of this experiment will involve us confronting, once again, the friction of formats. Computational approaches require computable information, and it turns out that print books aren't. Or at least, they aren't yet. This project brings us yet another way to think about getting material from one format into another.

The Nitty Gritty

Collectively, we will finish building a dataset of all of Hemingway's stories, novels, and nonfiction. (Say "Thanks!" to my previous classes for getting us started.) Individually, you will be scanning a number of pages from one or two of his books and then processing those scans with optical character recognition (OCR) software.

Scanning

It turns out that books can be kind of hard to scan, since there's all that pesky page-turning to deal with. We're going to simplify things by making these books less booklike and removing their bindings.

- You will scan the pages that you are assigned, *turning the pages into PDFs*. If you have selections from multiple books, please scan each book separately, creating a different file for each.
- There are three printers around the Jesse Knight Building that have automatic feeders and that can scan both sides of the page. You can find them in 3003C, 4073 East, and 4016 West. I estimate that it will take you five minutes to do the scanning. The scanners will email you the file.
- Before scanning, you need to make four changes to the default settings:
  - The default is to only scan one side of the page. You need to make sure you scan *two sides*.
  - Set the scanner to work in *grayscale* rather than color.
  - The default resolution on the scanners is 300 dpi, *but you should set it to 200 dpi*, as it will result in a smaller file.
  - The default file type on the scanners is a compact PDF. This will produce poor output. Instead, *you need to change the file type to PDF*.
- When you have received a file, check it to *make sure you got both sides of the page*. Then rename it to lastname-bookabbreviation-pages; for example, croxall-FWBT-75–254.pdf. If you're working with two different books, please make sure you've saved them as two different files. *Upload a copy of the PDF(s) to the class Google Drive folder.*

OCR

- To do the OCR work, you will need to bring your PDFs to one of several computers in the Joseph F. Smith Building (JFSB) that have the Prizmo OCR software Installed on them.
- When opening Prizmo, choose "New Document" and then drag-and-drop your PDF onto the window.
- Make sure that "Abc" is selected in the upper left and that the language is set to English. You shouldn't have to make any other adjustments to the settings.
- Select all of the pages in your file by clicking on a single page image and choosing "Edit > Select All" (⌘A).

- Then click "Recognize."
- Sit back and relax as Prizmo processes all of your text.
- As you look through each page of the text, do the following:
  - First, make sure that only the body of the text is selected on the page.
-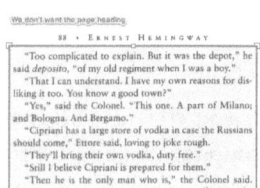
  - Second, check for misspellings and correct them. They will have red underlines; if the word is spelled correctly and will repeat regularly throughout your pages (like a character's name, a place name, or a foreign word), you can right-click and tell Prizmo to ignore that word moving forward.
  - Third, check for random characters such as numbers or strange punctuation marks and correct them. Prizmo won't catch these with red underlines most of the time. Just glance around the page. You'll be surprised how good the human eye is at seeing misplaced characters.
-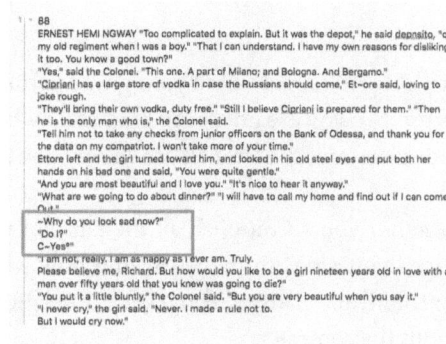
  - Remember: *I'm not asking you to read through each and every single word.*
- When you've finished all of your pages, choose "Export" and set the Format to "Regular Text." Make sure you include all pages. Click "Export to File," and then save the file.
- Name your file lastname-bookabbreviation-pages; for example, croxall-SAR-100–286.txt, and *email me the file.*
- If you have pages from more than one book, you will have to go through this process for each book. But don't worry: I made the number of pages equal for everyone.

- *Important: Please do not spend any more than five hours on the OCR, even if you don't finish.*
- You need to get me all of your files *no later than 3:00 P.M. on Friday, 15 December.* This will give me the chance to compile everything in time for the final.

Final

- For the final exam, we will again use our old friend Voyant to find patterns in the Hemingway data set. You will work in groups again and have free range of the tools. Since we won't have read everything, your experience asking questions and drawing conclusions will be much different than working with Duffy's poetry. Who knows, maybe even the word collocates will be interesting this time!
- In your groups, you will write an eight-hundred-word (minimum) blog post about the patterns that you've found and the interpretations that you derived from them. Finally, your group will also give a brief presentation on the work that you've done.
- Then we'll all high-five each other and ride off into the sunset.

Grading

This project, including the final, is worth 10 percent of your grade in the class. As this is an experimental class project, you are not being graded on what you and your group find about Hemingway's work. After all, we simply don't know what we'll find—if anything.

Instead, you'll be graded on whether you accomplish all the parts of the assignment (pass/fail); how engaged you are with the work; and how well you apply the methods of screwing around and pattern recognition/interpretation we've been embracing throughout the semester.

Credits

This assignment was designed by Brian Croxall in 2014 and is licensed with a Creative Commons BY (CC BY 4.0). Special props to Stewart Varner for telling me to stop thinking about Whitman; David Mimno and Ted Underwood for encouragement; and Paul Fyfe and Jason B. Jones for an idea that I gleefully ripped off. None of this would be possible without the fantastic resource of Voyant Tools, which Stéfan Sinclair and Geoffrey Rockwell have developed for years amid constant pestering from me for new features.

Appendix H

Digital Resources for Teaching Hemingway

Compiled by Lisa Tyler

Drawn from Lisa Tyler's essay in this collection, "Virtual Papa: Ernest Hemingway's Digital Presence," below is a list of diverse digital resources that can help teachers prepare lessons and activities for their Hemingway students.

Baker, Allie. *The Hemingway Project: Collecting Stories about the Enduring Influence of Ernest Hemingway.* Wendy Simpson, 2016.

Baker, Carlos. "A Search for the Man As He Really Was." *The New York Times,* 26 July 1964, www.nytimes.com/books/99/07/04/specials/hemingway-search.html.

Blume, Lesley M. M. "The Vindication of Pauline Hemingway, Ernest's Second (and Most Vilified) Wife." *Vogue,* 8 June 2016, www.vogue.com/article/pauline-hemingway-forgotten-wife.

"Depicting Hemingway: Guy Harvey Sketches 'The Old Man and the Sea.'" *Key West Art and Historical Society,* 2016, www.kwahs.org/exhibitions/depicting-hemingway.

Didion, Joan. "Last Words." *The New Yorker,* 9 Nov. 1998, www.newyorker.com/magazine/1998/11/09/last-words-6.

Diliberto, Gioia. "A Marriage Unraveled." *Chicago Tribune,* 1 July 2011, articles.chicago tribune.com/2011-07-01/opinion/ct-oped-0701-hemingway-20110701_1_hadley-richardson-ernest-hemingway-marriage.

Donaldson, Scott. "The Jilting of Ernest Hemingway." *Virginia Quarterly Review,* vol. 65, no. 4, Autumn 1989, www.vqronline.org/essay/jilting-ernest-hemingway.

"Early Years: Ernest and Marcelline Hemingway in Oak Park." *Illinois Digital Archives,* Illinois State Library and Illinois Secretary of State, www.idaillinois.org/ui/custom/default/collection/default/resources/custompages/bin/edi.php?collection=p16614coll27&startrec=251.

"Ernest Hemingway." *Simon & Schuster,* 2017, www.simonandschuster.com/authors/Ernest-Hemingway/1792713.

"Ernest Hemingway in His Time: An Internet Source Page and Online Exhibition from the University of Delaware Library, Newark, Delaware." *Special Collections Department,* University of Delaware, 11 May 2012, www.lib.udel.edu/ud/spec/exhibits/hemngway/.

"Ernest Hemingway's *Kansas City Star* Articles." *The Kansas City Star,* 28 July 2007, www.kansascity.com/entertainment/arts-culture/article294962/Ernest-Hemingways-Kansas-City-Star-stories.html.

Hemingway, Grace Hall. "Mother's Scrapbooks." *Ernest Hemingway Audio-visual Materials,.* John F. Kennedy Presidential Library and Museum, www.jfklibrary.org/Research/The-Ernest-Hemingway-Collection/Hemingway-Audiovisual-Materials.aspx.

Federal Bureau of Investigation. "Ernest Hemingway." *FBI Records: The Vault.* vault.fbi.gov/ernest-miller-hemingway.

"Featured Author: Ernest Hemingway." *The New York Times,* 1999, www.nytimes.com/books/99/07/11/specials/hemingway-main.html.

Garcia Marquez, Gabriel. "Gabriel Garcia Marquez Meets Ernest Hemingway." *The New York Times,* 26 July 1981, www.nytimes.com/books/99/07/04/specials/hemingway-marquez.html.

Gumbel, Andrew. "Transsexual Son Haunts Hemingway Clan." *The Independent,* 27 Sept. 2003, www.independent.co.uk/news/world/americas/transsexual-son-haunts-hemingway-clan-88844.html.

Hemingway, Ernest. "Ernest Hemingway—Banquet Speech." *Nobelprize.org: The Official Website of the Nobel Prize,* 2017, www.nobelprize.org/prizes/literature/1954/hemingway/speech/.

———. "Hemingway Reports Spain." *New Republic,* 27 Apr. 1938, newrepublic.com/article/89502/hemingway-spain-spanish-civil-war.

———. "Italy, 1927." *New Republic,* 18 May 1927, newrepublic.com/article/79268/italy-1927.

"Hemingway in Key West." Key West Art and Historical Society, 2016, www.kwahs.org/exhibitions/ernest-in-key-west.

Hemingway, Mary [Welsh]. "At Harry's Bar in Venice." *Holiday,* June 1968. Reprinted in *The Astounding World of Holiday,* Josh Lieberman, 27 June

2012, holidaymag.wordpress.com/2012/06/27/harrys-bar-in-venice-by-mary-hemingway-june-1968/.

"The Hemingway Papers." *The Toronto Star*, 1996–2012, ehto.thestar.com/.

Hemingway-Pfeiffer Museum and Educational Center. Arkansas State University, hemingway.astate.edu/.

Hotchner, A. E. "Hemingway in Love." *Smithsonian*, Oct. 2015, www.smithsonianmag.com/arts-culture/ernest-hemingway-in-love-180956617/.

Jones, Josh. "The (Urban) Legend of Ernest Hemingway's Six-Word Short Story: 'For Sale, Baby Shoes, Never Worn.'" *Open Culture*, 24 Mar. 2015, www.openculture.com/2015/03/the-urban-legend-of-ernest-hemingways-six-word-story.html.

"Julian Barnes Reads 'Homage to Switzerland' by Ernest Hemingway." *The Guardian*, 7 Dec. 2010, www.theguardian.com/books/audio/2010/dec/08/julian-barnes-ernest-hemingway-podcast.

Landau, Elizabeth. "Hemingway Family Mental Illness Explored in New Film." *CNN*, 23 Jan. 2013, www.cnn.com/2013/01/21/health/hemingway-film/index.html.

Lovett, D. F. "Six Things Hemingway Never Said." *What Would Bale Do*, 10 July 2015, whatwouldbaledo.com/2015/07/10/six-things-hemingway-never-said/.

Lyman, Rick. "Martha Gellhorn, Daring Writer, Dies at 89." *New York Times*, 17 Feb. 1998, www.nytimes.com/1998/02/17/arts/martha-gellhorn-daring-writer-dies-at-89.html.

Marano, Lou. "The Hemingway Suicide Curse." *UPI*, 10 Oct. 2001, www.upi.com/The-Hemingway-suicide-curse/60461002739993/.

Meyers, Jeffrey. "The Quest for Hemingway." *Virginia Quarterly Review*, vol. 61, no. 4, Autumn 1985, www.vqronline.org/essay/quest-hemingway.

Mitgang, Herbert. "Mary Hemingway Dies at 78; Wrote of Life with Novelist." *New York Times*, 28 Nov. 1986, www.nytimes.com/1986/11/28/obituaries/mary-hemingway-dies-at-78-wrote-of-life-with-novelist.html.

O'Toole, Garson. "For Sale, Baby Shoes, Never Worn." *Quote Investigator*, 28 Jan. 2013, quoteinvestigator.com/2013/01/28/baby-shoes/.

"Paula McLain on Reviving Hemingway and *The Paris Wife*," *YouTube*, uploaded by Penguin Random House Canada, 8 Feb. 2011, www.youtube.com/watch?v=mR6bfEvYLEo.

Plimpton, George. "Ernest Hemingway, The Art of Fiction No. 21." *Paris Review*, no. 18, Spring 1958, www.theparisreview.org/interviews/4825/the-art-of-fiction-no-21-ernest-hemingway.

"Publications by Members." *Michigan Hemingway Society*, 2017, www.michiganhemingwaysociety.org/articlelinks/articlelinks.htm.

Reynolds, Michael. "Ringing the Changes: Hemingway's *Bell* Tolls Fifty." *Virginia Quarterly Review*, vol. 67, no. 1, Winter 1991, www.vqronline.org/essay/ringing-changes-hemingway's-bell-tolls-fifty.

Ross, Lillian. "The Moods of Ernest Hemingway: The Writer, Unenthusiastically, Visits New York." *The New Yorker*, 13 May 1950, www.newyorker.com/magazine/1950/05/13/how-do-you-like-it-now-gentlemen.

Sanford, Marcelline Hemingway. "At the Hemingways: Ernest Returns from War." *The Atlantic*. Reprinted as "Hemingway Goes to War." *The Atlantic*, Aug. 2014, www.theatlantic.com/magazine/archive/2014/08/hemingway-goes-to-war/373437/.

Scribner, Charles III. "Ernest Hemingway: A Publisher's Perspective." *Charles Scribner III*. Charles Scribner, charlesscribner.com/ernest-hemingway.html.

Stoppard, Tom. "Reflections on Ernest Hemingway." *American Masters*. PBS, 14 Sept. 2005, www.pbs.org/wnet/americanmasters/ernest-hemingway-reflections-on-ernest-hemingway/629/.

Thurber, James. "A Visit from St. Nicholas (in the Ernest Hemingway Manner)." *The New Yorker*, 24 Dec. 1927, www.newyorker.com/magazine/1927/12/24/a-visit-from-saint-nicholas-in-the-ernest-hemingway-manner.

Tyler, Lisa. *Virtual Hemingway*, 2018, virtualhemingway.hcommons.org/.

White, E. B. "Across the Street and into the Grill." *The New Yorker*, 14 Oct. 1950, www.newyorker.com/magazine/1950/10/14/across-the-street-and-into-the-grill.

Works Cited

Adorno, Theodor. "Late Style in Beethoven." *Essays on Music*. University of California P, 2002, pp. 564–68.
Aiken, Conrad. "William Faulkner: The Novel as Form." 1939. *William Faulkner: The Critical Heritage,* edited by John Bassett, Routledge & Kegan Paul, 1975, pp. 243–50.
Adamson, Glenn. *Fewer, Better Things: The Hidden Wisdom of Objects*. Bloomsbury, 2018.
Amdon, Stephen. "I Didn't Like Sex at All." *Salon,* 12 Aug. 2016, www.salon.com/2006/08/12/gellhorn/.
Arnold, Lloyd. *Hemingway: High on the Wild*. Grossett & Dunlap, 1976.
Baker, Allie. *The Hemingway Project*. Wendy Simpson, 2016, thehemingwayproject.com.
Baker, Carlos. "A Search for the Man As He Really Was." *The New York Times,* 26 July 1964, www.nytimes.com/books/99/07/04/specials/hemingway-search.html
———. *Ernest Hemingway: A Life Story*. Scribner, 1969.
———. *Hemingway: The Writer as Artist*. Princeton UP, 1972.
Bakhtin, Mikhail. *Problems of Dostoevsky's Poetics,* edited and translated by Caryl Emerson, U of Minnesota P, 1984.
Barbour, George. "Barbour George (Professor) Collection." *British Imperial War Museums,* www.iwm.org.uk/collections/search?query=red%20cross%20italian%20front&items_per_page=10.
Barnard, Rita. "Modern American Fiction." *The Cambridge Companion to American Modernism,* edited by Walter Kalaidjian, Cambridge UP, 2005, p. 46.
Barry, Robert L. *Breaking the Thread of Life: On Rational Suicide*. Transaction, 1996.
Bartlett's Familiar Quotations, 11th ed., edited by Christopher Morley and Louella D. Everett, Collier, 1937.
———, 18th ed., edited by Geoffrey O'Brien, Little, Brown, 2012.
Bass, Randall. "Story and Archive in the Twenty First Century." *College English,* vol. 61, no. 6, 1999, pp. 259–70.
Bauerlein, Mark. *The Dumbest Generation: How the Digital Age Stupefies Young Americans and Jeopardizes Our Future (Or, Don't Trust Anyone Under 30)*. Penguin, 2008.
Bear, John. *The #1 New York Times Best Seller: Intriguing Facts about the 484 Books That Have Been #1 New York Times Bestsellers Since the First List, 50 Years Ago*. Ten Speed Press, 1992.

Benfer, Emily A., and Colleen F. Shanahan. "Educating the Invincibles: Strategies for Teaching the Millennial Generation in Law School." *Clinical Law Review*, vol. 20, no. 301, Fall 2013, pp. 1–39. Loyola U of Chicago School of Law Research Paper No. 2013-021.

Benstock, Shari. *Women of the Left Bank: Paris, 1900–1940.* U of Texas P, 1984.

The Best of Bad Hemingway: Choice Entries from the Harry's Bar & American Grill Imitation Hemingway Competition. Houghton Mifflin, 1989.

Bimberg, Edward L. *The Moroccan Gourms: Tribal Warriors in a Modern War.* Greenwood P, 1999.

Blouin, Francis X., Jr. "History and Memory: The Problem of the Archives." *Publications of the Modern Languages Association of America*, vol. 119, no. 4, 2004, pp. 296–98.

Blume, Lesley M. M. "The Vindication of Pauline Hemingway, Ernest's Second (and Most Vilified) Wife." *Vogue*, 8 June 2016, www.vogue.com/article/pauline-hemingway-forgotten-wife.

Boreth, Craig. *The Hemingway Cookbook.* Chicago Review P, 1998.

Botnik. *Botnik,* botnik.org.

———. "Harry Potter." *Botnik,* botnik.org/content/harry-potter.html.

Bowman, Peter, and Suzanne W. Churchill, eds. *Index of Modernist Magazines,* 2018, Davidson College, modernistmagazines.org.

Brasch, James D., and Joseph Sigman. *Hemingway's Library: A Composite Record.* 1981. Electronic ed., 2000, John F. Kennedy Presidential Library and Museum, jfklibrary.libguides.com/ld.php?content_id=38785340.

Brian, Denis. *The True Gen: An Intimate Portrait of Hemingway by Those Who Knew Him.* Grove P, 1988.

"Broom: An International Magazine of the Arts." *Blue Mountain Project: Historic Avant-Garde Periodicals for Digital Research,* Princeton U, July 15, 2014, library.princeton.edu/sites/default/files/IAML 2014 BMP handout 140715.pdf.

Bromwich, Jonah Engle. "Life on the Meme Council: Meet the Internet's Gatekeepers." *The New York Times*, 15 Dec. 2017, www.nytimes.com/2017/12/15/style/know-your-meme.html.

Burdick, Kelly, et al. "Hemingway Is Bull." *Digital Humanities Fall 2017,* 20 Dec. 2017, dh17.dralexlyman.net/uncategorized/hemingway-is-bull/.

Busch, Frederick. "Reading Hemingway without Guilt." *The New York Times*, 12 Jan. 1992.

Campugan, Belen H. *A Realia Approach in Teaching Interdisciplinary Concepts.* Thesis. St. Peters College, 2013, Iligan Independent Publishers, 2013.

Caquard, Sébastien. "Cartography I: Mapping Narrative Cartography." *Progress in Human Geography*, vol. 37, no. 1, 2014, pp. 135–44.

Carr, Nicholas. *The Shallows: What the Internet Is Doing to Our Brains.* Norton, 2010.

Carroll, Allen, and Rupert Essinger. "Tell Your Story Using a Map." *The ArcGIS Book,* 2017, learn.arcgis.com/en/arcgis-book/chapter3/.

Carson, Chris. "A Closer Look at the Decline in Hunter Participation." *Big Game Logic,* 12 Jan. 2015, www.biggamelogic.com/Articles-News/ArticleType/Article View/ArticleID/603.

Center for Disease Control. "Remembering the 1918 Influenza Pandemic." *CDC Features,* 7 May, 2018, www.cdc.gov/features/1918-flu-pandemic/index.html.
Cirino, Mark, *Reading Hemingway's* Across the River and into the Trees: *Glossary and Commentary.* Kent State UP, 2016.
Cirino, Mark, and Mark P. Ott, eds. *Ernest Hemingway and the Geography of Memory.* Kent State UP, 2010.
Clarke, Arthur C. "The Power of Compression." *Greetings, Carbon-Based Bipeds! Collected Essays, 1934–1998,* edited by Ian T. MacAuley, St. Martin's P, 1999, pp. 353–55.
CliffsNotes. Houghton Mifflin Harcourt, 2016, www.cliffnotes.com,
Comley, Nancy R., and Robert Scholes. *Hemingway's Genders: Rereading the Hemingway Text.* Yale UP, 1994.
Conrad, Joseph. *Heart of Darkness.* Bedford / St. Martin's, 1996.
Crawford, Matthew B. *The World beyond Your Head: On Becoming an Individual in an Age of Distraction.* Farrar, Straus, & Giroux, 2015.
Croxall, Brian. *Introduction to Digital Humanities,* 2017, www.briancroxall.net/f17dh/.
Croxall, Brian. "Tired of Tech: Avoiding Tool Fatigue in the Classroom." *Writing and Pedagogy,* vol. 5, no. 2, 2013, pp. 249–68.
Curnutt, Kirk. *Coffee with Hemingway.* Duncan Baird, 2007.
———. *Reading Hemingway's* To Have and Have Not: *Glossary and Commentary.* Kent State UP. 2017.
Daiker, Donald A. "The Pedagogy of *The Sun Also Rises.*" *Ernest Hemingway's* The Sun Also Rises, edited by Harold Bloom. New ed., Infobase, 2011, pp. 165–78.
Darici, Katiuscia. "'To Draw a Map Is to Tell a Story': Interview with Dr. Robert T. Tally, Jr. on Geocriticism." *Universitat Pompeu Fabra,* 15 June 2015, www.raco.cat/index.php/Forma/article/view/294989.
Davidson, Shelbi, et al. "DIGHT215Group3FinalExam." *Google Docs,* 20 Dec. 2017, docs.google.com/document/d/1DU6DDjVwf-MnWPzbesDPnX_KTiONn3kc6Kx1cb7fD30/edit?ts=5a3ae8e6#.
Daw, Tim M. "Shifting Baselines and Memory Illusions: What Should We Worry about When Inferring Trends from Resource User Interviews?" *Animal Conservation,* vol. 13, no. 6, 2010, pp. 534–35.
Dawkins, Richard. The Selfish Gene. Oxford UP, 1976.
de Certeau, Michel. *The Practice of Everyday Life,* translated by Steven Rendall, U of California P, 1988.
Dearborn, Mary. *Ernest Hemingway: A Biography.* Knopf, 2017.
DeFazio, Albert J. III. "Skillful Teaching of *The Sun Also Rises* in Secondary Schools." Hays, *Teaching Hemingway's* The Sun Also Rises. pp. 67–87.
del Gizzo, Suzanne. "'Glow-in-the-Dark Authors': Hemingway's Celebrity and Legacy in Under Kilimanjaro." *The Hemingway Review,* vol. 29, no. 2, 2010, pp. 7–27.
DeLand, Adam. "Hipster." *Know Your Meme,* 10 Apr. 2011, knowyourmeme.com/memes/cultures/hipster.
"Depicting Hemingway: Guy Harvey Sketches 'The Old Man and the Sea.'" *Key West Art and Historical Society,* 2016, www.kwahs.org/exhibitions/depicting-hemingway.

Derrida, Jacques. *Of Grammatology*, translated by Gayatri Chakravorty Spivak, Johns Hopkins UP, 1976.

———. "Violence and Metaphysics: An Essay on the Thought of Emmanuel Levinas." *Writing and Difference*, translated by Alan Bass, U of Chicago P, 1978, pp. 79–153.

Didion, Joan. "Last Words." *The New Yorker*, 9 Nov. 1998, www.newyorker.com/magazine/1998/11/09/last-words-6.

Diliberto, Gioia. "A Marriage Unraveled." *The Chicago Tribune*, 1 July 2011, articles.chicago tribune.com/2011-07-01/opinion/ct-oped-0701-hemingway-20110701_1_hadley-richardson-ernest-hemingway-marriage.

Dirda, Michael. Introduction to *ABCs of Reading* by Ezra Pound. 1934. New Directions, 2010, pp. 1–8.

Donaldson, Scott. "The Jilting of Ernest Hemingway." *Virginia Quarterly Review*, vol. 65, no. 4, Autumn 1989, www.vquonline.org/essay/jilting-ernest-hemingway.

———. *By Force of Will: The Life and Art of Ernest Hemingway*. Viking, 1977.

Dos Passos, John. *The Best Times: An Informal Memoir*. New American Library, 1966.

———. *The Fourteenth Chronicle: Letters and Diaries of John Dos Passos*, edited by Townsend Ludington, Gambit, 1973.

Drew, Joshua, et al. "Collateral Damage to Marine and Terrestrial Ecosystems from Yankee Whaling in the 19th Century." *Ecology and Evolution*, vol. 6, no. 22, 2016, pp. 8181–92.

Dubus, Andre III. "Ernest Hemingway: Why His Work Matters Now More than Ever, a Love Letter from the Digital World." *The Hemingway Review*, vol. 32, no. 1, Fall 2012, pp. 7–15.

Earle, David M. *All Man! Hemingway, 1950s Men's Magazines, and the Masculine Persona*. Kent State UP, 2009.

"Early Years: Ernest and Marcelline Hemingway in Oak Park." *Illinois Digital Archives*. Illinois State Library and Illinois Secretary of State, www.idaillinois.org/ui/custom/default/collection/default/resources/custompages/bin/edi.php?collection=p16614coll27&startrec=1&startrec=1.

Eby, Carl P. *Hemingway's Fetishism: Psychoanalysis and the Mirror of Manhood*. SUNY P, 1999.

Eliot, T. S. *Collected Poems, 1909–1962*. Faber & Faber, 1963.

———. *Selected Essays, 1917–1932*. Harcourt, Brace & World, 1932.

Emerson, Ralph Waldo. "Self-Reliance." *Emerson's Essays*. Harper & Row, 1951, pp. 31–66.

eNotes. eNotes.com, 2018, www.enotes.com.

"Ernest Hemingway, 'Across the River and into the Trees,' Caorle, Venice, Italy." *YouTube*, uploaded by Caorle Channel + Venice, 7 Sept. 2012, www.youtube.com/watch?v=D8P9q-k34yw.

"Ernest Hemingway Collection." Hemingway LTD, 2014, www.ernesthemingwaycollection.com/.

"Ernest Hemingway in His Time: An Internet Source Page and Online Exhibition from the University of Delaware Library, Newark, Delaware." *Special Collections Department*, University of Delaware, 11 May 2012, www.lib.udel.edu/ud/spec/exhibits/hemngway/.

"Ernest Hemingway's Nobel Prize Acceptance Speech." *JFK Presidential Library and Museum,* www.jfklibrary.org/asset-viewer/ernest-hemingways-nobel-prize-acceptance-speech-1954.

"Ernest Hemingway Photograph Collection: Media Gallery." John F. Kennedy Presidential Library and Museum, www.jfklibrary.org/Research/The-Ernest-Hemingway-Collection/Media-Galleries/Hemingway-Chronologically.aspx.

"Ernest Hemingway. Reading." *Youtube,* uploaded by nagusd, 5 Jan. 2014, www.youtube.com/watch?v=3Zv-EzQxyWg.

"Ernest Hemingway." *Simon & Schuster,* 2017, www.simonandschuster.com/authors/Ernest-Hemingway/1792713.

"Ernest Hemingway." *Wikipedia,* 5 Nov. 2017, en.wikipedia.org/wiki/Ernest_Hemingway.

"The Ernest Hemingway Collection Media Galleries." *JFK Presidential Library and Museum,* www.jfklibrary.org/Research/The-Ernest-Hemingway-Collection/Media-Galleries.aspx.

"Ernest Hemingway's Kansas City Star Articles." *The Kansas City Star.* Knight-Ridder/McClatchy, 28 July 2007, www.kansascity.com/entertainment/arts-culture/article294962/Ernest-Hemingways-Kansas-City-Star-stories.html.

"1930s." *Esquire Classic Archive,* archive.esquire.com/issues/1939.

Fantina, Richard. *Ernest Hemingway: Machismo and Masochism.* Palgrave, 2005.

Farrah, Andrew. *Hemingway's Brain.* U of South Carolina P, 2017.

"Featured Author: Ernest Hemingway." *The New York Times,* 1999, www.nytimes.com/books/99/07/11/specials/hemingway-main.html.

Frabetti, Federica. "Rethinking the Digital Humanities in the Context of Originary Technicity." *Culture Machine,* vol. 12, 2011, pp. 1–22

Federal Bureau of Investigation. "Ernest Hemingway." *FBI Records: The Vault,* vault.fbi.gov/ernest-miller-hemingway.

Feldman, Brian. "The Hot New Meme Is Giving in to Your Worst Impulses." *New York,* 24 Aug. 2017, http://nymag.com/intelligencer/2017/08/the-guy-checking-out-a-girl-meme-explained.html.

Fitch, Noel. *Walks in Hemingway's Paris: A Guide to Paris for the Literary Traveler.* St. Martin's, 1989.

Flannery, Eóin. *Ireland and Ecocriticism: Literature, History, and Environmental Justice.* Routledge, 2016.

Frank, Joseph. "Spatial Form in Modern Literature." *The Idea of Spatial Form.* Rutgers UP, 1991, pp. 31–66.

Franklin, Benjamin. *The Autobiography of Benjamin Franklin,* edited by Edmund S. Morgan, 2nd ed., Yale UP, 2003.

Frey, David. *Papa's Planet,* davidmfrey.com/papas-planet/.

Fyfe, Paul. "How to Not Read a Victorian Novel." *Journal of Victorian Culture,* vol. 16, no. 1, 2011, pp. 84–88.

Fyfe, Paul, and Richard Menke. "Data Copperfield: A Pedagogical Experiment in Distributed Collaboration." *Journal of Victorian Culture,* vol. 21, no. 4, 2016, pp. 559–66.

Gajdusek, Robert. *Hemingway's Paris.* Scribners, 1978.

Gallo, Carmine. "Re-Think PowerPoint, Don't Ditch It." *Forbes*, 30 July 2015, www.forbes.com/sites/carminegallo/2015/07/30/rethink-powerpoint-dont-ditch-it/#49a6bda013fe.

García Márquez, Gabriel. "Gabriel Garcia Marquez Meets Ernest Hemingway." *The New York Times*, 26 July 1981, www.nytimes.com/books/99/07/04/specials/hemingway-marquez.html.

Gellhorn, Martha. "Eichmann and the Private Conscience." *The Atlantic*, vol. 209, no. 2, Feb. 1962, pp. 52–59, www.theatlantic.com/past/docs/issues/62feb/eichmann.htm.

———. "High Explosive for Everyone." *Collier's*, 1937. Reporting America at War. WETA, 2003, www.pbs.org/weta/reportingamericaatwar/reporters/gellhorn/madrid.html.

———. "Is There a New Germany?" *The Atlantic*. vol. 213, no. 2, Feb. 1964, pp. 69–76, www.theatlantic.com/past/docs/issues/64feb/germany.htm.

"Giants of San Fermin Dance." *YouTube*, uploaded by Sanferminencierro, 16 Apr. 2012, *www.youtube.com/watch?v=8acOgX6HOfI*.

Gil, Paul. "What Is a Meme?" *Lifewire*, 9 Dec. 2017, www.lifewire.com/what-is-a-meme-2483702.

Godfrey, Laura. "Hemingway and Cultural Geography: The Landscape of Logging in 'The End of Something.'" *The Hemingway Review*, vol. 26, no. 1, Fall 2006, pp. 47–62.

———. *Hemingway's Geographies: Intimacy, Materiality, and Memory*. Palgrave Macmillan, 2016.

Godfrey, Laura, and Bruce Godfrey. "Mapping Hemingway in Idaho." *Inside Idaho*, www.insideidaho.org/stories/hemingway-in-idaho/index.html?appid=8372c1acd90749a489cd937795d788a5.

Gold, Matthew K. "Digital Humanities." *The Johns Hopkins Guide to Digital Media*, edited by Marie-Laure Ryan et al., Johns Hopkins UP, 2014, pp. 143–49

———, ed. *Debates in the Digital Humanities*. U of Minnesota P, 2012.

The Great War. "Italy in World War 1: The Great War Special." *YouTube*, uploaded by The Great War, 13 July 2015, www.youtube.com/watch?v=JzjjBQlofuo.

Green, John. "Archdukes, Cynicism, and World War 1: Crash Course World War History #36." *YouTube*, uploaded by Crash Course, 27 Sept. 2012, www.youtube.com/watch?v=_XPZQoLAlR4.

Greenberg, Paul. "A Fish Tale." *The New York Times*, 12 Aug. 2007, www.nytimes.com/2007/08/12/books/review/Greenberg-t.html

Grimes, Larry E. "Even the Darkness Is Light? Or, Does the Sun Also Rise? Approaches to Teaching Religious Dimensions of The Sun Also Rises." Hays, *Teaching Hemingway's* The Sun Also Rises, pp. 149–65.

Gumbel, Andrew. "Transsexual Son Haunts Hemingway Clan." *The Independent*, 27 Sept. 2003, www.independent.co.uk/news/world/americas/transsexual-son-haunts-hemingway-clan-88844.html.

Hanazaki, Natalia, et al. "Evidence of the Shifting Baseline Syndrome in Ethnobotanical Research." *Journal of Ethnobiology and Ethnomedicine*, vol. 9, no. 1, 2013, 75.

Hays, Peter L. "Hemingway's Playboy Interviews: Are They Genuine?" *Fifty Years of Hemingway Criticism*. Methuen, NJ: Scarecrow P, 2003. 215–19.

———, ed. *Teaching Hemingway's* The Sun Also Rises. Kent State UP, 2007.
Heim, Michael. *The Metaphysics of Virtual Reality.* Oxford UP, 1993.
Hemingway, Ernest. *Across the River and into the Trees.* Scribner's, 2003.
———. "Advice to a Young Man." *Playboy,* vol. 11, Jan. 1964, 153, 225–27.
———. *By-Line Ernest Hemingway: Selected Articles and Dispatches of Four Decades,* edited by William White. New York: Scribner, 1985.
———. *The Complete Short Stories of Ernest Hemingway.* Finca Vigía Edition. Scribner's, 1987.
———. *Conversations with Ernest Hemingway,* edited by Matthew J. Bruccoli, U of Mississippi P, 1986.
———. *Dateline: Toronto. The Complete* Toronto Star *Dispatches, 1920–1924,* edited by William White, Scribner, 2002.
———. *Death in the Afternoon.* New York: Scribner's, 1932.
———. "Ernest Hemingway—Banquet Speech." *Nobelprize.org: The Official Website of the Nobel Prize,* 2017, www.nobelprize.org/prizes/literature/1954/hemingway/speech/.
———. *Ernest Hemingway: Selected Letters, 1917–1961,* edited by Carlos Baker, Scribner's, 1981.
———. *A Farewell to Arms.* New York: Scribner's, 1929.
———. *For Whom the Bell Tolls.* Scribner's, 1940.
———. *Green Hills of Africa.* Scribner's, 1935.
———. *Hemingway on Fishing,* edited by Nick Lyons, Simon & Schuster, 2012.
———. *Hemingway on Hunting,* edited by Séan Hemingway, Scribner, 2003.
———. "Hemingway Reports Spain." *New Republic,* 27 Apr. 1938, newrepublic.com/article/89502/hemingway-spain-spanish-civil-war.
———. "In Harry's Bar in Venice," *YouTube,* uploaded by Ernest Hemingway—Topic, 13 Mar. 2015, https://www.youtube.com/watch?v=c1hN3xtWrCg.
———. "Italy, 1927." *New Republic,* 18 May 1927, newrepublic.com/article/79268/italy-1927.
———. *The Letters of Ernest Hemingway,* vol. 2, *1923–25,* edited by Sandra Spanier, Albert J. DeFazio III, and Robert W. Trogdon, Cambridge UP, 2013.
———. *The Letters of Ernest Hemingway,* vol. 3, *1926–29,* edited by Rena Sanderson, Sandra Spanier, and Robert W. Trogdon, Cambridge UP, 2015.
———. "A Man's Credo," *Playboy,* vol. 10, Jan. 1963, 120, 124, 175.
———. *A Moveable Feast.* New York: Scribner's, 1964.
———. *A Moveable Feast: The Restored Edition.* Scribners, 2009.
———. "A Natural History of the Dead." *Complete Short Stories,* pp. 335–41.
———. "Notes on the Next War: A Serious Topical Letter." *Esquire,* Sept. 1935, 19, 156.
———. "On Writing." *The Nick Adams Stories.* Scribner's, 1972.
———. "Saturday Night at the Whorehouse in Billings, Montana." *YouTube,* uploaded by Ernest Hemingway-Topic, 13 Mar., 2015, https://www.youtube.com/watch?v=1AG94UMoDfc.
———. *Selected Letters 1917–1961,* edited by Carlos Baker, Scribner Classics, 2003.
———. "The President Vanquishes: A Bimini Letter." *Esquire,* July 1935: 23, 167.
———. *The Nick Adams Stories,* edited by Philip Young, Scribner's, 1972.

———. *To Have and Have Not.* Scribner's, 1937.

———. *The Garden of Eden.* Scribner's, 1995.

———. "The Gambler, the Nun, and the Radio." *Complete Short Stories,* pp. 355–68.

———. *The Old Man and the Sea.* Scribner's, 2003.

———. *The Sun Also Rises.* New York: Scribner's, 1926.

———. "The Three-Day Blow." *Complete Short Stories,* pp. 85–93.

Hemingway, Grace Hall. "Mother's Scrapbooks." *Ernest Hemingway Audiovisual Materials.* John F. Kennedy Presidential Library and Museum, www.jfklibrary.org/Research/The-Ernest-Hemingway-Collection/Hemingway-Audiovisual-Materials.aspx.

Hemingway, Jack. *Misadventures of a Fly Fisherman: My Life with and without Papa.* McGraw-Hill, 1986.

Hemingway, Mary Welsh. *How It Was.* Knopf, 1976.

———. "At Harry's Bar in Venice." *Holiday,* June 1968. Reprinted in T*he Astounding World of Holiday.* Josh Lieberman, 27 June 2012, holidaymag.wordpress.com/2012/06/27/harrys-bar-in-venice-by-mary-hemingway-june-1968/.

Hemingway, Patrick. Foreword to *Hemingway on Hunting,* pp. xiii–xviii.

———. Introduction to *True at First Light,* by Ernest Hemingway. Scribner's, 1999, pp. 7–11.

"Hemingway in Key West." *Key West Art and Historical Society,* 2016, www.kwahs.org/exhibitions/ernest-in-key-west.

"The Hemingway Papers." *The Toronto Star,* 1996–2012, ehto.thestar.com/.

Hemingway-Pfeiffer Museum and Educational Center. Arkansas State University, hemingway.astate.edu/.

"Hemingway's Oak Park Roots." *The Ernest Hemingway Foundation of Oak Park,* www.hemingwaybirthplace.com/hemingway-and-oak-park/.

Hendrickson, Paul. *Hemingway's Boat: Everything He Loved in Life, and Lost.* Knopf, 2011.

Heppler, Jason. What Is Digital Humanities? 2015, whatisdigitalhumanities.com.

"Highsmith (Carol M.) Archive." *Library of Congress,* www.loc.gov/pictures/collection/highsm/item/2010638629/.

Holmes, Burton. *Seeing Paris: Part One: On the Boulevards.* 1920. Internet Archive, archive.org/details/6113_Seeing_Paris_Part_One_On_the_Boulevards_00_00_59_05.

Hotchner, A. E. "Hemingway in Love." *Smithsonian,* Oct. 2015, www.smithsonianmag.com/arts-culture/ernest-hemingway-in-love-180956617/.

———. *Papa Hemingway: A Personal Memoir.* Bantam, 1967.

Howard, Michael. *The First World War.* Oxford UP, 2002.

Ilgunas, Ken. *Walden on Wheels: On the Open Road from Debt to Freedom.* New Harvest, 2013.

"Italian Forces during World War I. Lot 6941." *Library of Congress,* www.loc.gov/pictures/search/?q=LOT%206941&fi=number&op=PHRASE&va=exact&co!=coll&sg=true&st=gallery.

Jackson, Jeremy B. C., et al. "Historical Overfishing and the Recent Collapse of Coastal Ecosystems." *Science,* vol. 293, no. 5530, 2001, pp. 629–37.

Jolas, Eugene. "Proclamation: The Revolution of the Word." *transition*, vol. 16–17, 1929, 13.
Jones, Jason B. "How to Read 3 Victorian Novels in 2.5 Hours." *The Salt-Box*, 27 Mar. 2008, www.jbj.wordherders.net/2008/03/27/how-to-read-3-victorian-novels-in-25-hours.
Jones, Josh. "The (Urban) Legend of Ernest Hemingway's Six-Word Short Story: 'For Sale, Baby Shoes, Never Worn.'" *Open Culture*, 24 Mar. 2015, www.openculture.com/2015/03/the-urban-legend-of-ernest-hemingways-six-word-story.html.
———. "Hear Hemingway Read Hemingway and Faulkner Read Faulkner (90 Minutes of Classic Audio)." *Open Culture*, 15 Jan. 2015, www.openculture.com/2015/01/hear-hemingway-read-hemingway-and-faulkner-read-faulkner.html.
"Julian Barnes Reads 'Homage to Switzerland' by Ernest Hemingway." *The Guardian*, 7 Dec. 2010, www.theguardian.com/books/audio/2010/dec/08/julian-barnes-ernest-hemingway-podcast.
June, Audrey Williams. "The Best and Worst Part of Being a Professor: Students." *The Chronicle of Higher Education*, 18 Sept. 2018, www.chronicle.com/article/The-Best-Worst-Part-of/244669.
Kahler, Erich. *The Inward Turn of Narrative*. Trans. Richard Winston and Clara Winston. 1970. Princeton UP, 1973.
Keese-Hamm, Natalie. Personal interview with Laura Godfrey, 5 Sept. 2018.
Kirschenbaum, Matthew G. "Digital Humanities As/Is a Tactical Term." Gold, *Debates in the Digital Humanities*, pp. 415–28.
———. "What Is Digital Humanities and What's It Doing in English Departments?" *ADE Bulletin*, no. 150, 2010, pp. 55–61.
———. "What Is 'Digital Humanities,' and Why Are They Saying Such Terrible Things about It?" *differences*, vol. 25, no. 1, 2014, pp. 46–63.
Krebs, Natalie. "Why We Suck at Recruiting New Hunters, Why It Matters, and How You Can Fix It." *Outdoor Life*, 18 Jan. 2018, www.outdoorlife.com/why-we-are-losing-hunters-and-how-to-fix-it.
King, Darryn. "Ermahgerddon: The Untold Story of the Ermahgerd Girl." *Vanity Fair*, 15 Oct. 2015, www.vanityfair.com/culture/2015/10/ermahgerd-girl-true-story.
Knickerbocker, Scott. "Skiing with Papa." In *Teaching Hemingway and the Natural World*, edited by Kevin Maier, Kent State UP, 2018.
Koizumi, Rie. "Relationships between Text Length and Lexical Diversity Measures: Can We Use Short Texts of Less Than 100 Tokens?" *Vocabulary Learning and Instruction*, vol. 1, no. 1, 2012, pp. 60–69.
Kotecki, K. "Mapping Hemingway's 'The Killers': Text Mapping as Modelling." *DHSI 2015 Blog*. 12 June 2015, textmappingasmodelling.wordpress.com/2015/06/12/mapping-hemingways-the-killers/.
Kurzweil, Ray. *The Singularity Is Near: When Humans Transform Biology*. Penguin, 2005.
Landau, Elizabeth. "Hemingway Family Mental Illness Explored in New Film." *CNN*, 23 Jan. 2013, www.cnn.com/2013/01/21/health/hemingway-film/index.html.
Latham, Aaron. "A Farewell to Machismo." *The New York Times*, 16 Oct. 1977, pp. 52–53, 55, 80, 82, 90, 92, 94, 96, 98–99.

Lauter, Paul. "Modernism and the Self." *The Heath Anthology of American Literature,* vol. 2, edited by Paul Lauter. Heath, 1990, pp. 851–55.

Lefebvre, Henri. *The Production of Space,* translated by Donald Nicholson-Smith, Blackwell, 1991.

———. *Writings on Cities,* edited and translated by Eleonore Kofman and Elizabeth Lebas, Blackwell, 1996.

Leff, Leonard. *Hemingway and His Conspirators: Hollywood, Scribners, and the Making of American Celebrity Culture.* Rowman & Littlefield, 1997.

Lewis, Paul. "'Our Minds Can Be Hijacked': The Tech Insiders Who Fear a Smartphone Dystopia." *The Guardian,* 6 Oct. 2017, theguardian.com/technology/2017/oct/05/smartphone-addiction-silicon-valley-dystopia.

"Library Acquires Rare Films: Prelinger Collection Features Ephemeral Films." *Library of Congress Information Bulletin,* vol. 61, no. 10, Oct. 2002, www.loc.gov/loc/lcib/0210/prelinger.html.

The Little Review. The Modernist Journals Project, Brown U and U of Tulsa, www.modjourn.org/render.php?view=mjp_object&id=LittleReviewCollection.

Lottick, Kenneth V. "The Filmstrip: A Guide to A-V's Work Horse." *The Clearing House,* vol. 26, no. 6, Feb. 1952, 325–27.

Lovett, D. F. "Six Things Hemingway Never Said," *What Would Bale Do,* 10 July 2015, whatwouldbaledo.com/2015/ 07/10/six-things-hemingway-never-said/.

Loy, Mina. *The Lost Lunar Baedeker: Poems of Mina Loy,* edited by Roger L. Conover, Macmillan, 1996.

Lunden, Ingrid. "6.1b Smartphone Users by 2020, Overtaking Basic Fixed Phone Subscriptions," *TechCrunch,* 2 June 2015, techcrunch.com/2015/06/02/6-1b-smartphone-users-globally-by-2020-overtaking-basic-fixed-phone-subscriptions/.

Lyman, Alex. "Botnik Story." *Digital Humanities Fall 2017,* 20 Dec. 2017, dh17.dralexlyman.net/uncategorized/botnik-story/.

Lyman, Rick. "Martha Gellhorn, Daring Writer, Dies at 89." *The New York Times,* 17 Feb. 1998, www.nytimes.com/1998/02/17/arts/martha-gellhorn-daring-writer-dies-at-89.html.

Lynn, Kenneth. *Hemingway.* Simon & Schuster, 1987.

Lyon, Rachel. Personal Interview with Laura Godfrey. 17 July 2017.

Macdonald, Dwight. "Ernest Hemingway." *Encounter,* Jan. 1962, pp. 115–21.

———. "Masscult and Midcult." *Masscult and Midcult: Essays against the American Grain,* edited by John Summers, *New York Review of Books,* 2011, pp. 3–70.

Macrorie, Ken. *The I-Search Paper.* Revised ed. of *Searching Writing,* Heinemann, 1988.

"Magazine Archive." *Poetry Foundation,* 2018, www.poetryfoundation.org/poetrymagazine/archive.

Maher, Susan Naramore. *Deep Map Country: Literary Cartography of the Great Plains.* U of Nebraska P, 2014.

Maier, Kevin. "Hunting." *Ernest Hemingway in Context,* edited by Debra Moddelmog and Suzanne del Gizzo, Cambridge UP, 2015, pp. 267–76.

Marano, Lou. "The Hemingway Suicide Curse." *UPI,* 10 Oct. 2001, www.upi.com/The-Hemingway-suicide-curse/60461002739993/.

Martin, Lawrence. "Ernest Hemingway, Gulf Stream Marine Scientist: The 1934–35 Academy of Natural Sciences Correspondence." *The Hemingway Review*, vol. 20, no. 2, Spring 2001, pp. 5–15.

McAuliffe, Mary. *When Paris Sizzled: The 1920s Paris of Hemingway, Chanel, Cocteau, Cole Porter, Josephine Baker, and Their Friends*. Rowman & Littlefield, 2016.

McCarthy, Cormac. *The Sunset Limited*. Vintage, 2006.

McFarlane, Robert. *The Wild Places*. Penguin, 2008.

McGonigal, Jane. *Reality Is Broken: Why Games Make Us Better and How They Can Change the World*. Penguin, 2011.

McLain, Paula. *Love and Ruin: A Novel*. Ballantine, 2018.

McLuhan, Marshall. *Understanding Media*. MIT P, 1994.

Messent, Peter. *Ernest Hemingway*. St. Martin's P, 1992.

Meyers, Jeffrey. *Hemingway: A Biography*. Da Capo, 1999

———. "The Quest for Hemingway." *Virginia Quarterly Review*, vol. 61, no. 4, Autumn 1985, www.vqronline.org/essay/quest-hemingway.

Michaels, Walter Benn. *Our America: Nativism, Modernism, and Pluralism*. Duke UP, 2002.

Michener, James A. Introduction to *The Dangerous Summer*, by Ernest Hemingway, Scribner's, 1985, pp. 3–40.

Miller, Henry. *Conversations with Henry Miller*, edited by Frank L. Kersnowski and Alice Hughes, U of Mississippi P, 1994.

Mitgang, Herbert. "Mary Hemingway Dies at 78; Wrote of Life with Novelist." *The New York Times*, 28 Nov. 1986, www.nytimes.com/1986/11/28/obituaries/mary-hemingway-dies-at-78-wrote-of-life-with-novelist.html. Moretti, Franco. *Distant Reading*. Verso, 2013.

———. *Graphs, Maps, Trees*. Verso, 2005.

Myers, Ransom, and Boris Worm. "Rapid Worldwide Depletion of Predatory Fish Communities," *Nature*, no. 423, 15 May 2003, pp. 280–83.

@NatTowsen. "It's not automated! We have a team of writers who all use the Botnik predictive text keyboard. We trained keyboards on all 7 books and had a big writing jam. Then I took the best pieces of copy, arranged them into a narrative, and wrote some copy to fill in the gaps." *Twitter*, 12 Dec. 2017, 1:40 p.m., twitter.com/NatTowsen/status/940652654925111296.

National Endowment for the Arts. "Survey of Public Participation in the Arts," 2013, www.arts.gov/news/2013/national-endowment-arts-presents-highlights-2012-survey-public-participation-arts.

"New Hemingway Materials from Cuba Made Available for First Time at JFK Library." *JFK Presidential Library and Museum*, 11 Feb. 2014, www.jfklibrary.org/About-Us/News-and-Press/Press-Releases/2014-Hemingway-Cuba-Documents.aspx.

North, Michael. "Visual Culture." *The Cambridge Companion to American Modernism*, edited by Walter Kalaidjian, Cambridge UP, 2005, pp. 177–94.

O'Toole, Garson. "For Sale, Baby Shoes, Never Worn." *Quote Investigator*, 28 Jan. 2013, quoteinvestigator.com/2013/01/28/baby-shoes/.

———. *Hemingway Didn't Say That: The Truth behind Familiar Quotations*. Little A, 2017.
Ockerbloom, John Mark, ed. "The Dial." *The Online Books Page*, U of Pennsylvania, onlinebooks.library.upenn.edu/webbin/serial?id=thedial.
Ong, Walter. *Orality and Literacy*. Routledge, 2003.
The Open Syllabus Project. *The Open Syllabus Project*, opensyllabusproject.org/.
Owens-Murphy, Katie. "Hemingway's Pragmatism: Truth, Utility, and Concrete Particulars in *A Farewell to Arms*. *The Hemingway Review*, vol. 29, no. 1, 2009, 87–102.
Palin, Michael. "Walk Like the Man: Go for a Stroll through the City's Vibrant Left Bank, the Hemingway Way." *Time Out*, 13 Apr. 2017, www.timeout.com/paris/en/walks-tours/walk-like-the-man.
———. *Michael Palin's Hemingway Adventure*. PBS, www.pbs.org/hemingwayadventure/index.html.
"The Paris Wife—Paula McLain." *YouTube*, uploaded by W. H. Smith, 1 Mar. 2012, www.youtube.com/watch?v=A190EM_Z3dk.
Paul, Steve. "Quotation Controversy: Writing and Bleeding." *The Hemingway Society*, 27 May 2016, www.hemingwaysociety.org/quotation-controversy-writing-and-bleeding.
"Paula McLain on Reviving Hemingway and The Paris Wife," *YouTube*, uploaded by Penguin Random House Canada, 8 Feb. 2011, www.youtube.com/watch?v=mR6bfEvYLE0.
Pauly, Daniel. "Anecdotes and the Shifting Baseline Syndrome of Fisheries." *Trends in Ecology and Evolution*, vol. 10, no. 10, 1995, p. 430.
Pew Research Center. "Millennials in Adulthood." *Pew Research Center Social and Demographic Trends*, 7 Mar. 2014, www.pewsocialtrends.org/2014/03/07/millennials-in-adulthood/.
———. "Mobile Fact Sheet." *Pew Research Center Internet and Technology*, 5 Feb. 2018, www.pewinternet.org/fact-sheet/mobile/.
Pilsch, Andrew. *Transhumanism: Evolutionary Futurism and the Technologies of Utopia*. U of Minnesota P, 2017.
Pinnegar, John K., and Georg H. Engelhard. "The 'Shifting Baseline' Phenomenon: A Global Perspective." *Reviews in Fish Biology and Fisheries*, vol. 18, no. 1, 2008, pp. 1–16.
Plimpton, George. "Ernest Hemingway, The Art of Fiction No. 21." *The Paris Review*, no. 18, Spring 1958, www.theparisreview.org/interviews/4825/the-art-of-fiction-no-21-ernest-hemingway.
Postman, Neil. *Amusing Ourselves to Death: Public Discourse in the Age of Show Business*, Penguin, 1986, pp. 64–80.
———. *Technopoly: The Surrender of Culture to Technology*. Knopf, 1992.
Postman, Neil, and Charles Weingartner. *Teaching as a Subversive Activity*. Delacorte P, 1970.
Pottle, Russ. "Key West as Carnival: Hemingway and the Commodification of Celebrity." *Key West Hemingway: A Reassessment*, edited by Kirk Curnutt and Gail D. Sinclair, UP of Florida, 2009, pp. 285–98.

Pound, Ezra. *The Cantos of Ezra Pound*. 1970. New Directions, 1996.
———. *The Literary Essays of Ezra Pound*, edited by T. S. Eliot, Faber & Faber, 1954.
Prensky, Marc. "Digital Natives, Digital Immigrants." *On the Horizon*, vol. 9, no. 5, Oct. 2001, pp 1–6.
"Publications by Members." *Michigan Hemingway Society*, 2017, www.michiganhemingwaysociety.org/articlelinks/articlelinks.htm.
Puga, Rafael, et al. "Vulnerability of Nearshore Tropical Finfish in Cuba: Implications for Scientific and Management Planning." *Bulletin of Marine Science*, vol. 94, no. 2, 2017, pp. 1–16.
Raeburn, John. *Fame Became of Him: Hemingway as Public Writer*. Indiana UP, 1984.
Ramsay, Stephen. "The Hermeneutics of Screwing Around; or What You Do with a Million Books." *Pastplay: Teaching and Learning History with Technology*, edited by Kevin Kee, U of Michigan P, 2014, pp. 111–20.
Ray, Rick. "Black and White Footage of the Parade of Giants at the San Fermin Fiesta in the 1920s." Shutterstock, www.shutterstock.com/video/clip-4145197-stock-footage--s-black-and-white-footage-of-the-parade-of-giants-at-the-san-fermin-fiesta-in-the-s.html.
Reeve, Jonathan Pearce. "Does 'Late Style' Exist? New Stylometric Approaches to Variation in Single-Author Corpora." *Digital Humanities* 2018, dh2018.adho.org/does-late-style-exist-new-stylometric-approaches-to-variation-in-single-author-corpora/.
Remembering Hemingway in Central Idaho. Produced by Mary Tyson. Film prepared for The Community Library, Ketchum, Idaho, 2015, www.comlib.org/regionalhistory/.
Reynolds, Michael. *Hemingway: The Final Years*. Norton, 1999.
———. *Hemingway: The 1930s*. Blackwell, 1996.
———. *Hemingway's First War: The Making of "A Farewell to Arms."* Princeton UP, 1976.
———. *Hemingway: The 1930s through the Final Years*. Norton, 2000.
———. *Hemingway's Reading: An Inventory*. Princeton UP, 1981, John F. Kennedy Presidential Library and Museum, www.jfklibrary.org/~/media/assets/Archives/Documents/Ernest%20Hemingway/Ernest%20Hemingway%20PDFs/Hemingways%20Reading.pdf.
———. "Ringing the Changes: Hemingway's Bell Tolls Fifty." *Virginia Quarterly Review*, vol. 67, no. 1, Winter 1991, www.vqronline.org/essay/ringing-changes-hemingway's-bell-tolls-fifty.
Rockwell, Geoffrey, and Stéfan Sinclair. *Hermeneutica: Computer-Assisted Interpretation in the Humanities*. MIT P, 2016.
Rockwell, Geoffrey, et al. *Text Analysis Portal for Research*, tapor.ca/home.
Rogal, Samuel J. *For Whom the Dinner Bell Tolls: The Role and Function of Food and Drink in the Prose of Ernest Hemingway*. International Scholars Publications, 1997.
Romano, Aja. "Hopepunk, the Latest Storytelling Trend, Is All about Weaponized Optimism." *Vox*, 27 Dec. 2018, www.vox.com/2018/12/27/18137571/what-is-hopepunk-noblebright-grimdark?fbclid=IwAR2xUOnOomVGjpdACF6PFPkYvLwsVevhmAKigK5orJfWc8mon5qwrg3gp8k.

Roorda, Randall. "Deep Maps in Eco-Literature." *Michigan Quarterly Review*, vol. 40, no. 1, 2001, pp. 257–72.

Ross, Lillian. "How Do You Like It Now, Gentlemen?" *The New Yorker*, 13 May 1950, www.newyorker.com/magazine/1950/05/13/how-do-you-like-it-now-gentlemen.

Rott, Nathan. "Decline in Hunters Threatens How U.S. Pays for Conservation." *NPR*, 20 Mar. 2018, www.npr.org/2018/03/20/593001800/decline-in-hunters-threatens-how-u-s-pays-for-conservation.

Rusche, Harry. *Lost Poets of the Great War*, www.english.emory.edu/LostPoets/.

Ryden, Kent. *Mapping the Invisible Landscape: Folklore, Writing, and the Sense of Place*. U of Iowa P, 1993.

Said, Edward. *On Late Style: Music and Literature against the Grain*. Pantheon, 2006.

Samuel, Alexandra. "Yes, Smartphones Are Destroying a Generation, but Not of Kids." *JSTOR Daily*, 8 Aug. 2017, daily.jstor.org/yes-smartphones-are-destroying-a-generation-but-not-of-kids/.

Sanford, Marcelline Hemingway. "At the Hemingways: Ernest Returns from War." Atlantic. Reprinted as "Hemingway Goes to War." *The Atlantic*, Aug. 2014, www.theatlantic.com/magazine/archive/2014/08/hemingway-goes-to-war/373437/.

Schindler, Marcel. "The Old Man and the Sea." *Vimeo*, 30 Mar. 2012, vimeo.com/39473645.

Scribner, Charles III. "Ernest Hemingway: A Publisher's Perspective." *Charles Scribner III*. Charles Scribner, charlesscribner.com/ernest-hemingway.html.

Seymour, David. "David Seymour (CHIM) Photograph Collection: War and Social Documentary Subjects, ca. 1935–1955." *Library of Congress*, 18 Mar. 2015, www.loc.gov/rr/print/coll/david-seymour-photograph-collection.html.

"Shitposting Is Modern Dadaism." *Reddit*, r/psidechannel, 6 Apr. 2016, www.reddit.com/r/pbsideachannel/comments/4dnqu7/idea_shitposting_is_modern_dadaism/.

Silverman, Aaron, and Molly Maguire. *The Ernest Hemingway Adventure Map of the World*. Scb Distributors, 1986.

Sinclair, Stéfan, and Geoffrey Rockwell. "Mandala." *Voyant Tools Help*, voyant-tools.org/docs/#!/guide/mandala.

Smith, Paul. "Hemingway's Early Manuscripts: The Theory and Practice of Omission." *Journal of Modern Literature*, vol. 10, 1983, pp. 274–88.

———. "1924: Hemingway's Luggage and the Miraculous Year." *The Cambridge Companion to Ernest Hemingway*, edited by Scott Donaldson. Cambridge UP, 1996.

———. "The Trying-out of *A Farewell to Arms*." *New Essays on* A Farewell to Arms, edited by Scott Donaldson. Cambridge UP, 1990, pp. 27–52.

Solnit, Rebecca. *The Faraway Nearby*. Penguin, 2014.

SparkNotes. SparkNotes.com, 2018, Sparknotes.com.

Spilka, Mark. *Hemingway's Quarrel with Androgyny*. U of Nebraska P, 1990.

Stoneback, H. R. "From the Rue St. Jacques to the Pass of Roland to the 'Unfinished Church on the Edge of the Cliff.'" *The Hemingway Review*, vol. 6, no. 1, Fall 1986, pp. 2–29.

———. *Reading Hemingway's* The Sun Also Rises: *Glossary and Commentary*. Kent State UP, 2007.

Stoppard, Tom. "Reflections on Ernest Hemingway." *American Masters.* PBS, 14 Sept. 2005, www.pbs.org/wnet/americanmasters/ernest-hemingway-reflections-on-ernest-hemingway/629/.
Streetlight Manifesto. "Here's to Life." *Everything Goes Numb*, 2003.
Tate, Allen. "Hard-Boiled." *Hemingway: The Critical Heritage*, edited by Jeffrey Meyers. Routledge & Kegan Paul, 1982, pp. 93–95.
Tavernier-Courbin, Jacqueline. *Ernest Hemingway's* A Moveable Feast: *The Making of Myth.* Northeastern UP, 1991.
"Ten Greatest Waterfowling Quotes." *Sporting Classics Daily*, 29 June 2015, sporting classicsdaily.com/ten-greatest-waterfowling-quotes/.
Thorne-Murphy, Leslee, and Michael C. Johnson. "The Victorian Short Fiction Project: A Web-Based Undergraduate Research Assignment." *Journal of Victorian Culture*, vol. 16, no. 1, pp. 101–11.
ThugNotes. Wisecrack, Inc., 2018, www.wisecrack.co/thug-notes/.
Thurber, James. "A Visit from St. Nicholas (in the Ernest Hemingway Manner)." *The New Yorker*, 24 Dec. 1927, www.newyorker.com/magazine/1927/12/24/a-visit-from-saint-nicholas-in-the-ernest-hemingway-manner.
Trodd, Zoe. "Hemingway's Camera Eye: The Problem of Language and an Interwar Politics of Form." *The Hemingway Review*, vol. 26, no. 2, Spring 2007, 7–21.
Trogdon, Robert. *The Lousy Racket: Hemingway, Scribners, and the Business of Literature.* Kent State UP, 2007.
Turchi, Peter. *Maps of the Imagination: The Writer as Cartographer.* Trinity UP, 2004.
Turkle, Sherry. *Alone Together: Why We Expect More from Technology and Less from Each Other.* Basic Books, 2011.
Twenge, Jean. *iGen: Why Today's Superconnected Kids Are Growing Up Less Rebellious, More Tolerant, Less Happy—and Completely Unprepared for Adulthood.* Simon & Schuster, 2017.
———. "Have Smartphones Destroyed a Generation?" *The Atlantic*, Sept. 2017, theatlantic.com/magazine/archive/2017/09/has-the-smartphone-destroyed-a-generation/534198/.
Tyler, Lisa. *Virtual Hemingway*, virtualhemingway.hcommons.org/.
United States, Congress, House. United States Code. Office of the Law Revision Counsel, 30 July 2018, uscode.house.gov.
Verduin, Kathleen. "Hemingway's Dante: A Note on Across the River and into the Trees." *American Literature*, vol. 57, no. 4, 1985, pp. 633–40.
Veremeulen, Timotheus, and Robin van der Akker. "Notes on Metamodernism." *Journal of Aesthetics and Culture*, vol. 2, no. 1, 2010, 1–14.
Vernon, Alex. "ENGL 465—Ernest Hemingway Seminar." *Alex Vernon*, 2016, static1.squarespace.com/static/51b5f68fe4b0b6f800420ca4/t/57f6c2c2ebbd1a9b34f40c29/1475789508536/465_desc_syl_f16.pdf.
Vonnegut, Kurt. *Slaughterhouse-Five, Or, The Children's Crusade, a Duty Dance with Death.* Delacorte P, 1969.
Voss, Frederick, and Michael Reynolds. *Picturing Hemingway: A Writer in His Time.* Yale UP, 1999.

Waldmeir, Joseph J., and Frederic J. Svoboda, eds. *Hemingway: Up in Michigan Perspectives*. Michigan State UP, 1995.
Weber, Ronald. *Hemingway's Art of Non-Fiction*. Palgrave Macmillan, 1990.
Whitaker, Dane. "The Truth According to Hemingway." *Digital Humanities,* 19 Dec. 2017, dh.danewhitaker.com/uncategorized/the-truth-according-to-hemingway/.
White, E. B. "Across the Street and into the Grill." *The New Yorker,* 14 Oct. 1950, www.newyorker.com/magazine/1950/10/14/across-the-street-and-into-the-grill.
Wickes, George. *Americans in Paris*. Doubleday, 1969.
Williams, Tennessee. "A Writer's Quest for Parnassus." *The New York Times Magazine,* 13 Aug. 1950, www.nytimes.com/books/00/12/31/specials/williams-parnassus.html.
Williams, William Carlos. *The Collected Poems of William Carlos Williams*. 3 vols., edited by A. Walton Litz and Christopher MacGowan. New Directions, 1991.
Wimsatt, W. K. *The Verbal Icon: Studies in the Meaning of Poetry*. U of Kentucky P, 1954.
Young, Philip. Review of *Byline: Ernest Hemingway: Selected Articles and Dispatches of Four Decades,* edited by William White. 1967. *Ernest Hemingway: The Critical Heritage*. London: Routledge, 1982, pp. 516–18.

Contributors

Ricky Baldridge is currently working toward his MA in English with a literature emphasis at the University of Idaho. He is currently working on exploring how the emerging genre of cli-fi (climate fiction) can use utilize techniques of narrative empathy to elicit awareness in its readership.

Lee J. Brainard is an undergraduate student at the University of Idaho. He is enjoying a successful career in law enforcement, and after raising his children, he returned to the classroom in 2014 to complete his formal education.

Nicole J. Camastra (PhD, University of Georgia) is an upper school teacher and English department head at The O'Neal School in Southern Pines, North Carolina. Her research and teaching interests include American literature, literature and music, and modernist fiction. She has published several essays on American authors and coedited *Elizabeth Madox Roberts: Essays of Discovery and Recovery* (2008). Currently, she is completing a book, provisionally titled "Acoustic Longing: Ernest Hemingway, F. Scott Fitzgerald, and Romantic Music."

Jordan Cissell is a PhD student in the Department of Geography at the University of Alabama. His research integrates field- and remote sensing–based methods to explore human-environment interactions and environmental conservation in tropical coastal landscapes, particularly those in Latin America.

Brian Croxall is assistant research professor of digital humanities at Brigham Young University, where he designs and manages computational research projects and teaches courses on technology and American literature. His recent articles appear in *American Imago, Journal of Digital Humanities, Writing and Pedagogy, Neo-Victorian Studies,* and the forthcoming *Digital Pedagogy in the Humanities*. He is the coeditor (with Rachel A. Bowser) of *Like Clockwork: Steampunk Pasts, Presents, and Futures* (2016) and a contributing author for the group blog *ProfHacker*.

Kirk Curnutt is professor and chair of English at Troy University, where he has taught since 1993. He is the author of *A Reader's Guide to Hemingway's* To Have and Have Not, as well as recent studies of William Faulkner and F. Scott Fitzgerald, and the editor of *American Literature in Transition: 1970–1980*.

Mark Ebel, professor of Spanish and film at Chipola College, has presented and participated at several major Hemingway conferences. His latest article is "The Last Volley in

Across the River and into the Trees" in the 2016 edition of *Florida Council of Teachers of English*. Mark is an avid outdoorsman and athlete who has run with the bulls at Pamplona.

Allison Gneckow is an English major at the University of Idaho in Coeur d'Alene. During her time as an undergraduate, she has taken special interest in literary modernism, including the works of Ernest Hemingway. She has served as moderator at and contributed her writing to the Northwest Undergraduate Conference in the Humanities.

Bruce R. Godfrey is geographic information systems librarian at the University of Idaho Library. He has published on geospatial data management and web-based geospatial infrastructures, as well as on the creation and maintenance of geospatial documentation, in the *Journal of Web Librarianship, PNLA Quarterly, Journal of Map and Geography Libraries, Library Trends,* and *Information Technology and Libraries*.

Laura Godfrey is associate professor and assistant chair of the Department of English and Humanities at North Idaho College. She has published widely on American literature and on Hemingway in journals such as *Western American Literature, Arizona Quarterly, Critique,* and *The Hemingway Review* as well as in edited collections. Her first book, *Hemingway's Geographies*, was published in 2016.

Richard Hancuff is manager of online learning systems and is on the English faculty at Misericordia University. He holds a PhD in English from George Washington University and a BS in secondary education from Pennsylvania State University. He specializes in national identity formation through and against competing and intersecting discourses primarily of race and ethnicity, particularly in African American and American literature.

Rebecca Johnston teaches at Santa Fe College in Gainesville, Florida, and is the co-vice president of the Florida Hemingway Society. Rebecca was the 2016 recipient of the Lewis-Reynolds-Smith Founder's Fellowship and one of the 2017 recipients of the JFK Hemingway research grants. She has published on Twain and Hemingway.

Michelle E. Moore is professor of English at the College of Dupage. Her book, *Chicago and the Making of American Modernism: Cather, Hemingway, Faulkner, and Fitzgerald in Conflict*, was published in 2019. She has published in *Cather Studies, Faulkner Journal,* and *Literature/Film Quarterly*. In addition, she has published chapters on teaching Henry James and the film director Todd Solondz.

Kelly Owens is an undergraduate student at the University of Idaho, majoring in English with an emphasis in literature. She was the recipient of both the Virginia Johnson Award for Outstanding Critical Writer at North Idaho College and an honorable mention for Best Critical Writing Paper at the Northwest Undergraduate Conference in the Humanities in 2017.

Marshall J. Palmer is a nontraditional senior at the University of Idaho, pursuing a degree in professional writing. His unusual religious upbringing has led to a writing focus on religious fundamentalism and its precipitating causes, as well as fundamentalism's influence on the US political landscape. His other interests include linguistics in the areas of theoretical semantics and lexicography.

Michael K. Steinberg is associate professor of New College and geography at the University of Alabama. His research is focused on the human-dimensions of environmental conservation, endangered species, and conservation mapping. He is the author of *Stalking the Ghost Bird: The Elusive Ivory-Billed Woodpecker in Louisiana* (2008) and *Dangerous Harvest: Drug Plants and the Transformation of Indigenous Landscapes* (2004). His work has also been published in several journals.

Lisa Tyler, professor of English at Sinclair Community College in Dayton, Ohio, is the author or editor of four books: *Student Companion to Ernest Hemingway* (2001), *Teaching Hemingway's* A Farewell to Arms (2008), *Understanding Marsha Norman* (2019), and *Wharton, Hemingway, and the Advent of Modernism* (2019). She serves on the editorial advisory board of *The Hemingway Review* and has published more than forty essays in academic journals and edited collections. She received Sinclair's Distinguished Faculty Scholar Award in 2017.

Index

Page numbers in italics refer to illustrations.

ABC, 15
ABCs of Reading (Pound), 44
Academy of Natural Sciences, 29
Across the River and into the Trees (Hemingway novel), 57; Barone Alvarito, 99, 103; the "boatman/poler," 94–97, 99, 101–4; decoys in, 97–98; digital analysis of, 75; duck hunting in, 92–100, 103; "hunting guide," 96–97; iceberg principle used in, 101; jacket patch in, 100–104; opening paragraphs, 94–95; Renata, 99–100; Richard Cantwell, 93, 94, 97, 99–100, 102–4; the "shooter," 94, 96, 100–102; war as a theme in, 104
Adams, Caroline, 86
Adamson, Glenn, 93–94
Adorno, Theodor, 89
"Advice to a Young Man" (Hemingway article), 40–41
"Age of distraction," 5
Ahmad, Maida, 86
Ahmed, Hana, 86
Aiken, Conrad, 42
Albrecht, Jacob, 86
Al-Jazeera, 15
Alone Together (Turkle), 1
An, David, 86
Anderson, Sadie, 86
Anderson, Sherwood, 143
Anita, 26
"Aphorisms of Futurism" (Loy), 43
ArcGIS StoryMaps, 121, 127, 131, 136
Aristotle, 1
Arnold, Lloyd, 138, 139, 141
"Art of Fiction, The" (Hemingway article), 17
"At Harry's Bar in Venice" (Mary Welsh Hemingway), 18
Atlantic, The, 18
Atlantic Game Fishing (Farrington), 29
Au, Joyce, 86
Austen, Jane, 62
Avenue de l'Opera, 153

Bacon, Savannah, 86
Baker, Carlos, 18, 57, 58, 83, 155–56
Bakhtin, Mikhail, 20, 47–48
"Banal Story" (Hemingway short story), 40
Barnard, Rita, 132
Barnes, Julian, 19
Bartlett's Familiar Quotations (Bartlett), 37
Bashō, 1
Bass, Randal, 161
Battle of Caporetto, 150
BBC, 16
Benstock, Shari, 41, 125
Bergman, Ingrid, 139
Berra, Yogi, 41
Best of Bad Hemingway, The, 83
Best Times, The (Dos Passos), 53
"Big Two-Hearted River" (Hemingway short story), 4, 45, 60; Bubblelines tool, 69; deep mapping, 132–33, 151; digitizing, 69; iceberg principle used in, 43, 54; Nick Adams, 43, 133, 151; Rinaldi, 43
Big Wood River, 136
Billfish, 24–25, 27; conservation, 25–26, 30–31
"Black Ass at the Cross Roads" (Hemingway short story), 61
Blackboard, 53
Blake, William, 62
Bledsoe, Thomas, 58
Bloch, Daniella, 86
Blouin, Francis X., Jr., 161
Bluefin tuna, 24, 25
Book-of-the-Month Club, 131
Boreth, Craig, 20
Botnik, 83
Boyle, Kay, 44
Breit, Harvey, 58
Brezel, Elyssa, 86
Brigham Young University, 86, 87
Briones, Nathan, 86
British Imperial War Museum, 152, 155
Brohan, Bill, 134

224

Broom (magazine), 160
Brown University, 86
Bunker, Paul, 86
Burdick, Kelly, 72, 86
"Burnt Norton" (Eliot poem), 42
"Butterfly and the Tank, The" (Hemingway short story), 61

Cadwalader, Charles, 29
Café des Amateurs, 121–22
Calder, Maddie, 86
Cameras, 6
Cantos (Pound), 42
Canvas, 53
Carte de visite, 6
Casseday, Matt, 86
Cather, Willa, 2, 145
"Cat in the Rain" (Hemingway short story), 60
CBC, 16
CBS, 15
Center for Disease Control, 156
Champs Élysées, 153
Charles Scribner's & Sons, 72, 109
"Che Ti Dice la Patria" (Hemingway short story), 148
Chicago Tribune, 15, 18
Christian Science Monitor, 15
Chronicle of Higher Education, 93
Chuang Tzu, 1
Chung, Nancy, 86
Cirino, Mark, 93, 120
Clarke, Arthur C., 54
"Clean, Well-Lighted Place, A" (Hemingway short story), 39
CliffNotes, 19
Close reading, 5, 60
Cluny, 121–22
CNN, 15
Collected Poems (Eliot), 42
Collier's magazine, 18
Comley, Nancy, R., 87
"Common readers," 19
Complete Short Stories, The (Hemingway short story collection), 60–61; digital analysis of, 73
Conrad, Joseph, 143
Cooper, Gary, 134, 139
Copyright law, 17, 24, 87–88
Cordell, Ryan, 87
Covarrubias, Miguel, 34
Crane, Hart, 44
CrashCourse, 152
Crawford, Matthew, 1, 5
Critical thinking, 105–6
Crosby, Harry, 44
C-SPAN, 16

Cuauhtemoc Moctezuma Brewery, 48
Cuba, 22, 23, 29, 34, 35, 119, 150; commercial fishing off, 25; images of, 153; mapping, 151
Cuba Capitol on the Prado (Highsmith photograph), 154
Curnutt, Kirk, 154, 156
Curtis, Celia, 86

Daiker, Donald, 115
Dangerous Summer, The (Hemingway nonfiction): digital analysis of, 70; introduction, 89
David Copperfield (Dickens), 88
Davidson, Shelbi, 76, 86
Dawkins, Richard, 36, 37, 52
Death in the Afternoon (Hemingway nonfiction), 20, 71; bullfighting in, 71; digital analysis of, 70; iceberg principle, 42, 44, 101; quotes from, 39, 44
Debates in the Digital Humanities (Gold), 87
De Certeau, Michel, 123, 124
Deep maps/mapping, 129–45; creating, 131; digital, 131
DeFazio, Albert J., 114
Del Gizzo, Suzanne, 155
Derrida, Jacques, 124–25
Der Spiegel, 16
Dial, The, 160
Dichmann, Chris, 76, 86
Dickens, Charles, 88
Didion, Joan, 18
Dietrich, Marlene, 16
Digital age, 2
Digital editions, 62, 65
Digital humanities, 59, 61, 84, 87
"Digital Humanities As/Is a Tactical Term" (Kirschenbaum essay), 87
Digital Humanities Summer Institute, 132
Digital identity, 8
Digital immigrants, 4
Digital maps, 133–34, 139–44; immersive, 149–52; interactive, 134
Digital natives, 113
Diliberto, Gioia, 18
Dillman, Connor, 86
Dillon, Jeffrey, 86
Distant reading, 59–60, 61–62, 85–86, 88
Distant Reading (Moretti), 84
"Doctor and the Doctor's Wife, The" (Hemingway short story), 61
Dôme, The, 120
Donaldson, Scott, 18, 129
Dos Equis, 48, 49
Dos Passos, John, 44, 53
Drumm, Andrew, 86
Dubus, Andre, III, 7

226 INDEX

Duck hunting, 95–100; decoys, 96–98; dogs, 98; hunting guides, 96–97

Eastman, Max, 20
Eby, Carl P., 58, 85, 87
Eichmann, Adolf, 18
Einstein, Albert, 41
Eliot, T. S., 42, 43
Emerson, Ralph Waldo, 111
Emory University, 3, 86, 87
Encounter, 133
"End of Something, The" (Hemingway short story), 61, 130
ENotes, 19
Environmental literature, 22–31
Epic Fail!, 36
Ermahgherd Girl, 36
Ernest Hemingway (Messent), 87
Ernest Hemingway Adventure Map of the World (Silverman and Maguire), 131
Ernest Hemingway and the Geography of Memory (Cirino and Ott), 120
Ernest Hemingway Collection, 148–49
Ernest Hemingway Foundation of Oak Park, 159
Ernest Hemingway in Context (Maier), 99
Ernest Hemingway: Machismo and Masochism (Fantina), 87
"Ernest Hemingway, Reading" (Hemingway album), 161
Ernest Hemingway's A Moveable Feast (Tavernier-Courbin), 127
Esquire, 26, 37, 44, 160; "Monologue to the Maestro," 6–7; "The President Vanquishes," 53
Esri Story Map, 137
Essential Questions, 112, 115
Etsy, 20
"Even the Darkness Is Light?" (Grimes), 114
Everett, Louella D., 37
Evil Kermit, 36

Facebook, 34, 106
Fantina, Richard, 87
Farewell to Arms, A (Hemingway novel), 149–50, 155; Catherine Barkley, 45, 51; deep mapping in, 130, 149–50; digital analysis of, 75; Frederic Henry, 45, 51, 130, 143, 146–50, 152, 156; geography, 148, 150; quotes from, 16, 45
"Farewell to Machismo, A" (Latham), 87
Farnsworth, Miles, 76, 86
Farrington, Kip, 29
Faulkner, William, 42
FBI, 17, 32
Fenton, Charles, 57, 58, 83, 123
Films on Demand, 112
Filmstrips, 32–33, 52–53

Finca Vigía, 34, 35, 50, 159
Fitch, Noel, 131
Fitzgerald, F. Scott, 114, 119
Forum, The, 40
For Whom the Bell Tolls (Hemingway novel): deep mapping in, 130, 131, 151; digitizing, 65; quotes from, 45; Robert Jordan, 45, 78, 130, 146, 151, 156
For Whom the Dinner Bell Tolls (Rogal), 90–91
Fowler, Henry W., 29
Fox News, 15
Frank, Joseph, 42
French Revolution, 122
Frey, David, 132
"From the Rue St. Jacques to the Pass of Roland to the 'Unfinished Church on the Edge of the Cliff'" (Stoneback), 114
Fyfe, Paul, 87, 88, 91

Gajdusek, Robert, 119, 120
"Gambler, the Nun, and the Radio, The" (Hemingway short story), 110
Gaming behaviors, 2
García Márquez, Gabriel, 18
Garden of Eden, The (Hemingway novel), 16, 87; David Bourne, 110; digital analysis of, 72
Gender stereotypes/roles, 51–52, 60
Generational divisions, 8–9
Gesang, Tiffany, 86
Glenn, Ashley, 86
Godfrey, Laura, 119, 120, 122–23
"God Rest You Merry, Gentlemen" (Hemingway short story), 60
Gold, Matthew K., 87
Goldman, Jonathan, 48
Gonzales, Angelica, 86
Google, 24, 37, 47, 106, 113, 161; Earth, 142, 149, 150, 154; Maps, 121, 126–28, 149–51, 155; Suite for Education, 126
Gorizia, 149, 150
Goumiers, 101
Gran Hotel, 149
Graphical user interface (GUI), 65
Gray, Anita, 134–35, 139, 140–41
Great Gatsby, The (film), 114
Great Gatsby, The (Fitzgerald), 114
Green Hills of Africa (Hemingway nonfiction), 27–28, 44; digitizing, 70; syllabi, appearances in, 85
Greetings, Carbon-Based Bipeds! (Clarke), 54
Grimes, Larry, 114
Grumpy Cat, 36
Guardian, The, 19; "'Our Minds Can Be Hijacked': The Tech Insiders Who Fear a Smartphone Dystopia," 113
Gulati, Adriti, 86

Gutierrez, Carlos, 26
Guy Checking Out a Girl, 36

Hancuff, Richard, 156
Harper, Elizabeth, 76, 86
Harriman, Averell, 139
Harry Potter and the Portrait of What Looked Like a Large Pile of Ash, 82–83
Hays, Peter, 40–41, 114
Heart of Darkness (Conrad), 143
Heim, Michael, 5
Hemingway, Ernest: alcoholism, 49–50; analyses of writings, regarding, 57–58; autographical details in stories, 146–47, 152, 156; Bahamas, 22, 25; caricatures of, 34; celebrity and, 21; character names, reusing of, 77–78; Cuba, 22, 23, 29, 34, 35, 119, 150; digital presence, 15–20; estate, 16; experiencing while recording, 6–7; fan pages, 20; FBI file, 17; fishing, 22–31, 34, 53; fishing photos, 23, 24, 25, 26, 28, 29, 30, 34, 35; hunting, 95, 147; iceberg principle of writing, 42–44, 54, 60, 100, 136–37; Idaho, 119, 131–42; image as a sportsman, 22–31; internet searches for, 15–16, 19; Italy, 17, 147; Key West, 22, 26, 30, 119; letters, 8, 158; memes, 8, 32–52; Nobel Prize speech, 17, 110, 161; Oak Park, 119, 123; Paris, 119–28, 147; PEN keynote address, 7; plane crash, 48–49, 53; public identity and masculinity, 15–31, 34, 35, 48–51, 60–61, 146, 156–57; quotes, 16, 37–40, 46; quotes, misattributed/manufactured, 16, 38, 41, 47, 53–54; safari, 48, 49, 147; sentence structure and length, 71–72; Spain, dispatches from, 17; suicide/death, 17, 50–51, 58, 139; tattoos of, 34, 36; and theories regarding his writing, 58–59, 81, 83–84, 87, 119
Hemingway, Grace Hall, 17, 159, 162
Hemingway, Gregory "Gigi," 17, 28
Hemingway, Hadley, 18, 20, 51, 119, 121, 123, 147
Hemingway, Jack "Bumby," 17, 25, 28, 34, 140
Hemingway, Mariel, 17
Hemingway, Martha Gellhorn, 18
Hemingway, Mary Welsh, 18, 34, 48, 139, 140
Hemingway, Patrick "Mouse," 19, 25, 89, 99
Hemingway, Pauline Pfeiffer, 17, 28
Hemingway, Séan, 19
Hemingway and Gellhorn, 18
Hemingway Cookbook, 18
Hemingway Didn't Say That (O'Toole), 41
Hemingway Festival, 134
Hemingway Literary Festival, 20
Hemingway Look-Alike Contest, 20, 119
Hemingway Memorial, 136, 139
Hemingway on Hunting (Hemingway nonfiction), 99
Hemingway Pfeiffer Museum and Educational Center, 18
Hemingway Project, 19
Hemingway Society: blog, 16; Hemingway Letters Project, 158
Hemingway: The Final Years (Reynolds), 57
Hemingway Trails and Quizzes App, 154
Hemingway's Art of Non-Fiction (Weber), 128
Hemingway's Fetishism (Eby), 85, 87
Hemingway's Genders (Comley and Scholes), 87
Hemingway's Geographies (Godfrey), 120
Hemingway's Paris (Gajdusek), 119
Hemingway's Quarrel with Androgyny (Spilka), 87
Hemingway's Reading 1910–1940 (Reynolds), 161
Heppler, Jason, 87
Hermeneutica (Rockwell and Sinclair), 66
Hickock, Guy, 148
High on the Wild (Arnold), 139
"Hills Like White Elephants" (Hemingway short story), 34, 60, 80; Jig, 39; quotes from, 39
"History and Memory the Problem of the Archives" (Blouin), 161
Holiday (magazine), 18
Holmes, Alias Burton, 153
"Homage to Switzerland" (Hemingway short story), 19
Hotchner, A. E., 16, 17
"How Do You Like It Now, Gentlemen?" (Ross article), 17
How to Not Read a Victorian Novel course, 88, 90
Hudson, W. H., 109
Huffington Post, 15

Idaho, 119, 131–35; deep mapping, 135–38; Hemingway stories, 138–44
Imagism, 42
Imperial War Museum, 152
"In Another Country" (Hemingway short story), deep mapping of, 133
Index of Modernist Magazines, 160
"Indian Camp" (Hemingway short story), 42
Information-action ratio, 112
In Our Time (Hemingway short story collection), 43, 88
Instagram, 106, 114
International Game Fish Association, 28–29
Introduction to Digital Humanities course, 10, 84, 86, 87
iPads, 59
I-Search Paper project, 110–11, 114
Islands in the Stream (Hemingway novel), 69; digital analysis of, 72, 78, 80; Thomas Hudson, 78, 146
Isonzo Front, 152

Jhol, Shilpa, 86
John F. Kennedy Presidential Library, 17, 123, 161; digital archives, 152; Hemingway Archive/Collection, 17, 22–23, 24, 29, 54, 155; photographs, 159
Johns Hopkins Guide to Digital Media, The, 87
Johnson, Michael C., 88
Jolas, Eugene, 44
Jones, Jason B., 87, 88

Kahler, Erich, 42
Kansas City Star, 17
Karsh, Yousuf, 34, 36, 49, 51
Kazi, Omair, 86
Ketchum Community Library, 134, 136, 139
Keuler, John, 86
Key West Art and Historical Society, 18–19; "Depicting Hemingway" exhibit, 19; "Hemingway in Key West" exhibit, 19
"Killers, The" (Hemingway short story), 61; deep mapping, 132; Nick Adams, 42
Kim, Mike, 86
Kirschenbaum, Matthew G., 87
Knickerbocker, Scott, 5
Know Your Meme, 37
Kronfeld, Lily, 86
Krebs, Natalie, 92–93

Lanham, Charles "Buck," 100
Lao Tzu, 1
"Last Good Country, The" (Hemingway short story), 130
"Late Style Beethoven" (Adorno and Said), 89
Latham, Aaron, 87
Lauter, Paul, 7–8
Lee, Harper, 134
Leeds, Bill, Jr., 53
Lefebvre, Henri, 124, 125
Le Monde, 16
Levine, David, 34
Levine, Eryn, 86
Lewis, Paul, 113
Library of Congress, 152–55; Carol M. Highsmith Archive, 153–54; Prelinger Collection, 153
Lim, Abe, 86
Lim, Daniel, 86
"Literary cartography," 143
Little Review, The, 88, 160
Lo, Mitchell, 86
Look Magazine, 48
Lost Poets of the Great War (Rusche, website), 3
Lottick, Kenneth, 52–53
Lowe, Joe, 26
Loy, Mina, 43
Luhrmann, Baz, 114

Lycée Henri Quartre, 122
Lyman, Alex, 72, 83, 86
Lynn, Kenneth, 87
Lyon, Rachel, 145

Macdonald, Dwight, 45, 133
Macrorie, Ken, 110–11
Maguire, Molly, 131
Maier, Kevin, 99
"Man's Credo, A" (Hemingway article), 40–41
Mapping Hemingway in Idaho, 131, 134, 138, 140–41, 145
Marlin, 23, 26, 53
Maxwell, Aymer, 100
Mayo Clinic, 135
McAuliffe, Mary, 125
McCarthy, Cormac, 113
McClain, Paula, 18
McGill University, 65
McGonigal, Jane, 1
McLuhan, Marshall, 106
Memes, 8, 32–52; context, 39–40; humorous, 47–48; inspirational, 46–47; *The Old Man and the Sea*, 46; origin of concept, 36–37, 52; quotation, 16, 38, 41, 47, 48; replicability of, 47
Menke, Richard, 88
Menocal, Mayito, 48
Men without Women (Hemingway short story collection), 39–40; "Banal Story," 40
Messent, Peter, 87
Metamodernism, 7
Metaphysics of Virtual Reality, The (Heim), 5
Meyer, Wallace, 58
Meyers, Jeffrey, 18
Michael Palin's Hemingway Adventure, 122, 131–32, 147
Michaels, Walter Benn, 114
Michener, James A., 89
Michigan Hemingway Society, 18
Microsoft Windows 95, 33
Miller, Henry, 52
Mindfulness, 5–6
Mishima, Yukio, 50
Mizener, Arthur, 58
Modernism, 42, 45, 119, 132, 143, 160
Modernist Journals Project, 160
"Monologue to the Maestro" (Hemingway article), 6–7
Monroe County Courthouse, 134
Moretti, Franco, 57, 59, 84
Morley, Christopher, 37
Moscow High School, 145
Moscow Times, 16
Most Interesting Man in the World, 48, 49, 147
Moveable Feast, A (Hemingway nonfiction book), 39, 43, 51, 119–21, 123; digitizing, 70;

"A Good Café on the Place St.-Michel," 121–22, 126; iceberg principle used in, 43; mapping, 121–28; quotes from, 51; "Secret Pleasures," 125
"Mr. and Mrs. Elliot" (Hemingway short story), 60
Mrs. Dalloway (Woolf), 145
MSWord, 53
Murphy, Leslee Thorne, 88
"My Old Man" (Hemingway short story), 44

Nation, 51
National Book Award, 18
"Natural History of the Dead, A" (Hemingway short story), 110
Nature Conservancy, 140
NBC, 15
Neatline, 132
New Criticism, 127
New Republic, 17
New York Times, 15, 17, 18, 36, 53, 92; "Featured Writers," 16
Nick Adams Stories, The (Hemingway short story collection), 43, 110
Nicomachean Ethics (Aristotle), 1
"Night before Battle, The" (Hemingway short story), 154
Nobel Prize, 110, 161; website, 17
North, Michael, 6
North Idaho College, 1, 3, 134, 144
"Now I Lay Me" (Hemingway short story), 60; analyzing, 151–52; Bubblelines tool, 69; digitizing, 69; Nick Adams, 152
NPR, 15–16
Nurse-McLeod, Justine, 86

Oak Park Library, 159
O'Connor, Matt, 86
Of Grammatology (Derrida), 124
Old Man and the Sea, The (Hemingway novel), 19, 22, 26, 45; Bubblelines tool, 69; deep mapping, 151; digital analysis of, 69, 74–75, 78, 80, 82; quotes from, 38, 46; reviews of, 57; Santiago, 147, 151, 156; stop-action video, 19; visual aids for teaching, 153
Ong, Walter, 110
On Late Style Music and Literature against the Grain (Adorno and Said), 89
Openculture, 161
Open Syllabus Project, The, 85
Optical character recognition (OCR) software, 63–64, 86, 88
Orality/oral projects, 111–12
O'Toole, Garson, 41, 53–54
Ott, Mark, 120
Our America (Michaels), 114

"Out of Season" (Hemingway short story), 43, 94; iceberg principle, 54; Peduzzi, 43

Palin, Michael, 122, 131, 147–49
Panthéon, 121–22, 126
Papa Hemingway (Hotchner), 16
Papa's Planet (Frey), 132
Paris, 119–25, 153; Left Bank, 125
Paris Review, 17, 53
Paris Wife, The (McClain), 18
"Paterson" (Williams poem), 43
Paul, Steve, 16
PBS, 147; *Reporting America at War*, 18; WETA, 18
PDF files, 62–63
Penney, Erin, 86
Perkins, Maxwell, 8
Pew Research Center, 3
"Physical and Virtual Environments" (class), 1
Pickrell, Liz, 72, 86
Pilar, 22, 29, 35
Place Contrascarpe, 121
Plath, Sylvia, 50
Playboy, 40; "Advice to a Young Man," 40–41; "A Man's Credo," 40–41
Plimpton, George," 17, 53
Poetry, 160
Poetry Foundation, 160
Posner, Miriam, 87
Postman, Neil, 105, 106, 111, 112
Postmodernism, 132
Pottle, Russ, 19–20
Pound, Ezra, 41, 42, 43, 44, 143, 160
PowerPoint, 33, 37, 38, 48, 52, 53, 112, 155
Pownall, Brandon, 86
Practice of Everyday Life, The (de Certeau), 123
Predictive keyboard, 83
Prensky, Marc, 4
"President Vanquishes, The" (Hemingway article), 53
Pretty Good Bad Hemingway, 83
Prezi, 112
Princeton University, Blue Mountain Project, 160
Prizmo, 63–64
"Proclamation: The Revolution of the Word" (Jolas essay), 43–44
Production of Space, The (Lefebvre), 125
Professor's House, The (Cather), 2, 145
Project-based learning, 112
Project Gutenberg, 62, 88
Purple Land, The (Hudson), 109

Qureshi, Heba, 86

Rackleff, Stephen, 72, 86
Raeburn, John, 16, 18

Ramsay, Stephen, 84
Reading Hemingway's Across the River and into the Trees (Cirino), 93
"Reality augmentation," 5
Reality Is Broken (McGonigal), 1–2
Reeve, Jonathan Pearce, 89
Remembering Hemingway in Central Idaho, 134
"Remembering the 1918 Influenza Pandemic" (CDC), 156
Reuters, 16
Reynolds, Michael, 18, 57, 148, 161
Rive Droite, 125
Rive Gauche, 125
Rockwell, Geoffrey, 65–67, 81, 86, 89
Rogal, Samuel J., 90–91
Roosevelt, Theodore, 98
Ross, Lillian, 17
Rossetti, Dante Gabriel, 62
Rowling, J. K., 83
Running from Crazy, 17
Rusche, Harry, 3
Russell, Joe "Sloppy Joe"/"Josie," 26
Ryden, Kent, 129–30, 143

Said, Edward, 89
Sailfish, 30
Salon, 18
Sample, Mark, 87
Sampson, Tara, 86
Samuel, Alexandra, 113
Sanford, Marcelline Hemingway, 17
Saviers, George, 135
Schindler, Marcel, 19
Scholes, Robert, 87
Schreiber, Abby, 86
Scribner, Charles, III, 17
Scribner Paperback Fiction series, 89
Sculpin, 29
"Sea Change, The" (Hemingway short story), 60
Seeing Paris: Part One: On the Boulevards, 153
Select, The, 120
Selfhood, digitally influenced, 2
Selfish Gene, The (Dawkins), 36
Shakespeare, William, 62
Shakespeare & Company, 127
Sharks, 27, 35, 53
She, Nicholas, 86
"Shitposting," 8
"Short, Happy Life of Francis Macomber, The" (Hemingway short story), 94
Siddiqi, Noreen, 86
Silver Creek Preserve, 136, 140–41
Silverman, Aaron, 131
Simon & Schuster, 19
"Simple Enquiry, A" (Hemingway short story), 60

Simpson, Wendy, 19
Sinclair, Stéfan, 65–67, 81, 86, 89
Slaughterhouse-Five (Vonnegut), 59
Slideshow presentations, 34
Sloppy Joe's bar, 119
Smartphones, 3, 133
Smith, Jayme, 86
Smith, Paul, 148
Snapchat, 106, 114
"Snows of Kilimanjaro, The" (Hemingway short story), 34, 61
"Soldier's Home" (Hemingway short story), 143
Solnit, Rebecca, 129
Spanish Earth, The, 152
SparkNotes, 19
Spilka, Mark, 87
Spotify, 161
Stechmann, Cara, 86
Stein, Gertrude, 143
St.-Étienne-du-Mont, 122
Stoneback, H. R., 109, 113–14
Stoppard, Tom, 18
"Story and Archive in the Twenty-First Century" (Bass), 161
Story maps, 137–38, 141
Strater, Mike, 53
"Summer People" (Hemingway short story), 61
Sun Also Rises, The (Hemingway novel), 2, 4, 58, 119, 152; Avenue de l'Opera, 153; Bill, 114; blindness and sight as themes in, 106–9; Brett Ashley, 7, 39, 51, 76–77, 107–8, 114–15; Champs Élysées, 153; connecting students to, 8; deep mapping, 133, 144, 151, 154; digital analysis of, 75, 76–77, 82; Frances, 106–7; Jake Barnes, 7, 51, 76, 105–10, 113–15, 153, 156; language and communication as themes in, 107–10, 114; Pedro Romero, 39; point of view in, 108–9; quotes from, 39, 51; research projects based on, 112; review of, 51; Robert Cohn, 106–10, 114; San Fermin procession, 153; syllabi, appearances in, 85; teaching in the digital age, 105–15; Voyant Trends tool, 67; word cloud, 66
Sunset Limited, The (McCarthy), 113
Sun Valley Lodge, 134, 135
Sy, Lloyd Kevin, 86

Tally, Robert, 132, 143
TAPoR, 88
Tate, Allen, 51
Tattoos, Hemingway, 34, 36
Tavernier-Courbin, Jacqueline, 127
Teaching Hemingway's The Sun Also Rises (Hays), 114
Teetor, Hannah, 86
Thiesen, Earl, 48

Thiriot, Clarissa, 76, 86
Thoreau, Henry David, 2
ThugNotes, 19
Thurber, James, 16
To Have and Have Not (Hemingway novel): deep mapping, 151; digital analysis of, 75, 82; Harry Morgan, 45, 151, 154; quotes from, 45; visual aids for teaching, 153
To Kill a Mockingbird (Lee), 134
Toronto Star, 17, 160; "A Veteran Visits the Old Front," 147
Torrents of Spring, The (Hemingway novella): digital analysis of, 73, 76, 78, 80; Scripps, 76; syllabi, appearances in, 85; Yogi, 76
"Tradition and the Individual Talent" (Eliot essay), 43
Trail Creek Cabin, 134, 139–40
Trail Creek Road, 138, 141–42
Trail Creek Summit, 136
Transatlantic Review, 160
True at First Light (Hemingway nonfiction), 16; digital analysis of, 70; introduction, 89
Turkle, Sherry, 1, 2–3
Twain, Mark, 41
Twenge, Jean, 92

Under Kilimanjaro (Hemingway nonfiction), 89
Undine, 150
United States Copyright Law, 88
United States Fishing and Wildlife Service, 92–93
University of Alberta, 65
University of Delaware Library, 18
University of Idaho Library, 134, 136
University of Iowa, 62
University of Nebraska–Lincoln, 62
University of Virginia Scholar's Lab, 132

Vanity Fair, 36
Valerstain, Dennis, 86
VCR tapes, 32–33
Veneto, Italy, 92, 95, 98
Verduin, Kathleen, 93
Vernon, Alex, 85
"Very Short Story, A" (Hemingway short story), 61
Vite, Amanda, 72, 86
Vocabulary density, 70, 72
Vogue, 18
Vonnegut, Kurt, 59
Voyant, 65, 91; Bubblelines tool, 69, 70, 89; Cirrus tool, 66, 68, 89; Contexts tool, 68;
default view, 68; drinking and eating references, 78, 79, 80; gender references, 81–82; Mandala tool, 81, 82; stop words, 66, 73, 89–90; Summary tool, 66, 68, 70, 72, 73; Trends tool, 66, 67–68, 73–81; truth references, 82

Walden (Thoreau), 2
Walks in Hemingway's Paris (Fitch), 131
Ward, William Arthur, 41
Washington Post, 15
Washington State University, 3
Waste Land, The (Eliot), 42, 43
Weber, Ronald, 127–28
Weiss, Jonathan, 86
What Is Digital Humanities? (Heppler), 87
"What Is Digital Humanities and What's It Doing in English Departments?" (Kirschenbaum essay), 87
"What is 'Digital Humanities' and Why Are They Saying Such Terrible Things about It?" (Kirschenbaum essay), 87
When Paris Sizzled (McAuliffe), 125
Whitaker, Dane, 81–82, 86
White, E. B., 16
Whitman, Walt, 62
Wickes, George, 119
Williams, James, 106, 113
Williams, Tennessee, 92
Williams, William Carlos, 43
Wilson, Edmund, 87
Wimsatt, W. K., 42
Winner Take Nothing (Hemingway short story collection), 110
Wisdom Foundation, 41
Wisdom: The Magazine of Knowledge and Education, 41
Women of the Left Bank, Paris 1900–1940 (Benstock), 125
Woodworth, Ben, 86
Woolf, Virginia, 19, 50, 145
Word clouds, 66, 88, 89
World beyond Your Head, The (Crawford), 1
World War I, 119, 122, 147, 148, 151–52; digital images of, 152
World War II, 100–101, 146
Writings on Cities (Lefebvre), 125

Young, Philip, 37, 43, 57–58, 83, 87
YouTube, 33, 52, 134, 152–55

Zeng, Saier, 86

www.ingramcontent.com/pod-product-compliance
Lightning Source LLC
Chambersburg PA
CBHW020650230426
43665CB00008B/377